PRENTICE-HALL
FOUNDATIONS OF MODERN SOCIOLOGY S

Alex Inkeles, Editor

INDUSTRIAL SOCIOLOGY
   Ivar Berg

INTRODUCTION TO SOCIAL RESEARCH, Second Edition
   Ann Bonar Blalock/Hubert M. Blalock, Jr.

RACE AND ETHNIC RELATIONS
   Hubert M. Blalock, Jr.

THE LIFE COURSE: A Sociological Perspective
   John A. Clausen

DEVIANCE AND CONTROL
   Albert K. Cohen

MODERN ORGANIZATIONS
   Amitai Etzioni

SOCIAL PROBLEMS
   Amitai Etzioni

AGING AND OLD AGE: New Perspectives
   Anne Foner

LAW AND SOCIETY: An Introduction
   Lawrence M. Friedman

THE FAMILY, Second Edition
   William J. Goode

SOCIETY AND POPULATION, Second Edition
   David M. Heer

WHAT IS SOCIOLOGY? An Introduction to the Discipline and Profession
   Alex Inkeles

GENDER ROLES AND POWER
   Jean Lipman-Blumen

THE SOCIOLOGY OF SMALL GROUPS, Second Edition
   Theodore M. Mills

SOCIAL CHANGE, Second Edition
   Wilbert E. Moore

THE SOCIOLOGY OF RELIGION, Second Edition
   Thomas F. O'Dea/Janet O'Dea Aviad

THE EVOLUTION OF SOCIETIES
   Talcott Parsons

FOUNDATIONS OF MODERN SOCIOLOGY, Fourth Edition
   Metta Spencer/Alex Inkeles

SOCIAL STRATIFICATION: The Forms and Functions of Inequality, Second Edition
   Melvin M. Tumin

THE LIFE COURSE

THE LIFE COURSE

THE LIFE COURSE

A Sociological
Perspective

JOHN A. CLAUSEN
University of California, Berkeley

Prentice-Hall   Englewood Cliffs, New Jersey 07632

Library of Congress Cataloging-in-Publication Data

Clausen, John A.
  The life course.

  (Prentice-Hall foundations of modern sociology series)
  Includes index.
  1. Life cycle, Human—Social aspects. I. Title.
II. Series.
HQ799.95.C55 1986   305   85-19388
ISBN   0-13-535907-4

Editorial/production supervision: Linda Benson
Manufacturing buyer: John B. Hall

Printed in the United States of America

10 9 8 7 6 5 4 3 2 1

ISBN   0-13-535907-4   01

Prentice-Hall International (UK) Limited, *London*
Prentice-Hall of Australia Pty. Limited, *Sydney*
Prentice-Hall Canada Inc., *Toronto*
Prentice-Hall Hispanoamericana, S.A., *Mexico*
Prentice-Hall of India Private Limited, *New Delhi*
Prentice-Hall of Japan, Inc., *Tokyo*
Prentice-Hall of Southeast Asia Pte. Ltd., *Singapore*
Editora Prentice-Hall do Brasil, Ltda., *Rio de Janeiro*
Whitehall Books Limited, *Wellington, New Zealand*

For Suzanne

CONTENTS

PREFACE, xiii

CHAPTER 1

THE LIFE COURSE AND ITS DETERMINANTS, 1

The Life Course, Aging, and Time Frames, 2
The Biological Component, 4
The Sociocultural Context, 6
Historical Time and Cohort Influences, 7
Determinants of Life-Course Outcomes, 9
Methodological Issues, 11

CHAPTER 2

THEORIES AND THEMES IN THE STUDY OF THE LIFE COURSE, 16

General Perspectives on the Life Course, 17
Stage Theories of Development, 19
Role Sequences and Transitions, 26
Themes in the Study of the Life Course, 32
General Questions to be Addressed, 35
Concluding Comments, 39

CHAPTER 3

INFANCY AND EARLY CHILDHOOD, 42

The Human Organism, 43
Maturation of the Infant and Young Child, 47
Language and the Attainment of Selfhood, 50
What Society Expects of Parents and of Infants, 53
The Importance of Infancy and Early Childhood, 58

CHAPTER 4

LATER CHILDHOOD, 64

Physical Development in the Preadolescent Years, 65
Cognitive Development in Childhood, 67
Early Socialization in the Family, 72
Peer Relationships, 76
School and the Student Role, 77
Developmental Tasks and Stages in Childhood, 78
Social Structural Influences on Development, 81

CHAPTER 5

ADOLESCENCE AND YOUTH, 85

Physical Growth after Puberty, 88
Cognitive Development in Adolescence, 90
The Society and Culture of Adolescence and Youth, 92
Sexual Expression in Adolescence, 94
Educational Attainment and Occupational Choice, 96
Identity: The Self in Adolescence, 101
The Transition from Adolescence to Adulthood, 103

CHAPTER 6

THE ADULT YEARS: OCCUPATIONAL CAREERS, 109

Occupational Choice, 113
Career Lines: Some Examples, 118

CHAPTER 7

MARRIAGE AND THE FAMILY CYCLE, 129

Antecedents to Forming a Family, 131
The Transition to Marriage, 134
Children in the Home, 136
Divorce and Remarriage, 143
Interrelationships of Work and Family Roles, 144

CHAPTER 8

THE MIDDLE YEARS, 151

Middle Age and Its Transitions, 152
Physiological Change in the Middle Years, 153
Intellectual Capacities in the Middle Years, 156
Role Involvement in the Middle Years, 158
Personality in the Middle Years, 167

CHAPTER 9

THE LATER YEARS, 174

Physical and Psychological Change in the Later Years, 177
Retirement: Theme and Variations, 180
Aspects of Successful Aging, 181
Last Act of All, 189
The Life Course—Looking Back, 191

NAME INDEX, 195
SUBJECT INDEX, 201

PREFACE

The human life course can hardly be the property of any single discipline, whether humanistic or scientific. In these pages I have tried to delineate the ways in which life in society gives substance to the individual life course. Societies and their cultural systems provide rough scripts and casts of characters whose interactions influence the development and behavior of other players in the drama of life. But many behaviors would be incomprehensible without some understanding of the processes of physical and psychological development. We are all organisms before we become persons, and the attributes of the organism have consequences for the persons we become. Among those attributes, physique, intellectual capacities and temperament are especially important; they not only represent potentials to be developed but to a large extent influence the social stimulus value we possess for others. I hope that the reader will view the life course as a constantly evolving product of the complex interactions among the biological, the psychological, and the sociocultural realms.

In the past two decades, our knowledge of the linkages between phases of the life course has been enormously increased by systematic research that has followed the same individuals over some period of years. I have tried to reflect the major findings of this research, most of it bearing on the life course in the United States. Some research has also drawn upon records from the past, to indicate what development was like one or two generations ago or even a hundred years ago. Historians have become interested in examining the life course in earlier eras just as other social scientists have been discovering the extent to which even short-term social change modifies the duration and character of the life course each new crop of babies can expect. Within the limits of space available, I have more often tried to document historical change than to draw comparisons with the life course in other societies, though the latter are equally illuminating of human development. I hope that enough comparative material has been included to make evident the vast range of possibilities that exist for the human life course. The reader is invited to make additional comparisons with the life courses of persons in other societies and those within other segments of American society.

My efforts to document the relationships, transitions, and problematic aspects of the life course in comtemporary America were greatly facilitated by the research program of the Institute of Human Development at the University of California, Berkeley, with which I have been affiliated for the past 25 years. I want to thank my associates there for their helpfulness and their efforts to broaden my perspectives. Dorothy Field, Hal Gelb, Norma Haan, Marjorie Honzik, Mary Cover Jones, Paul Mussen, and Arlene Skolnick each read one or more chapters and called to my attention new references, occasional errors, and awkward sentences. My former student, Shigeru Kojima, read the entire manuscript and made many useful suggestions. The writing of this book has also been facilitated by the current support of my research through grant AG 4178 from the National Institute of Aging.

I am much indebted to my secretary, Jane Rateaver, for her speed, precision, and good humor in melding successive fragments of chapters into the word processor. She has also helped with the index. Alex Inkeles made helpful suggestions all along the way but I thank him most of all for proposing that I write a book on the life course. My son Christopher pruned excess verbiage from several chapters. My greatest debt is to my wife, Suzanne, whose careful reading and thoughtful comments on each chapter were one more respect in which she has enriched my own life course for nearly half a century.

THE LIFE COURSE

THE LIFE COURSE

CHAPTER 1
THE LIFE COURSE AND ITS DETERMINANTS

No man is an island, entire of itself.
Each is a piece of the continent,
A part of the main,
—John Donne

On the average, a middle-class American born in the late twentieth century can expect to live to about the age of 70. Many will survive to 80 or 90, while others will die by 50. Each of us follows a unique course, the outcome of the interaction between our genetic makeup, the social placement of our families, the personalities of those who rear us, and the millions of events and experiences—scheduled or fortuitous—that affect us from the day we are born to the day we die. Nevertheless, we are all subject to the same laws that govern the unfolding of our genetic potentials in the course of physiological development and decline; each of us must prepare to take our place in a particular society, and the roles that are available to most of us, while numerous, are nevertheless limited. We actively seek out or carve out niches to occupy, but certain parts of our life histories have been roughly scripted for us by the society and the era in which we live.

The primary goal of this book is to describe and analyze the expectable life course and the elements that go into shaping it in one way or another. Our genetic heritage, for example, has a lot to do with whether we are likely to live to 80 or 90 or to die at 40 or 50. That heritage also very largely determines our appearance, stature, physique, and intellectual potential, all of which tend to influence the opportunities we find or the obstacles we must surmount to achieve our goals.

A basic premise of this book is that human life is purposive, that each of us sets goals, be they short-term or long-term, beginning in our early years. Those goals, and our sense of who we are and what we can do, are to a very large extent influenced by the beliefs of our culture and, to an even greater extent, by the beliefs and behaviors of those who guide us through the early years. The early years do not *determine* what we become. I shall argue that just as anatomy need not become destiny in the life histories of men and women, childhood experience need not markedly affect adult outcomes. This is not to say that early experience is unimportant. A major question to be considered in the coming chapters is whether the course of a human life tends to show continuity over time or flexibility and change in response to new experience.

The study of the life course cuts across many disciplines. It is the study of human development viewed biologically, psychologically, and culturally. It requires a historical perspective, because the expectable life course—its length, the influences affecting it, and the ages at which various events are expected to happen—varies tremendously even within a single century.

Until recently, we owed our most insightful analyses of the life course to the writings of great novelists, playwrights, and biographers. Great literature explores lives in process; we see the actor in the network of persons and social happenings that shape goals, that permit or interfere with the attainment of satisfactions, and that reaffirm or call into question the character's identity or integrity. Biography and autobiography in particular can give us insights into life sequences and the integration of the countless experiences that are part of a full life. Therefore we shall draw upon the riches of literature as well as on the research of social scientists.

THE LIFE COURSE, AGING, AND TIME FRAMES

The life course is, by definition, a progression through time. Aging or *life time* is the most obvious dimension in the study of the life course, and it is difficult to imagine any treatment of the course that does not in general follow the individual chronologically, from birth to death. The infant's early growth is phenomenally rapid, but first words and first steps require a considerable development of the nervous system beyond that present at birth. Chronological age is closely tied to biological maturing, though the two are not identical. Some boys and girls mature much earlier than others, and there are also great variations in the timing of the decline in vigor and strength that occurs in later life.

Chronological age has its social as well as its biological and psychological correlates, and *social time* affords another frame for analysis. Social time may be defined as the set of norms that specify when particular life transitions or accomplishments are expected to occur in a particular society or social milieu.[1] In American society, where so many of a person's rights, privileges, and duties are specified by law, one's birth date determines when one can be admitted to public school and, subsequently, when one may drive a motor vehicle, drink alcoholic beverages, marry without parental consent, vote for elected officials, and, ultimately, when one may retire with full Social Security benefits.

Social time is not, however, necessarily meshed with a fixed chronological age. In many instances, not law but custom in the form of informal expectations will specify when certain roles or responsibilities are to be taken on. Such expectations will vary considerably from one milieu to another. Until what age, for example, should youth continue to attend school? There are quite different expectations for working-class teenagers, most of whom will not go to college, and for middle-class teenagers, most of whom will. Linked with the age at which one might be expected to complete schooling is the age at which a person is expected to enter the labor market, or to marry.

There may be considerable variability in the ages at which individuals enter into new social roles, but this does not mean that social expectations are of negligible importance. Being "on time" counts for something. Except for those who have decided that marriage and a family are not for them, the man or woman who reaches 30 without having married (or having established a close intimate relationship with a member of the opposite sex) is likely to feel that s/he is behind schedule. The man who has not found his occupational niche by age 40 is even more likely to feel that something is amiss in his life.

Precocity, on the other hand, has different meanings for the young and the old. The boy or girl who takes on adult patterns of smoking, drinking, and sexual relations will be seen as "fast" in more than one sense. And to be fast may in this instance be frowned upon more seriously than to be slow, especially by one's elders. Social time, then, provides guidelines by which progress along the life course may be assessed in particular cultures or social milieus.

The life course is not merely lived out in abstract time. Every life is anchored not only in a particular sociocultural context and geographical region but in a particular *historical time*. Historical time mirrors societal change, epoch-making events and cultural eras. Each generation has a different experience with war and depression, cataclysms and great discoveries, and each generation tends to see the world through lenses colored by the values and issues that are dominant in the formative years of its members. Even the birth rate at any given time will influence the quality of life experienced by members of the new generation being born. The birth rate was low during the Depression of the 1930s but almost doubled at the end of World War II, then gradually dropped back again. Elementary-school students in the late 1940s and the 1950s experienced overcrowding in their schools, the flourishing of a new "adolescent culture," and the student revolts of the 1960s.[2] Except in areas where there had been a recent influx of population as a result of migration, students in the 1970s and early 1980s found that there were more than enough classrooms and teachers to meet their needs, though some of the classrooms were showing wear. Teachers on college faculties, particularly the younger ones without tenure, have experienced insecurity because there has been less demand for their services than there was a few years ago. One generation's opportunities may be problems for the next generation.

Thus it will be necessary for us to deal with several different dimensions of time as we examine the life course. The thread we shall follow in our presentation will be the process of chronological aging, but we shall try to note throughout this book the variations that occur in biological aging, and the norms or constraints that are provided by expectations as to appropriate timing in the life course. Beyond this, we shall periodically stop to ask, "How do lives in one historical era differ from those in another?" or "How do events that may shape or shake up a society impinge upon young persons or those of mature years, influencing the courses of their lives?"

THE BIOLOGICAL COMPONENT

Before we become persons, we are organisms. The distinction may seem obvious, yet it will bear keeping in mind. An individual's biological makeup sets limits to potentials, and such attributes as strength, beauty, or height may predispose the possessor to pursue particular activities and social roles. The groups we belong to as well as our ability to perform in various social roles will be influenced by our sex, our appearance, our temperament, and our intelligence, and all of these depend to a significant degree on our genetic constitution and our early physiological development.

Genetic Input

A sociological or psychological analysis of the life course does not require a detailed understanding of genetics or of physiological development, but it is important to understand how biological factors exert their influence. Except for identical twins, no two individuals have the same genetic makeup; each of us has a unique combination of the half million or so genes whose DNA contains the genetic code or program for the development of the organism.[3] That program is set at conception. It may call for exceptional physical stature, strength, or longevity, or it may call for malformation or organic malfunction, disease, and early death. Most of the time it produces a mixed bag of attributes that are not markedly divergent from the average of a particular population.

What we actually become is, of course, not determined by heredity alone, but by the interaction of heredity and environment. Moreover, environmental effects do not begin to operate at birth, but immediately after conception. Indeed, among the most potent environmental influences to which we are subject are those experienced while we are still in the womb. In Chapter 3 we shall discuss these intrauterine influences, which tend to be related to the mother's health, diet, and to such factors as smoking and drinking practices and medicines taken.

Although our genetic makeup is determined at conception, it is by no means evident at birth. The proclivities that are programmed in the genes will to a large degree only be apparent through the gradual developmental unfolding that is called maturation, about which we shall have much more to say in Chapter 3. Body build; early or late sexual maturing; what we will look like at 20, at 40, or at 60; and how fast we are likely to age are all programmed in the genes. The programs can be modified somewhat by diet, disease, and personal practices and events, but given an average, adequate environment, genetically programmed changes will be occurring all our lives. The author, for example, suddenly appeared in a new light to his father when the latter was 85: At 50 the son had come to resemble his grandfather's appearance at that age, though the resemblance had never seemed great before. Suddenly the older man experienced the somewhat eerie feeling that his father, dead for more than 40 years, was standing before him.

Physiological Development and Aging

We do not all mature at the same rate, nor do changes in physical and intellectual development occur at the same time. Early walkers are not necessarily early talkers, and the precocious attainment of sexual maturity bears little relationship to one's intellectual maturity. A child's very fast early growth may lead adults to hold unrealistic expectations for him/her. Early sexual maturing in a girl may lead to pressures from older males, pressures that she is unprepared to deal with. We shall want to examine the consequences of variations in physiological development both in the light of social expectations held for persons of a given age and sex and in the light of the adaptational problems that may be posed for such persons.

Physical characteristics and physiological development have powerful influences on our views of ourselves. Body build and energy level, for example, influence how we are seen by others and how we see ourselves and feel about ourselves. Throughout the life course, but especially early and late in life, we tend to compare the changes we observe in our own bodies with the changes we observe in others.[4]

Apart from the psychological and social meanings attached to developmental and aging processes, however, there are intrinsic, biological realities with which we should be acquainted. The infant at six months is incapable of walking and talking, and the eight-year-old is incapable of many of the feats that are easily accomplished by the young adult. Here again, there may be great differences among individuals, but we need to know something about average potentials in order to get some idea of what we may anticipate in our own lives.

Disease and Impairment

At any stage, from embryonic life in the womb to old age, normal development may be thwarted by disease or injury. A normal, expectable life course includes a number of illnesses, major and minor, but some persons are born with or acquire impairments that make this expectable life course impossible. Severe malformations at birth, either as a consequence of genetic mutations or of the intrauterine effects of drugs or of maternal illness may lead to early death or to a life of helpless dependency. Many infants who would have survived for a very short time in the past are now living well into the adult years. The courses of their lives are markedly influenced by their impairments, but to a considerable extent they are subject to the same general developmental processes as their unimpaired peers.

We shall consider the effects of disease or impairment on the life course only as we note the kinds of adaptational problems that may be posed at different stages of life. Some impairments, such as blindness, deafness, and mental retardation have been much more systematically studied than others, but their effects on the life course as a whole have seldom been examined. We shall note such evidence as exists for the light it may throw on how the various determinants of the life course operate within different historical and cultural contexts.

THE SOCIOCULTURAL CONTEXT

No one has phrased the effects of culture on the course taken by the developing person more eloquently than the anthropologist Ruth Benedict:

> The life history of the individual is first and foremost an accommodation to the patterns and standards traditionally handed down in his community. From the moment of his birth the customs into which he is born shape his experience and behavior. By the time he can talk, he is a little creature of his culture, and by the time he is grown and able to take part in its activities, its habits are his habits, its beliefs his beliefs, its impossibilities his impossibilities.[5]

A culture may be defined as the set of beliefs, values, and practices that are widely shared by members of a society at any given time. The beliefs and view of the world that are shared in a particular milieu provide the individual with his or her cognitive map for exploring the accessible world. That map will change with life experience, but to a large extent the basic goals toward which a person strives will be defined by cultural values and standards. From our culture, for example, we derive our beliefs as to whether the fruits of a good life are to be enjoyed in the living thereof, or are to be realized only in an afterlife or reincarnation.

Through the process of socialization—the process of learning the way of life of our society and learning to adapt our behavior to that of others—we develop controls, goals, skills, and a sense of self. We learn early that certain behaviors and certain words are acceptable when we are with our peers but not with our parents. We learn that what is expected of a five-year-old is not an adequate standard for a seven-year-old. The attributes with which parents most want to imbue their children are derived not only from the culture but from the parents' placement in the social system. Inequalities tend to be perpetuated in almost all societies, regardless of their political and economic systems (beyond the very simplest societies) by virtue of the ability of parents to pass on values, skills, and resources that make for success.

Intergenerational transmission of the cultural heritage is always selective and partial because it always involves many persons with different life experiences. In complex societies, culture is far from homogeneous, and the particular version that a person comes to incorporate by virtue of social class, ethnic group, and religion may influence that person's identity as much as does physical appearance. What dialect does one speak? Does one crave soul food, tacos and refried beans, rice, or continental cuisine? What life patterns, beliefs, and goals is one led to take for granted by one's parents and peers?

The life course is channeled by culture and social structure in other ways as well. At what ages may sexually mature males and females associate freely and intimately? In the People's Republic of China, until very recently adolescent and young adult men and women had little opportunity to be alone together. Asked about the low rate of births to unmarried Chinese girls (in contrast to the high rate among American girls), a physician in Shanghai replied: "Do you think we are such fools as to let adolescent boys and girls go alone into the parks?" Marriage of a man before his late twenties is frowned upon. Thus the life course may be scheduled in important respects by the requirements of authoritarian governments and bureaucratic organizations.[6]

Age norms are an important part of culture. "Act your age" is heard not merely from our parents or other adults when we are small but from our children and other folk when our hair has grayed and we are expected to be sedate and "mature." The fun-loving older woman who likes to dance and party may be accused of trying to act "kittenish"; the 70-year-old man who retains a keen interest in physical contact with the opposite sex may be seen as a "dirty old man." In some cultures the old are not only viewed as asexual but as once again innocent; in others it is assumed that older folks have been around, and older men and women may give expression to the most scatological humor. Whether a person is regarded as ready for the shelf at 65 or 70 or is revered as wise and distinguished depends as much on social norms as on individual attributes.

HISTORICAL TIME
AND COHORT INFLUENCES

Even in relatively stable, traditional societies, each generation has its unique themes and problems. A period of drought and famine is believed to have resulted in the abandonment of the great cities of the Mayan civilization nearly a thousand years ago. Those who were young at the start of this period must have gloried in the high culture of Mayan life and the prospects of even greater glory in the future. Their children's lives must have been very different, with starvation and social disintegration the basic facts of daily life.

In modern industrial society, with its rapid technological and social change, new generations regularly face situations vastly different from those that confronted their parents. My parents, born nearly two decades before automobiles began appearing on America's streets, later witnessed not only the airplane but the radio, television, satellites, and the era of the computer. Hand in hand with the products of technology came changes in values, from Victorian reticence surrounding sexuality to the blatant use of sex in advertising and entertainment and the easy sexuality of the late twentieth century. The expectations of a normal life course changed as much as did the modes of transportation and communication.

Since new generations are constantly replacing older ones, there are no sharp boundaries to generations. Moreover, social changes that make a profound difference for the life course are not spaced evenly; a single event such as a war, a drought, or a new invention can bring about such changes of perspective and practices, in government and in private life, that younger and older children in the same family seem to be living in different worlds. Therefore social scientists use the concept of the *cohort* rather than that of the generation when they want to specify the particular slice of time that a given group experiences.[7]

A *cohort* is a group that moves along together through the life course and thus experiences historical events at about the same age. The term was originally used by demographers to designate all persons born in a given time period (usually a year or a decade). An example will be helpful. The cohort of males born in 1920 in the United States experienced the Great Depression of the 1930s as adolescents and, when World War II came to the United States late in 1941, most of them were drafted into military service. By contrast, the cohort of males born in 1930 experienced the Great Depression as young children and were too young for military service in World War II. The meanings of the Depression and the war were very different for these two groups; the differences show up in their occupational and marital histories, as the sociologist Glen Elder has shown in his analysis of long-term longitudinal data.[8]

A cohort's placement in historical time tells us much about the opportunities and the constraints placed upon its members. But beyond the effects of particular historical events, there are more subtle influences that differentiate cohorts or generations. The great German sociologist Mannheim (1952) called attention to "the problem of generations," noting that particular periods in historical time have a distinctive *Zeitgeist* (literally "spirit of the time").[9] Individuals growing up at such times are predisposed to characteristic modes of thought and experience. Just as Benedict would say that the child and the developing adult are creatures of their culture, Mannheim would say that they are also creatures of their time. There is no contradiction here, for cultural change is manifest in changing values, beliefs, and actions. Cohorts thus experience somewhat different cultures or subcultures.

In the study of the life course, then, we must be attentive to biological givens, to developmental processes and the socialization of the person, to social and cultural contexts that not only define the meaning of life and the goals to be sought but the means available for the pursuit of one's goals, and finally to the historical context and the way in which the events and the spirit of a particular era shape the life experience of members of a given cohort. All these components are potentially in interaction. The human infant is not merely a passive recipient of experience but a struggling, striving creature who early begins to organize information about the influences upon it and selectively adapt to them. It sets goals and pursues them. Life outcomes are a product of the continual interactions of person and life experience.

DETERMINANTS
OF LIFE-COURSE OUTCOMES

In the next chapter we shall consider a number of theoretical formulations that attempt to explain or characterize the stages, the transitions, the sequences of social roles, and the sense of purpose and identity that go to make up a life course. Before doing so, it may be useful to examine more closely some of the larger components and contexts that we have thus far discussed in rather general terms. Biological, psychological, and social processes constantly interact, and they do so in describable ways even if the outcome of the interaction is not predictable.

In the first few weeks of life, it is almost impossible to determine which behavioral tendencies are biologically given and which are a product of sociocultural shaping except as specific genetic "markers" are associated with inborn tendencies.[10] Almost immediately after conception, there begins an interaction between genetic potential and the intrauterine environment (which is itself affected by the diet, drug use, and life regime of the mother-to-be). Therefore, in practice we cannot neatly distinguish the effects of the components and contexts we have discussed. As a consequence, we shall find it necessary to label the phenomena we are dealing with in terms that reflect more directly observable phenomena.

When we look at life histories, we can usually identify certain features of persons that had a bearing on the way others responded to them, and we can get a pretty good idea of how caretakers, settings, life events, and personal efforts went into shaping those lives at any given time. In my own work, I have found it useful to distinguish four classes of influences on the development of the life course and the individual's performance in the various roles that structure that course—son or daughter, student, spouse, parent, worker, friend, citizen, and so on. They are:

1. The person's own attributes, constitutionally given or developed—intelligence, appearance, strength, health, temperament.
2. The sources of socialization, support, and guidance that initially orient persons to the world in which they will function and subsequently assist them to cope with problems or offer emotional support when effective solutions are limited.
3. The opportunities available to the person or the obstacles that are encountered in the environment, as influenced by social class, ethnic group, age, sex, and social network; as well as the effects of war, depression, and other major social changes that affect particular birth cohorts differently; and, not least, the vagaries of chance.
4. Investments of effort that persons make in their own behalf (commitments) and the mobilization of resources to attain desired goals.

It is apparent that these components do not neatly coincide with the orientations of disciplines studying the life course. While personal resources are influenced significantly by biological givens, they are by no means biologically determined. The development of intelligence owes a great deal to the richness of stimuli and the intellectual challenges encountered in one's social environment. Whether we are strong or weak depends on our physique, on diet, and on how we choose to develop and use our physique. Even our appearance, though biologically given, is evaluated positively or negatively in terms of criteria of beauty held by members of a given society or segment of society. Moreover, personal resources are themselves subject to change—sometimes purposive change, such as comes about through education or training, and sometimes unwanted change, such as that resulting from illness, injury, or aging.

Much of culture is transmitted by our early caretakers and peers. Most often our parents are the ones who orient us to the world of places, things, and people. They give us a sense of whether the world is threatening or friendly, depending largely on how they have found it in their own experience. They let us know (not always accurately) which of our problems are our fault and which result from other people's actions. They console us (or blame us) when we are sad or confused. In short, they and other persons throughout the life course can help us over the rough spots or let us down when we need help. They can help us acquire skills and competence or discourage us from doing so. As one writer has recently put it, each of us has a "convoy" of persons who provide us with social and emotional support throughout our lives, though the makeup of the convoy changes as people move into or out of our lives.[11] This convoy or network of relationships is partly specified by the ways of our society, partly reflects where we are and who we are, and is subject to the influences of historical events and the uncertainties of all human life.

What we take for granted and what we encounter in our day-to-day experience will depend on our age, sex, race, social status, and cohort membership to a considerable extent. If we are born in an urban slum, we are unlikely to have an opportunity to prepare for Harvard Medical School. As children, we will be exposed to different grammatical constructions, have a more limited vocabulary, and have quite different aspirations for our adult years from children born to upper-middle-class professionals in a suburb. We slum children will have a shorter life expectancy. We will more often be discriminated against and be given less favorable treatment by teachers, police officers, physicians, and others than will our upper-middle-class suburban counterparts. Social structure and group membership help to determine what we can and what we can't do.

But social structure only *tends* to determine what we can do. Each of us is potentially an autonomous doer who can make things happen. We may have to work twice as hard to get into Harvard Medical School, but if we have the intellectual potential, the necessary guidance and support, and above all the will to persevere, we may be able to bring off the improbable, if not the impossible. As we develop and organize our personal resources and our experiences, we become "our own persons." We cannot always succeed, but unless we mobilize our efforts in the pursuit of goals to which we have committed ourselves, we are most unlikely to attain our goals. There is an element of intentionality in every life. We shall seek to understand how such an element is forged and how it helps to determine outcomes in later life.

METHODOLOGICAL ISSUES

From autobiographies or personal memoirs written in the later years, we learn how the writers have come to see themselves and how they assess the influences of other persons and events on the direction their lives have taken.[12] Varied motives lead to writing such documents: the wish to understand one's own development; the wish to set the record straight by giving a firsthand account of important historical events in which a person participated; self-justification, especially if one has earned the reputation of scoundrel; or perhaps merely the hope that one's reputation will be sufficient to sell a manuscript and bring in more income. Even a diary written for one's own later consultation may serve a number of motives. Just as "no man is an island, entire of itself," neither is any man or woman unbiased in reviewing his or her life course.

Nevertheless, the meaning of any life is most fully apparent to the person leading that life. Human behavior has its unconscious elements, but most of our actions are intentional, and the actor best knows the intent. To understand why a person married at a particular time, took or didn't take a particular job, we had best ask that person. Moreover, we had best ask them at the time, or very shortly thereafter, for cognitive processes have a way of recasting memories of past actions. We tend to see the past very much in the light of the present.

There are, then, a number of methodological issues that must be kept in mind in attempting to achieve accurate generalizations about the life course in a particular society and a particular time. One issue relates to the difference between first person or subjective accounts and more objective observations, especially systematic assessments, made by others. Another issue relates to the dangers of retrospective falsification, if one asks about events and intents in the distant (or even slightly remote) past. These are much more obvious in their effects than is another methodological issue that must concern us—the problem of disentangling age and cohort effects.

Age versus Cohort Effects

Suppose we take a public opinion survey of political attitudes and find that 60-year-olds are more conservative than 40-year-olds. We may be tempted to generalize that persons become more conservative as they grow older. But suppose we are fortunate enough to have information on the attitudes toward civil rights of 40-year-olds two decades earlier, and we find that they were already more conservative than 40-year-olds today? In this case we may note that there have been shifts over time in the general population, shifts in the direction of more liberal attitudes toward governmental provision for health and welfare, civil liberties, and other public issues. The effects we might have attributed to age turn out, instead, to be cohort differences. Actually, not only cohort and age differences but period effects (effects of current developments) are found in the case of political attitudes.[13] In some respects, for example, political attitudes in the United States have become far more conservative in the 1980s than they were in the 1960s. Older persons, if they have not changed, may actually be more liberal than younger ones on certain issues. Cohort differences are also linked with increasing levels of education among more recent cohorts, so that a number of variables have to be controlled (statistically) in order to make defensible generalizations about age differences even when we have data for different time periods.

Only when we have data based on comparable measures administered to the same persons on two or more occasions can we generalize with any accuracy about the effects of aging on particular beliefs or behaviors. Longitudinal studies entail periodic observations and measures on the same group of individuals, permitting us to assess individual change over time. Even here, our generalizations will be limited to persons of specified characteristics within a given historical period. In a study of a group of men and women who have been followed regularly for the past 50 years by the staff of the University of California Institute of Human Development, we found that while men with blue-collar jobs or lower white-collar jobs had tended to become more conservative over the years, professionals had become somewhat more liberal.

Dealing with Retrospective Bias

Unfortunately, there have been few long-term longitudinal studies, and therefore we must frequently make the best use we can of data derived from asking about the past. Even in a longitudinal study, we cannot secure information about every important event at the time of its occurrence, so we must always depend to some extent on retrospective data. And always, we shall want to maintain a healthy skepticism about reconstructions of the past.

Perhaps the most thorough study of the process of long-term retrospective recall was made by a social psychologist, Marian Radke Yarrow, and her associates at the National Institute of Mental Health.[14] They located a nursery-school research unit that had for many years interviewed mothers of enrolled children to secure information about the children's behavior and development, mother-child relationships, and so on. The research staff went back to the mothers a number of years later and interviewed some whose children had been in the school fairly recently (3 to 8 years previously), an intermediate group enrolled 9 to 17 years previously, and those whose children had been in the school more than 18 years before. The mothers were asked many of the same questions that had been put to them originally at the school: Was the child easily upset? When had it begun to walk and talk? What kinds of problems had there been with the child as a preschooler?

Mothers whose children attended the school most recently recalled the child's early personality and their child-rearing practices somewhat more accurately than those who were more remote from the early years, but even at three to eight years there were many discrepancies. In general, what the mothers reported retrospectively differed markedly from what they had reported when the child was in school, except for such questions as whether or not the child had been separated from the father for a year or more in the early years, age of first tooth, first walking and first talking, and the child's relative physical status (height, weight) when in nursery school. Recollections of the child's personality and the early mother-child relationship were strongly influenced by the warmth of the *current* relationship and by the child's *current* personality at the time of the interview. That is, mothers who had a warm relationship with the child at the time of the interview (when the child might be anywhere from eight to 35 years old) remembered the nursery-school-aged child's attributes more favorably than they had reported them to be when the child was at the school. Conversely, those who now had a poor relationship with the child remembered the child less favorably. If the child currently seemed shy, the mother was more likely to remember shyness as a preschool characteristic, and vice versa. Recent relationships and characteristics colored recollections of the past to such a degree that acceptance of current reports as "facts" would often lead to very wrong inferences about the effects of early rearing and early personality on adolescent and adult personality. The events of later years rewrite the remembrance of things past.

We create myths to provide continuity between past and present. One of Yarrow's most interesting findings was obtained from interviews with some of the children themselves. Their recollections of early childhood were strongly influenced by their mother's recollections. Indeed, there was a closer resemblance between the child's and the mother's retrospective reports than between the child's recollections and the actual data secured when the child was in the nursery school. Some of us recognize the extent to which our early memories depend on what we have been told we were like, but we nevertheless tend to accept what we have been told as "the way it was."

Sometimes it is possible to secure information on past attitudes and life events from diaries and letters. Indeed, much of our information on the typical life course in past times comes from such sources. Family historians and demographers have been particularly resourceful in examining such materials according to the age and circumstances of the writers.[15] In trying to reconstruct an individual's subjective life history, letters and diaries can serve as a corrective for some retrospective biases. When we read letters we wrote many years ago, we are frequently amazed to find out how much our views—which we thought quite stable—have changed. Often it is the times that have changed, and we have changed with them, quite unaware of how differently we once saw particular issues.

When our objective is to learn about past life transitions or rites of passage, those socially ritualized passages from one life stage or status to another,[16] the use of multiple informants can also help to arrive at a more accurate account, since different individuals tend to experience such transitions in very distinct ways. Sometimes one can use official or unofficial statistics as guideposts for attempting to delineate typical ages for certain events, as in the case of marriage and the birth of a first child.

The use of public opinion surveys based on carefully selected samples of the population goes back only to the 1930s. Such surveys give us some baseline data for persons of specified characteristics. Follow-up of a previously studied group—called a *panel survey*—is a much more recent social-science technique, but one that is beginning to give us an approximation to longitudinal data on some topics. For example, there have now been a number of such studies which bear on the process of "status attainment" or occupational attainment in the early years.[17] Such studies permit us to ascertain what attributes influence one's chances of achieving high attainment independent of the advantages or disadvantages of one's family background. They also permit examination of the effects of early marriage or childbearing on a man's or a woman's ultimate social status.

The student who seeks to understand research on the life course need not be greatly concerned about the technical aspects of methodology, but should keep in mind that it is easy to confound age and cohort differences, and it is dangerous to accept retrospective accounts as gospel. Indeed, even the most admirably moral, intellectually gifted, and well-meaning persons may be quite unable to reconstruct the past in an unbiased manner, or even to remember it accurately. Forewarned, we can be skeptical of personal recitals of past influences and yet be sensitive to the present meanings of such accounts.

NOTES

1. For a good discussion, see Bernice Neugarten, "Time, Life and the Life Cycle," *American Journal of Psychiatry,* 136, no. 7 (July 1979), 887–93.
2. For an overview, see *Youth, Transition to Adulthood,* Report of the Panel of Youth of the President's Science Advisory Committee (Chicago: University of Chicago Press, 1974).
3. Our knowledge of genetics has been greatly advanced by recent biochemical discoveries relating to the structure of DNA, but researchers have mapped only a tiny proportion of the effects of particular gene combinations.
4. No one has more vividly commented on this process than the French writer Marcel Proust in his *Remembrance of Things Past* and especially in *The Past Recaptured.*
5. Ruth Benedict, *Patterns of Culture* (New York: Houghton Mifflin, 1934), pp. 2–3.
6. Most obviously in such respects as compulsory education, compulsory military service at a given age, and compulsory retirement.
7. A superb discussion is given in Norman Ryder, "The Cohort as a Concept in the Study of Social Change," *American Sociological Review,* 30 (1965).
8. Glen Elder, *Children of the Great Depression* (Chicago: University of Chicago Press, 1974).
9. Karl Mannheim, "The Problem of Generations," in Karl Mannheim, *Essays on the Sociology of Knowledge* (London: Routledge, Keagan and Paul, 1952).
10. A genetic marker is an objectively verifiable behavioral or structural feature that indicates the presence of a particular gene (allele) or gene combination.
11. Robert Kahn, "Aging and Social Support," in Matilda White Riley, ed., *Aging from Birth to Death* (Boulder, CO: Westview Press, 1979), pp. 79–90.
12. Issues in the use of personal documents for research purposes are discussed in Norman Denzin, *The Research Act* (Chicago: Aldine, 1970), Chapter 10, "The Life History Method."
13. On this point see Norval Glenn, *Cohort Analysis* (Beverly Hills, CA: Sage Publications, 1977).

14. Marian Radke Yarrow et al., "Recollections of Childhood: A Study of the Retrospective Method," *Monographs of the Society for Research in Child Development,* 35, no. 5 (Serial No. 138), 1970.

15. See, for example, either *Daedalus* for Spring 1968 ("Historical Population Studies") or John Demos and Sarane Boocock, eds., *Turning Points: Historical and Sociological Essays on the Family* (Chicago: University of Chicago Press, 1978).

16. Examples of rites of passage are baptism or confirmation (entry into the religious community), graduation ceremonies, engagement and marriage, and retirement ceremonies.

17. One of the best of these is reported in William Sewell and R. Hauser, *Education, Occupation and Earnings: Achievement in the Early Career* (New York: Academic Press, 1975).

CHAPTER 2
THEORIES
AND THEMES
IN THE STUDY
OF THE
LIFE COURSE

*There is nothing so practical
as a good theory.*
—Kurt Lewin

Theories are systematic efforts to formulate explanations of natural phenomena, to make sense out of what one observes or experiences. The philosopher of science Abraham Kaplan neatly phrases the function of a theory: "A theory is more than a synopsis of the moves that have been played in the game of nature; it also sets forth some idea of the rules of the game, by which the moves become intelligible."[1] Note that Kaplan specifies "some idea" and not necessarily an elegant and complete explanation.

Theories of the life course come in varied sizes and shapes. Some try to deal with the whole span of life; others seek to explain some stage or aspect of life. There are and long have been those persons who believe that our destinies are written in the stars. Astrology is perhaps the most elaborately formulated attempt to account for individual character and life experience, doing so on the basis of the position of heavenly bodies at the exact time of a person's birth. But once astronomers gave us an adequate theory of the movement of the stars and planets, the assumptions of astrologists were no longer tenable. Most of our current theories of the life course are much more modest; they seek to identify general tendencies or sequences of growth and social experience that derive from the nature of the human organism and the processes of physical, cognitive, and psychosocial development.

GENERAL PERSPECTIVES
ON THE LIFE COURSE

Less focused than attempts at explanation are general perspectives that afford a way of looking at the life course. The *developmental perspective,* for example, assumes a degree of "unfolding" of potentials that exist in the organism as it grows to maturity. From this perspective, one looks for typical processes of growth as well as for circumstances that influence the rate and qualities of growth. Once the organism has attained maturity, however, the developmental perspective tends to lose its focus. It is no longer clearly evident that growth goes on, except as an accretion of experience, and the delineation of typical processes becomes problematic at the very least.

The human animal exceeds all others in ability to learn, and this ability underlies the elaboration in human society of institutionalized modes of teaching that prepare individuals to function as members of society. As noted in Chapter 1, such teaching and learning is called *socialization.* Socialization is a lifelong process, the process of transmitting the skills and knowledge needed to perform roles that one will (or may) occupy as one moves along the life course. Much socialization effort is directed toward the developing child: providing the child with knowledge of its surroundings, the behavior expected of it, and the life goals that are deemed most important in a given society. But socialization goes on long after physical maturity has been achieved, and the *socialization perspective,* when focused on the adult life course, stresses the importance of the demands that other members of the society make upon the individual.[2] Such demands continue to shape interests, attitudes, and life goals, as well as providing motivation for learning new skills.

Closely akin to the perspective of adult socialization is that which views the life course as a sequence of adaptations to events and circumstances. One must adapt not only to the socially patterned demands of others, but also to one's growth and developmental problems, to changing life conditions and relationships, to frustrations and losses, to illness, and, if we survive long enough, to declining strength and abilities. An *adaptational perspective* leads us to examine how persons seek to cope with events and circumstances that demand responses different from habitual routines and require some modification of our existing strategies for getting along.[3]

Any adequate theory of the life course must incorporate elements of all of these perspectives since the life course so patently entails development, socialization, and adaptation. How the elements are to be combined and how they interact at various periods is perhaps the major issue in seeking a theory of the life course.

As noted above, beyond the years of physical growth, the developmental perspective loses much of the cogency that it derives from the regularities of physical maturation and cognitive development. Full body size and strength may be attained a bit later than full cognitive power, but men and women do not generally show much physical growth except in girth once they have passed their early twenties, and while they may gain knowledge, wisdom, and perhaps even wit, they gain mental power only by specialized learning, not by increased cognitive capacities. Nevertheless, the effort to achieve a developmental framework that will accommodate the middle years has brought into being two competing perspectives that we shall examine in greater detail as we proceed. One of these perspectives has been called the "timing-of-events" model and the other the "normative-crisis" model.

The Timing-of-Events Model

The *timing-of-events model* is based on the concept of social time that we encountered in the last chapter. In a given society (or sector of a complex society) at a given time, according to this perspective, there is an expected time for making major life transitions—for finishing the learning tasks of childhood and adolescence and taking on adult occupational and familial roles, for becoming self-sufficient, for marrying, for having children, and for becoming a responsible, respected member of the community. The expected times may not be sharply defined, but they are well enough defined within a band of years so that a person has a feeling of being on schedule, early, or late. I well recall how a colleague, unmarried at 40, regarded himself in the mirror of our shared hotel room, patted his somewhat rotund middle, and asked, "Do you think I'm too old to marry?" He had undoubtedly been asked hundreds of times in the previous 10 to 15 years, "Bill, when are you going to get married?" No one had to tell him that the average age for a male to marry in American society was then in the mid-twenties.

Being off schedule can be a source of stress to the extent that the norms relating to timing are clearly defined in the society. Where there are well-defined age norms for many events in adult life, the general contour of life transitions is given by the culture (the belief system of the society) rather than by biological processes. Adaptation is most urgently demanded when a person is unable or unwilling to make transitions at an expected time or when a person is confronted with disruption of an expected state (such as widowhood or premature forced retirement). The timing-of-events model provides one potential framework, then, for viewing the major transitions of adult life, predicting expectable sequences, and identifying certain types of life crisis.[4]

The Normative-Crisis Model

Quite a different framework is provided by the *normative-crisis model,* which assumes that even in the adult years there are certain tasks that must be accomplished somewhat in sequence if the person is to continue to grow, psychologically and socially.[5] Such tasks give rise to expectable stages; and theories that incorporate this perspective, such as those of Erikson and of Levinson—soon to be examined—assume that the life course is a sequence of such stages. At each stage (or, in Levinson's theory, age level), a person confronts a major task which poses a kind of crisis in that failure to accomplish the task threatens future achievement. Hence the label "normative crisis." One must expect life to pose a series of critical problems demanding resolution.

In childhood and adolescence, the tasks to be accomplished are those relating to the achievement of competence and autonomy, while in the adult years tasks have more to do with a person's relationships to others and with the acceptance of one's own life story and identity. Thus developmental, socialization, and adaptational perspectives are again incorporated, but the nature of the demands for adaptation is quite different from that in the timing-of-events model.

With these general considerations in mind, we turn now to more specific formulations.

STAGE THEORIES OF DEVELOPMENT

A stage may be defined as a single step or period in a progression or sequence. *Stage* may be primarily a descriptive term, useful for designating what tends to be going on at a particular developmental period; or the term may embody a theoretical explanation of what is going on. Infancy, childhood, and adolescence, for example, are simply descriptive terms for periods in the aging process; they have come to symbolize quite different constellations of physical, psychological, and social development, but the terms themselves do not explain anything.

As an explanatory tool, the concept of *stage* carries the implication that attainment of one level of functioning or set of competencies rests on the prior mastery of a lower level and is necessary for progression to a higher level. Consider this sequence: sit—walk—run. Children must be able to sit and to coordinate the motions of their heads and arms before they can walk without falling down, and they must be able to walk before they can run. We can easily see a direct relationship between the subsidiary skills necessary for the stage of sitting and those that are required for walking and running. On the other hand, even though most children learn to walk before they learn to swim, there is no necessary connection between the two, and in fact the infant can be taught to swim long before it is capable of walking. Therefore it would mean little to talk of a swimming stage.

Stages of Physiological Development

Normal physical development or maturation follows a highly predictable course. As Kagan has aptly put it, the script "guarantees that we will crawl before we run and babble before we speak."[6] The child's assimilation of early experience and hence its psychological and social development in the early years will rest upon its maturational stage. Thus, to a considerable extent, the stages of cognitive and personality development that may be discerned in the early years are linked with its physiological development.

Phases of biological development set broad limits to the social roles that persons occupy, and they cannot be ignored in any theory of the life course. Charlotte

Buhler, one of the first modern students of the life course, distinguished five major biological phases:[7]

1. A period of progressive growth without reproductive ability (0–15+).
2. A period of progressive growth with the onset of reproductive ability (approximately 15–22).
3. A period of reproductive ability without further growth (22–45+).
4. A period of beginning decline, with loss of reproductive ability by the female early in the period (45–65 or 70).
5. A period of sharper decline, often with loss of reproductive ability in both sexes (65 or 70 to death).

These periods can be roughly dated by age, but it is at once obvious that the boundaries are very approximate, especially at the upper levels of age. Some 80-year-olds are as vigorous as other 60-year-olds. But everyone who survives long enough goes through these stages, and to a degree at least, these are socially recognized age categories in modern societies.

Biology thus sets limits to physical and mental abilities. Even if these limits are only roughly linked to chronological age, they are very definitely linked to our conceptions of ourselves as we move along the life course. We shall see just how in subsequent chapters.

Stages of Cognitive Development

How do we come to perceive and make sense of the world that surrounds us? A century ago, William James wrote that the baby, "assailed by eyes, ears, nose, skin and entrails at once, feels that all is one great blooming, buzzing confusion."[8] Now we know that what the infant is experiencing is quite different from what the adults on the scene are experiencing, while at the same time we know that the infant is from the first engaged in sorting out and organizing its responses to what is going on around it. We owe our most cogent formulation of the way in which the child comes to know its world to the great Swiss scholar Jean Piaget, who spent more than 50 of his 84 years in observation and systematic theorizing about the ways in which infants and children interact with their environments and organize their experiences.[9]

Piaget saw the infant and child as actively striving to come to grips with and make sense of everything with which s/he comes into contact. In the beginning, the infant is a bundle of reflexes, reflexes that permit him/her to touch, taste, and in general manipulate the objects with which s/he is in contact. Reflexes quickly become coordinated, and the infant's responses become purposively exploratory rather than merely being reactive.

We shall discuss the central features of Piaget's theory of cognitive development in the next chapter. It is not a theory of the life course, but a formulation of developmental stages that no theory of the life course can disregard, for cognitive processes are basic to human functioning. Piaget found evidence for four major stages in cognitive development: the sensorimotor, during the first 18 months, when reflexes are coordinated and experience is organized without the primary use of symbols (i.e., prelinguistic thought); the preoperational stage (from about 18 months to about 6 years), in which the child uses symbolic referents but has not yet developed the ability to reason back and forth, invoking the examination of opposite possibilities; the stage of concrete operations (about 6–12 years), in which logical principles are mastered but are bound to concrete objects and events; and finally, the stage of formal, operational thought in which abstract properties and relationships can be invoked and hypotheses formulated about them. Each of the stages is dependent on attainment of the previous stage, and indeed, each stage contains substages that build upon previous attainment. Except for formal, operational thought, they are stages that all normal persons go through, and are only slightly influenced by the nature of the milieu in which the infant and child is reared, according to Piaget. But they are not entirely a reflection of biological maturation, for they depend upon the child's opportunity to interact with its environment.

Although not everyone attains the stage of formal operational thought, those who do so are likely to have developed this ability by adolescence. No further stages of development are postulated—not because cognitive growth stops, but because full capacity has been reached, and what a person does with his or her potentialities will determine the further elaboration of cognitive skills. Many developmental psychologists question parts of Piaget's formulations, but his basic postulates are generally accepted.

Closely related to Piaget's theory of cognitive development are theories that relate to stages of attainment in personality development and in moral judgment. We shall introduce these in later chapters.

Psychosocial Stage Theories

If we owe Piaget a great debt for his illumination of cognitive development, our debt to Sigmund Freud derives from his having revealed the less rational side of human behavior and its roots in early experience. Freud can hardly be said to have had a theory of the life course, but he had a theory of the origins of personality and especially of the problematic aspects of personality.[10] His formulations underlie almost all stage theories of psychosocial development.

Freud's Psychosexual Stages. Freud's view of human nature and its vulnerability was rooted in biology, particularly in the conflicts engendered in the infant by the imposition of social and cultural constraints on the expression of biological, particularly sexual, drives. For Freud, neurosis and other personality problems of the adult years were to be understood largely in terms of what had happened in infancy and early childhood. If all went well, the infant and child would pass through a series of stages of psychosexual development—oral, anal, and genital— each of which entailed securing bodily pleasure through these highly sensitive, "erogenous" zones of the body. But if as a consequence of parental anxieties or failure to achieve gratification through other channels the child became fixated on securing pleasure through oral or anal modes, Freud posited that particular personality attributes would be activated. Some persons would become "oral types," overeating and otherwise gaining satisfaction through the mouth. Others would become "anal types," hoarding and behaving in a constricted, constipated way.

Perhaps the keystone of psychoanalytic theory is the Oedipal resolution, through which the male child gives up his close ties with his mother and shifts his identification or sense of resemblance to his father. Identification entails not only feeling close to and sharing feelings with, but also wanting to resemble the person with whom one identifies. Because the mother is in most societies the basic caretaker and the provider of food and tender love, Freud assumed (correctly, it appears) that most infants and young children feel closer to their mothers than to anyone else. This early identification must clearly be shifted in the case of boys if they are to learn the skills and attitudes considered manly. Freud hypothesized (though he asserted his views more boldly than as a hypothesis) that little boys want to possess their mothers sexually. Thus they would become rivals to their fathers. But the powerful father is a fearsome figure, a potential castrator, and so as the better part of valor the little boy comes to identify with the aggressor rather than with the nurturing mother.

In predicting that boys are more likely to identify with a punitive than with a nurturing father, Freud was quite wrong. Many studies have demonstrated that boys are more likely to feel close to and want to resemble a father who is loving and accepting. Nevertheless, Freud seems to have been the first theorist to recognize the very important processes of early emotional development and to focus on the problem of the male child's coming to pattern himself on his father rather than his mother. His psychosexual stages have, moreover, become the point of departure for what has been the most influential theory of the life course yet formulated, that of Erik Erikson.

Erikson's Eight Stages of Man.   Clinically trained in psychoanalysis, Erikson built upon Freud's observations and formulations, but his writings draw also upon extensive cross-cultural experience and intensive biographical study of the lives of such titans as George Bernard Shaw, Gandhi, and Luther. Perhaps the most influential of the concepts Erikson has introduced is "psychosocial identity." In an autobiographical essay, Erikson (1970) described how he achieved his own sense of who and what he was as a young man.[11] The stepson of a Jewish pediatrician whom his mother married after being abandoned by her first (Danish) husband, Erikson early rebelled against the conventional standards and expectations of his parents. After finishing the German *Gymnasium,* he roamed Europe as an artist-wanderer until persuaded by a friend to join him as a teacher of young children in a small psychoanalytically oriented school in Vienna. Psychoanalytic training under Anna Freud prepared him as a child analyst. His association with other analysts, his interests and values as a professional, and his feeling of continuity and coherence in his own life all entered into his sense of identity. Subsequently, he observed children under study at the Institute of Human Development at Berkeley and, through short field trips with several outstanding anthropologists, he became acquainted at first hand with the cultures of the Sioux of South Dakota and the Yurok of Northern California. For Erikson, identity reflects not only one's feelings of uniqueness, but the realization of one's ties to others. It entails a sense of having grown yet of remaining the same through one's commitments and coherent history.

Erikson's theory of the life cycle derives, then, from a wide range of observation of human behavior informed by the psychoanalytic perspective. First presented in *Childhood and Society* (1950) as "eight stages of man," the formulation has been elaborated somewhat in later works, but the eight stages remain as originally stated.[12] The theory is epigenetic in that certain basic issues or behavioral propensities exist in some form from the start, but each becomes especially salient at a particular developmental stage. Each stage presents a challenging task that must be accomplished in order to permit further normal development. Each stage, in turn, leads to further differentiation of the personality, and each new accomplishment must be integrated in experience and drawn upon in meeting later developmental tasks. Erikson's stages are listed in Fig. 2-1. We shall discuss these in greater detail in subsequent chapters; here it is enough to note Erikson's belief that these issues or tasks must be dealt with in a particular order and that they are posed for the individual at age levels that reflect societal expectations.

The attainment of basic trust is a task for infancy. Loving, consistent care can produce trust in the child's first world, but disruption of care and tensions surrounding feeding, weaning, and the imposition of frustrating controls can lead to mistrust. The second stage—autonomy versus shame or doubt—Erikson links to the combined potentialities and consequences of muscular maturation, locomotion, and verbalization, as well as demands for toilet training and other controls.

As Fig. 2-1 indicates, five of Erikson's eight stages occur in the first third of life, the period in which the adult personality is coming into being. The tasks of the adult years are more difficult to formulate as developmental stages. One must have a sense of identity and a capacity for intimacy if one is to steer a somewhat autono-

Figure 2-1   Erikson's Eight Stages of Life

AGE LEVEL	TASK RESOLUTION
Infancy	Basic Trust vs. Mistrust
Early Childhood	Autonomy vs. Shame, Doubt
Play Age	Initiative vs. Guilt
School Age	Industry vs. Inferiority
Adolescence	Identity vs. Confusion
Young Adulthood	Intimacy vs. Isolation
Adulthood	Generativity vs. Stagnation
Old Age	Integrity vs. Despair

Adapted from Erik Erikson, *Childhood and Society* (New York: Norton & Company, Inc., 1950), p. 234.

mous course yet achieve a stable rewarding relationship with a mate and become a satisfactory parent. Beyond early adulthood, Erikson proposes generativity (becoming responsible for guiding the next generation) versus stagnation as the task for resolution in the middle years. Finally, in old age, coming to terms with the knowledge that death lies ahead entails the crisis of maintaining one's integrity versus despair. We shall consider the Eriksonian stages in greater detail at the appropriate times in our journey through the years from birth to death.

Levinson's Theory of the Life Course.   The most general, theoretical formulation relating to the patterning of adult development in American society—or, more accurately, the adult development of American males—is set forth in Daniel Levinson's *The Seasons of a Man's Life.*[13] Levinson postulates the evolution of an individual "life structure" through an orderly sequence of developmental periods. Periods of relative stability of aims and satisfactions alternate with transitional periods in which the previous structure is modified to a greater or lesser extent. As in Erikson's formulation, each period in the sequence presents certain developmental tasks to be accomplished. However, the structure of relationships and personal commitments through which the tasks of one period are accomplished may not serve the needs of self and society beyond that period.

The stages or periods of Levinson's "seasons" are closely linked to chronological age. In his twenties, the young man must make the transition into the adult world. This entails breaking his dependency on his parents and creating a stable life organization, while at the same time maintaining an exploratory stance toward the opportunities potentially available to him. In their twenties most men establish some measure of occupational commitment, marry, and become fathers. According to Levinson, however, the life structure of the twenties "is unstable, incomplete and fragmented." If he has not yet found a clear occupational direction or has not married, a man is likely to feel not only discontent but real distress. Even if a man has found an occupational niche and has made a sound marriage, in the late twenties he will feel the need for a change because some elements of his self will not have found expression in the first life structure. Consequently, there ensues a transitional period in which a man recognizes the need for greater investment in life goals, for "settling down" and building a structure that will establish his niche in society. This transitional period, according to Levinson, almost always comes between ages 28 and 32; a new structure will be in place or in process of development by 32, or disorganization and decline are foreseen.

The settling-down period is itself brought to a close by the midlife transition —often the midlife crisis—that occurs somewhere around age 40. As will be seen in Fig. 2-2, reproduced from Levinson, the stages that make up the seasons of a man's life have a ladderlike quality, and indeed the concept of climbing the ladder of success is a strong component in Levinson's formulation.

We shall examine Levinson's theory in greater detail when we consider the adult years. There are many interesting and provocative suggestions in *The Seasons of a Man's Life,* but there are discrepancies between the sequences and timing that

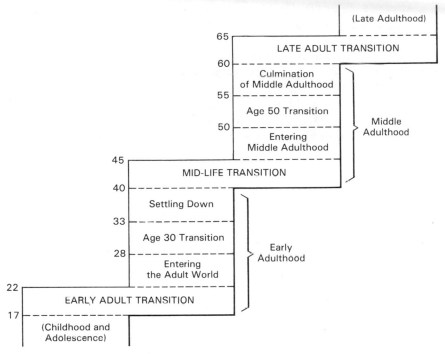

Figure 2-2 Levinson's Developmental Periods in Early and Middle Adulthood. (From *The Seasons of a Man's Life* by Daniel J. Levinson et al. Copyright © 1978 by Daniel J. Levinson. Reprinted by permission of Alfred A. Knopf.)

Levinson says we may expect to find and those that a careful reader can observe in the very cases Levinson presents. When one examines larger bodies of data, such as those derived from the major longitudinal studies, only a small proportion of men seem to fit Levinson's formulation.

Gould's Theory of Transformations.   Gould, like Erikson, anchors his formulation of the life course in psychoanalysis, but the stages he posits are more closely related to the adaptations entailed in taking on new social roles and responsibilities during the adult years. Gould derived his first formulation of stages from the problems patients of various ages presented when they sought psychotherapy at a psychiatric clinic.[14] In their late teens and early twenties, seekers of psychotherapy were most concerned with becoming independent of their parents. In their middle and late twenties, most of their energy was spent mastering what they were supposed to be, confident that they were growing and building for the future. The thirties, however, brought doubts; they now questioned what they were "supposed to" become. With the forties such questioning became more urgent; they questioned their own long-held beliefs and the meaning of life itself. These changing emphases—a series of transformations, in Gould's terminology—appeared also to be typical of members of the general population as they aged.

At each stage of life, Gould maintains, we are guided by unrealistic assumptions—myths—largely derived from our early childhood, when we were dependent and helpless. With each step toward and into adulthood, "the unfinished business of childhood intrudes, disturbing our emotions and requiring psychological work."[15] From adolescence to age 50, Gould maintains that we are steadily at work dismantling the false assumptions and protective devices that have derived from childhood consciousness. Ideally, we abandon unwarranted expectations, rigid rules, and inflexible roles, and "come to be the owners of ourselves."

The most common false assumptions that must be set aside emotionally as well as intellectually are, in Gould's view:

1. That we shall always live with our parents and be their child.
2. That our parents will always be there to help when we need them.
3. That life is simple and controllable, and that we do not have strong contradictory forces coexisting within us.
4. That there is no real death or evil in the world.[16]

"By the time we enter adulthood at the end of high school, we know that these assumptions are factually incorrect, yet they retain hidden control of our adult experience until significant events reveal them as emotional as well as intellectual fallacies," Gould writes.[17] The first-listed assumption must also be the first to be rejected, usually by our early twenties, and the second not much later. The "transformations" about which Gould writes are then the transformations of self that occur as assumptions are rejected emotionally through resolution of the conflicts engendered at particular life stages. These stages are not comparable to those posited by Erikson or Levinson, but there is again the notion of a series of normative crises to be surmounted.

Parts of Gould's formulation will probably apply to most persons in Western society, but thus far hardly any data exist to support the existence of the unrealistic assumptions that he sees as so important. Are the myths that Gould identifies the most salient ones in all walks of life? They seem to apply primarily to very protected upper-middle-class children.[18] We shall consider this issue in Chapter 5.

ROLE SEQUENCES AND TRANSITIONS

The stage theories we have just considered are based on aspects of physical development, the development of cognitive structures and skills, or the presumed emergence of certain critical developmental problems at particular age levels. They focus on the process of internal differentiation and the dynamics of development. They presuppose a more or less invariant order of stages, the attainment of each resting to a large degree on accomplishment of the prior stage. Individual development may be viewed within a social framework or context, but the context has little effect on the definition or delineation of stages.

Quite a different perspective is entailed in sociological theories that see the life course as structured very largely in terms of the social roles that people come to occupy. Entry into a major role may indicate attainment of a developmental stage, but even when this is the case, it is not assumed that the stages follow each other in an invariant order. Instead they are phases in sequences of relationships and commitments that can follow very different courses. The student role, for example, can overlap with marital and work roles. Stages defined by roles are descriptive categories, not theoretical explanations. The theoretical explanation is to be found in the processes of socialization, selection, and adaptation that underlie the assignment or taking on of social roles. This is the perspective that I personally find most congenial, and it will be the primary basis on which the following chapters are organized.

Long before social science came upon the scene, Shakespeare's character Jaques in *As You Like It* proclaimed the importance of social roles:

All the world's a stage,
And all the men and women merely players.
They have their exits and their entrances,
And one man in his time plays many parts,
His acts being seven ages.

The seven ages constitute the sequence of roles that might make up a life course, each role symbolizing age-appropriate behaviors.

At first the infant, mewling and puking in the nurse's arms; then the whining school boy with his satchel and shining morning face, creeping like snail unwillingly to school. And then the lover, sighing like furnace, with a woeful ballad made to his mistress' eyebrow. Then a soldier, full of strange oaths, and bearded like the pard, jealous in honor, sudden and quick in quarrel, seeking the bubble reputation even in the cannon's mouth. And then the justice, in fair round belly with good capon lined, with eyes severe and beard of formal cut, full of wise saws and modern instances; and so he plays his part. The sixth age shifts into the lean and slippered pantaloon, with spectacles on nose and pouch on side; his youthful hose well saved, a world too wide for his shrunk shank; and his big manly voice turning again toward childish treble, pipes and whistles in his sound. Last scene of all that ends this strange eventful history, is second childishness and mere oblivion; sans teeth, sans eyes, sans taste, sans everything.[19]

At the beginning and at the end, the organism is at center stage; life begins with helpless dependency and ends with the loss of those attributes that made competent participation in society possible and rewarding. But the course of life between these end points is defined in terms of major social roles. Roles provide general scripts of the responsibilities and privileges that go with occupying a given position or social category, such as infant, schoolboy, soldier, and so on. Roles may be defined as sets of norms or standards that apply to the expected behavior of categories of persons in their relationships with others. In the course of close, continuing relationships they become elaborated through informal negotiations and personal proclivities.[20]

For Shakespeare's Jaques, the infant role is one of total dependency on the nurse and others. Childhood is perhaps best represented by the role of student; the schoolboy must present himself in the classroom each morning despite his lack of enthusiasm for this enterprise. As adulthood is assumed, the male is expected to seek a mate, and each society has its expectations, often stereotyped, as to how a lover should behave. The role of soldier is most appropriate to the young adult male, who is expected to be daring and is allowed leeway in certain proprieties. But as the middle years often bring both a paunch and a greater concern with proprieties, the justice, with his proper dress and speech and his wise (if often trite) sayings, is a most appropriate role to symbolize middle age.

Each of us is born into a social organization whose members bear multiple relationships to one another and share a highly complex and reinforcing structure of expectations. These relationships and expectations set the frame of reference within which the individual defines and redefines goals, self-image, and investments of self. Certain possibilities exist for each of us as positions to be occupied, roles to be played. Moreover, to a large degree one role tends to link to another: Completion of high school makes possible entrance into college, and college graduation makes possible admission to law school and ultimately to a legal career. In such a sequence, failure in one role may preclude the assumption of others. This need not be the case, however, for there are several possible pathways to most positions in the social structure.

A life is made up of several subcycles of interlinked roles: student roles, family roles, career roles, community roles. A formal theory of the life course in terms of role sequences has not yet been attained, but we can specify some of the elements in such a theory and some of the consequences.[21] To do so, it will be useful to focus on certain generic aspects of role transitions in the early and later stages of life and then to examine the two major role sequences that tend to have greatest salience in giving a sense of continuity and coherence to the individual life course.

Early Socialization

The early developmental period is characterized by the most rapid growth and the most extensive learning experiences of the entire life course. We shall examine the process of early socialization in the next chapter; here we note the theoretical significance of the early interaction between genetic "givens," the ability of caretakers to orient the infant and child to the world in which that child must define and pursue goals and establish ties with others, and the subcultural and temporal themes that will color perceptions of the world and the possibilities it offers. Socialization is the general concept that refers to the processes of social interaction, teaching, and learning by which the child comes to take on the ways of a particular society. The term may also be used to designate the social apparatus by which such transmission takes place.[22]

In one sense the early years lay down a foundation of values; of physical, cognitive, and social skills; and of interests and personality tendencies upon which the adult life course will be built. But the concept *foundation* is too rigid; change in the most basic elements is always possible, though a considerable measure of stability is more usual. The timing of major life events, the sequence of roles occupied, and the level of a person's success in performing roles occupied depend to a large extent on the course of socialization.

Here, in barest outline, are some of the most important ways in which socialization shapes the life course:

1. Learning during childhood and adolescence prepares the person for social roles to be occupied as an adult, providing both general knowledge and skills that will be needed if one is to participate in cooperative activities with others and more specific information about the preparation that is required for performing particular adult roles.

2. Social structural placement (the parents' socioeconomic status, racial and ethnic membership, religious affiliation) and interpersonal processes influence the effective transmission of knowledge and the development of skills, so that some persons (e.g., those in the upper middle class, those of majority status, those in families that offer loving but firm guidance and consistent discipline) will be better prepared to make realistic choices and will have more resources for achieving their goals than others (e.g., persons in the lower class, deprived minority members, persons with overly permissive or rejecting parents).

3. Differences in educational attainments, interpersonal skills, and special talents acquired before the adult years, coupled with institutionalized selection processes, result in differential access to roles that entail the greatest potential for reward and power.

4. Values learned in childhood and the choices made on the basis of them influence both the scheduling of entry into an occupation, marriage, and having children, and the level of subsequent occupational attainment.

The transition from childhood and adolescence into adulthood entails moving from preparation to performance, from dependency to autonomy, from roles largely assigned by age, sex, family, and social origins to roles selected and achieved. Successful accomplishment depends on the adequacy of skills developed in the course of socialization, the accuracy of perceptions of opportunities available, and the degree of an individual's commitment to goals. To perform any role in a satisfactory way, a person must: (1) know what is expected, (2) be able to meet the role requirements, and (3) want to carry out the expected behaviors and pursue the goals appropriate to the role.[23] All three components—knowledge, abilities, and motivation—rest on socialization processes. Socialization does not end in childhood or adolescence; the life course continually presents new roles to be occupied even in the middle and later years, and many of them require preparation as well as on-the-job learning.

Two role sequences are especially likely to give substance and shape to the life course in the adult years: occupational careers and marital-family roles. Almost universally, people are not deemed adult until they are engaged in some form of productive work and have established families of their own. Both occupational activities and family role relationships involve sequential change, and both realms tend to be patterned in ways that help to explain the course of life.

Roles and the Family Cycle

For most people, family life provides the most intimate social relationships and the most lasting (if changing) commitments and responsibilities over the greater part of the life course. The personality is nurtured and shaped in the family of orientation, that is, the parental family that gives us our initial orientation to the world. But with adulthood and marriage comes a sequence (often called the family cycle) of stages as children are born to the married couple, grow from dependency to autonomy, and finally depart from the home (now an "empty nest"), ending with the married couple alone again. The family cycle is not merely a set of chronological stages in the course of family life; each stage entails coping with particular responsibilities posed by the requirements of the family as a whole as these intersect with other roles that must be filled simultaneously.[24]

The family cycle thus provides a framework within which we can examine the working out of the management of marital, parental, and occupational role involvements that place changing demands on men and women over a substantial portion of the life course. We shall examine phases of the family cycle in detail in Chapter 7.

Occupational Careers

In almost every society, a substantial part of human effort goes into providing oneself and one's dependents with food, shelter, and the necessities of life. In many societies the family is still the basic economic unit as well as the unit of procreation. In Western society, however, in the past several centuries the worlds of family and of work have been transformed by technological development. For the most part, occupational careers now take men and women outside the home and the family. For men, the occupational role has in many instances become the most important role in structuring the adult life course and in shaping the quality of family life and the sense of personal identity. Occupational roles have become more salient to many women as well, but women far less often invest themselves as heavily in occupational careers as in family roles.

The concept of career is one that will be useful in thinking about work roles and a number of other roles. Careers are sequences of related roles—social strands of a life course—in which persons invest themselves or are thrust.[25] A sharp change in occupation—from banker to painter in the South Seas, for example—may be seen as a change in careers, but in general the sequence of a man's or a woman's work roles will be referred to as their occupational careers. Careers may have great continuity and coherence, or they may entail many shifts or ups and downs in the course of the whole work life. Career continuity and coherence characterize the man or woman whose work life is devoted to a succession of increasingly respon sible jobs within the bureaucratic structure of a large corporation or a government agency.[26] Most professionals also have high coherence in their careers. Less-skilled workers, however, will more often shift types of work, especially in their early years, as will many persons displaced from their jobs by unemployment related to technological developments or shifts in industrial production.

The work career is a major source of providing continuity both in life-style and economic well-being and in the sense of who and what one is. Moreover, in societies that place a high premium on occupational and financial success, competition for high status and high earnings can become important goals in themselves. Career stages and demands can put heavy stresses on a person's relationships to spouse and children. Again, then, we have in the analysis of careers a tool for examining an important component in the organization of the individual life course.

Role Gain and Role Loss

The early years see us taking on an ever-increasing number of roles as group memberships increase and new positions are occupied. Some roles are tightly scripted, like jobs within a governmental agency, where the job description is spelled out in agonizing detail, specifying not only tasks to be carried out and technical skills to be applied, but also the degree of responsibility to others and supervisory arrangements. Many roles are much more open to creative negotiation, as in friendships.

The major roles taken on in the adult years tend to be institutionalized. That is, the positions occupied are located within organizations and institutions—family, business organization, religious order, and so on—that specify formal expectations for role performance. There is in general fairly good agreement on what constitutes effective or satisfactory performance. Such performance becomes a source of affirmation of the person, a part of identity.

As major roles are lost—through unemployment, the death of husbands and wives, retirement, or physical decline—major adaptations are demanded. Moreover, in the later years the positions that remain available are often of a different sort. They often lack clear definitions of expected behavior or of tasks to be accomplished. Many of these roles are tenuous rather than institutionalized, in that they represent positions outside formal organizations and institutions, social categories rather than parts of social structures.[27] Tenuously defined roles may be honorific (such as a Nobel laureate) or they may be devalued (widowhood, joblessness), but the devalued roles are more common in the later years. Norms to structure life tend to be lacking when the position that defines the role is a mere social category and not a functional part of an ongoing social enterprise.

Role gain and role loss are inevitable features of the life course, sometimes subject to individual choice, often not. When and how they occur has much to do with the contour of the life course. Several major studies and theoretical analyses of the life course have focused on role transitions.[28]

THEMES IN THE STUDY
OF THE LIFE COURSE

Sometimes we are unable to explain a particular phenomenon, but we can identify interesting aspects of it that can be studied as such. In a sense, we have just dealt with several factors that influence the sequencing structure of the life course. Because they provide a framework for attempting to explain aspects of the life course, we have dealt with role sequences and transitions as important elements in theories of the life course. But there are other aspects of the life course that are more in the nature of themes to be traced out than structural features. We shall touch briefly on three of these: goals and life purposes, life stress and adaptation, and the sense of identity through phases of the life course.

Goals and Life Purposes

To live is to strive. Culture and social placement influence the goals we strive toward, but to a large degree each of us chooses our objectives, short- and long-term. The process of goal setting was central to Charlotte Buhler's theorizing about the life course. Buhler noted that we establish our intents and interests gradually. Many people never come to formulate ultimate purposes, but nearly everyone at some time or other must ask, "What do I want? What am I living for?" Some purposively try to formulate goals that will provide an ultimate purpose in life. To connote this sense of searching for purpose or meaning, Buhler used the term *intentionality,* a theme that has been elaborated by Marjorie Fiske.[29]

Through setting goals and then striving to achieve them, humans seek self-fulfillment or self-realization, in the view of a number of humanistic psychologists.[30] The concept of self-realization is not easily defined, but it connotes the sense of having done one's best in the pursuit of goals deemed worthy, to which a person has committed himself or herself. It is probably safe to assume that persons who set praiseworthy goals and give their best efforts to achieving them will derive satisfaction from their striving if they are at least moderately successful. The concept of self-realization runs into difficulties when what had seemed to be praiseworthy goals fail to remain praiseworthy after achievement. Values and goals change in the process of striving. Also, how successful must a person be in order to feel fulfilled?

Apart from problems with the concept of self-realization or self-fulfillment, however, there is much to recommend looking at how goals and intentions are developed as a major theme in the study of the life course. Without some set of goals to pursue, whether short-term or more remote, there can be little sense of self-satisfaction. Persons who are at the edge of subsistence, struggling just to secure food and shelter, almost inevitably will have to give priority to more immediate physical needs than those who are free to contemplate manifold opportunities. But even for those who seldom if ever get to formulate explicitly their life purposes, one can discern interests and activities that become focal points for their

Investment of time and energy and sense of personal identity. Robert Dubin has proposed the concept of "central life interests" as "portion(s) of the individual's life space in which an affective investment is made."[31] They may be found in the work setting, the family, in games and sports, in art, or any one of a number of spheres. Central life interests are built up and become important definers of what is important to us as we allocate our energies.

The origins of early goal setting and central life interests are sometimes to be sought in childhood socialization, and especially in the values the child is exposed to, but often the critical socializing experiences come in adolescence and early adulthood. The development of intentionality becomes a core problem for theorizing on the life course.

Life Stress and Adaptation

If goal setting and the quest for meaning represent one major life theme, that theme has a counterpoint in adaptation. A person cannot always pursue chosen goals. One must adapt to and cope with events or circumstances that are not of one's choosing or liking. The agents of socialization demand changing standards of performance and may impose controls that are irksome and frustrating. There are also many unpredictable events and circumstances over which a person has no control, events that disrupt the normal flow of life and of relations with others and thereby demand adaptation. As a consequence, our lives often entail turmoil and stress.

When applied to the person, the concept of stress relates to a far more complex phenomenon than when applied to a physical structure such as a bridge.[32] Physical stress on a bridge is measured by the amount of external force placed upon it; that force produces strain, or a degree of deformation (bending, twisting, etc.) in the bridge. The stress of an onerous task, the loss of one's job, or the severe illness of a loved one can cause great strain on a person, but the external stress cannot be measured like the force on a bridge. The human mind interprets external events and evaluates their possible consequences. One person's source of stress may be another person's challenge. Therefore, it becomes very difficult to separate stress and resulting strain, and in the biomedical and psychological sciences it is common practice to use the word *stress* for the internal physical and psychological consequences of an external stressor.

If external stress is a general fact of life, coping with such stress and adapting more or less successfully to it must be an important element in the life course. As we shall see, there are various modes of attempting to defend against stressors as well as varied modes of coping.[33] In general, coming to grips with a problem and finding ways of overcoming it tends to have more favorable consequences for the individual than denying the existence of the problem or defending against it in other ways. We are beginning to learn, however, that for problems that cannot possibly be handled by the individual, defensive maneuvers such as denial may at times be useful. For example, denial of some of the deficits brought by old age may be less problematic for the person than dwelling on those deficits, about which nothing can be done.

How are effective coping mechanisms built up, and what are the consequences of various adaptational styles over the life course? Do early stressors that are successfully handled strengthen a person and make that person better able to handle stressors in the later years? Or does a heavy load of stress early on make one much more vulnerable in the later years? The answers to these questions are not yet in, though there is evidence suggesting that moderate early stressors may lead to more effective later functioning.[34]

This is another area in which we have partial explorations of causes and effects but no overarching theory (except as the psychoanalytic theory informs our knowledge of psychic mechanisms). However, research carried out in the past decade or two has given some provisional generalizations. Perhaps the nearest approach to a theoretical statement of the importance of adaptation in the life course is given by Vaillant in his book *Adaptation to Life.*[35]

A central thesis of Vaillant's work is that "if we are to master conflict gracefully and to harness instinctual strivings creatively, our adaptive styles must mature." In childhood we learn certain ways of protecting ourselves against the onslaught of events and situations that are painful to us. We may learn to repress or put completely out of mind the things that frighten us; we may engage in fantasy or project our fears or angry feelings upon others; or we may act out our fear and rage when we are very young, and such behavior will not necessarily get us into serious trouble. But ultimately we must develop more mature ways of coping with unacceptable or painful feelings. Unless we can modify immature or neurotic defenses, Vaillant maintains, we are likely to run into serious problems in handling our adult roles and in taking satisfaction from the goals we have pursued. In a sense, then, Vaillant's formulation is similar to Gould's theory of transformations, but without the implication that everyone shares a common set of myths that must be discarded. Instead, each person builds a unique set of strategies, conscious and unconscious, for coping.

Vaillant is primarily interested in understanding what makes for the combination of personal happiness and effective functioning that we call mental health. We shall be concerned less with mental health as such than with continuities and shifts in adaptive strategies, with the cumulative effects of stress and of social contexts, and with the costs and benefits of particular strategies of coping over the life course.

At the start of this section, adaptation was contrasted with goal seeking and the purposive pursuit of personal meanings. One is self-initiated, the other forced upon a person. But just as two musical themes may be combined in counterpoint, purposive commitment may be brought into the adaptive process. Both the particular goals to which a person is committed—for example, warm interpersonal ties, altruistic endeavors, personal achievement—and features of individual personality influence the kind of group supports that one will have for coping with severe stresses and the degree of threat that a given stressor poses.[36] Commitments, like defenses, are likely to change over time, and ultimately a degree of commitment to self-preservation tends to come into play.

Identity and the Life Course

For Erikson, the achievement of a firm sense of identity is the prime task of adolescence. The sense of being a unique self has roots in early childhood. Our feeling for who and what we are gives a source of continuity and coherence to our experience of our own life and yet is subject to subtle modifications over time. Sometimes identities are transformed; to the extent that major changes take place in a person's views of self, they constitute a set of markers for dividing up the life course.

Identity can be defined as a sense of who we are and what we stand for. It exists not as a thing but as a construct, a kind of theory about ourselves.[37] We are, and we stand for, many things, and the sense of identity is that more or less integrated set of perceptions we have of ourselves, our strengths, and our vulnerabilities, incorporating many components.

There is obviously a relationship between the goals to which we are committed and the view we have of ourselves. We tend to choose roles and relationships in terms of who we think we are and who we want to be. We get confirmations or we are confronted with discrepancies as we function in a role we have chosen or one thrust upon us. Discrepancies between what we have claimed to be and what we prove to be must be resolved by changing ourselves or our roles. Identity must entail a notion of what we may become—occupationally, as husbands, wives, or lovers; as parents; and as human beings in the broadest sense.

We shall want to examine those experiences that lead to positive feelings about self and those that lead to negative feelings. And as we get into the adult years, we shall want to look closely at what happens to identity in the face of success beyond one's wildest dreams or failure to achieve earlier aspirations. Much has been written of the midlife crisis which derives from finding that one's goals are less worthy than they had seemed and one's identity is no longer satisfying to oneself. How frequent are such crises? How are they managed and what happens to one's identity thereafter?

Again, the theme of identity merges in counterpoint with other themes or threads to be traced through the life course.

GENERAL QUESTIONS TO BE ADDRESSED

The theories and themes introduced in this chapter will be developed at much greater length in the following chapters, as we trace the life course from birth to death. They will both guide our analysis and illuminate facets of the life course. We shall draw upon available research in order to try to assess the validity of the various theories, the usefulness of the several perspectives, and their applicability to different populations and different times. Beyond this, we shall want to keep in mind certain general issues that have implications for the study of the life course or for policy decisions that relate to the life course. A number of these issues have already been introduced in Chapter 1. They will bear brief restatement here.

Continuity versus Discontinuity

The very expression, *life course,* suggests a certain continuity. A stream runs its course downhill, turning aside for rocks and avalanches, but subject to the constant force of gravity. The human life course is obviously very different, entailing growth, learning, the development of new skills and purposes, and adaptation to life's vicissitudes. There are nevertheless several sources of continuity. From childhood to late maturity there is in general much continuity of appearance and of manifest intelligence; the organism itself maintains considerable stability. Stability and continuity also reside in social networks, for most people. But how much continuity exists in the purposes that motivate our efforts, our styles in dealing with others, or our modes of coping with major adaptational problems? Does the shy, withdrawing child tend to produce a withdrawn adult? Does successful, satisfying occupational achievement in the twenties and thirties lead to greater satisfaction in the forties, or are midlife crises and discontinuity commonly encountered?

Both societies and individual lives are constantly in flux. Whether one chooses to emphasize continuity or discontinuity may be less important than asking what makes for greater versus less continuity. What makes for orderly life transitions as against disruptive ones? What features of the individual, of the individual's placement in society, of societal flux, and of institutional aids to adaptation make for greater stability or continuity in social roles, in life satisfaction, and in a sense of who and what a person is?

The Importance of Scheduling

The time at which various developmental transitions or later role transitions are expected is very much a cultural matter, varying tremendously across societies and over time in the same society. It is likely that the importance of being "on time" for any particular transition also varies from one society to another and from one time to another. Nevertheless, there is much evidence that the scheduling of such events as school leaving and marriage in Western society is consequential for subsequent attainments and satisfaction in the life course. We shall therefore look at the available data relating to the ordering of certain events such as school leaving, entry into a job, marriage, and having children both as these are reflective of earlier life orientations and as these tend to lead to particular outcomes in a given society at a given time.

The Validity of Stage Formulations

Closely related to scheduling is the discerning of stages in the life course. When we examine detailed life histories, do we find the stages that theorists have told us to expect? How are stages to be recognized? Are persons aware of the stages of their own lives? Where stages can clearly be said to exist, how closely are they linked to prior and subsequent stages, and to what extent do they enable us to make predictions about future developments in the life course?

Methodological developments in the study of event sequences and transitional states give promise of permitting more adequate tests of such global theories as those of Erikson, Gould, and Levinson.[38] In addition, less global formulations of person-situation interactions and of stages by which persons move through their lives, occupying particular states or statuses, have been proposed by William McKinley Runyan.[39] Delineating such sequences and theoretical formulations with sound empirical data will be a major task for large-scale, long-term longitudinal research.

The Role of Rites of Passage

As we noted in Chapter 1, some life transitions are symbolized by rites of passage. Formal ceremonies mark school graduation, induction into the military, marriage, retirement, and many other major transitions. The symbolic recognition of a change in status—of achievements that permit one to move on to other roles or of responsibilities undertaken or given up—promotes social solidarity through group celebration of the transition.

Societies differ considerably in the extent to which they ritualize transitions and in the particular transitions they choose to symbolize by formal rites of passage. In many societies, for example, attainment of puberty is formally recognized by rites of passage, while marriage itself is much less ritualized. How much difference does it make for the individual and for the society to have such rites? Do rites of passage always serve to promote continuity, feelings of belonging? How often do such rites become empty rituals because of social change? Conversely, are there situations in which the lack of any formal rites of passage makes transitions rougher than they need to be?

Integration of Personal Experience

Living entails constantly learning, but some lessons seem to have to be learned again and again. Sometimes we gain insights from our experiences and arrive at ways of solving problems that will be useful to us in the future, while other times we may be immobilized by a particular experience, quite unable to learn.

In the course of life we encounter many stressful situations, situations that we cannot change but must somehow adapt to. Successful adaptation is frequently called *coping*. An issue that we shall want to examine, insofar as possible, is how the child and the adult integrate and organize varied experiences. The product of such integration is, in the most general sense, personality. For some students of the life course, personality is indeed the primary and indeed almost exclusive focus of attention. While we shall want to know what personality theorists say about the course of personality change over the life span, we shall focus primarily on two aspects of the integration of experience: (1) on the formation of individual goals, commitments, and life-style; and (2) on strategies evolved for coping with life stresses and situations demanding adaptation.

Age versus Cohort Effects

As already noted, we shall try to assess the validity of theories by drawing upon the best available research. In dealing with empirical evidence bearing upon the relationships between aging and any attributes of persons or of their histories, we confront the issue of deciding whether effects are attributable to age *per se* or may be a consequence of differences between cohorts. As noted in Chapter 1, each generation or age group lives through a unique slice of human history. In the first half of the twentieth century in America, each succeeding generation has received substantially more schooling than the previous one. Younger persons are thus on the whole better educated than older persons. Increments in education are associated with superior scores on intelligence tests. Older persons have tended on the whole to score substantially less well than middle-aged ones, and middle-aged ones less well than young adults on standard intelligence tests. As a result, it was long assumed that intelligence tended to decline markedly with age, but we know now that the intergenerational difference was not a result of aging but of cohort educational differences. Several studies that have followed the same individuals for long stretches of the life span have found very little if any decline in intelligence prior to old age. Whether we attempt to interpret changes in IQ, in occupational patterns, or in sexual behavior with increasing age, we must attempt to disentangle historical or cohort effects from age effects.

Cultural and Social Structural Variations in Experience

Societies and segments of the same society at a given time will often differ even more than intergenerational cohorts. We have already noted the importance of one's placement in the social structure for the kind of socialization that is received and the kind of resources that one can call upon in planning one's life.[40] Greater differences in the patterning of the life course are associated with such variations in cultural values as the esteem with which older persons are held or the norms relating to sex roles within societies. The cohesiveness of the Japanese or Chinese family systems, both in Asia and in America, for example, and the honored roles occupied by aged parents, differ sharply from Anglo-American norms. Such features of culture markedly influence the transitions from adolescence to adulthood and from middle life to old age. This makes it difficult to formulate universally valid propositions about the life course; cultural variation is an essential feature of human social life. Therefore it is incumbent upon us to be aware of variations in the experiences of men and of women, of middle-class and working-class persons, of persons from highly developed technological societies and those from developing societies. The limits of space preclude close examination of societies other than American, but occasional contrasts will be noted.

CONCLUDING COMMENTS

It will by now be apparent why this chapter is entitled "Theories and Themes in the Study of the Life Course" and not "Theories of the Life Course." The life course can be approached from many perspectives. It cannot be explained by any one of them. The sequence of roles and experiences, the commitments and adaptations that the person makes over the years, the personality and identity that are evolved, the imprint of historical time—all these facets of the life course are subject to multiple influences and to group and individual variations in life events and in outcomes to be expected. To explain the life course would be to explain the fullness of life itself.

Instead, we must seek to understand how particular facets of the life course relate to other facets, or how particular strands of experience tend to be strung together. It is important to know the extent to which early experiences influence cognitive development or personality at some later period in life. It is also important to know how the timing and sequencing of role assumption in the adult years influences the level of accomplishment and the adaptational problems posed.

In our analysis we want to be able to establish the most general propositions that we can about phases or aspects of the life course, and at the same time to have some confidence that our propositions are valid. Overarching theories that attempt to explain the scheduling and sequencing of lives in all societies, or even over all the diverse ethnic groups and classes in our own society, are doomed to failure because there is no possibility of controlling for the many influences that differentiate groups and bear crucially on role-attainment processes.

Theories that deal with basic processes of human development—physical, cognitive, or emotional—will obviously have a greater probability of general validity (other things being equal) than will those that deal with role transitions in highly complex and diverse societies such as our own. We need to know how the basic processes operate, but we must also know how cultural, social structural, and historical influences modify the topography of the realm to be negotiated by persons in particular cultures, positions, or historical periods. Much of our evidence will be valid for only small segments of our own society, viewed in the context of recent history, since the systematic study of the life course is in its infancy. But as research becomes available for more diverse populations, it may be possible to discern general tendencies that extend to these populations. Shall we ultimately be able to formulate universally valid generalizations about the course of human life, generalizations more interesting and illuminating than those that come from the mere fact that we are all involved in humankind? Until then, it will be desirable to keep in mind the extent to which a given generalization is bound to a particular time and place and to examine facets and themes that can be studied systematically rather than speculating on more cosmic formulations.

NOTES

1. Abraham Kaplan, *The Conduct of Inquiry: Methodology for Behavioral Sciences* (San Francisco: Chandler, 1964), p. 302.
2. Orville G. Brim, Jr., "Adult Socialization," in J. A. Clausen, ed., *Socialization and Society* (Boston: Little, Brown and Company, 1968), pp. 183-226.
3. An excellent research report based on this perspective given by George Vaillant, *Adaptation to Life* (Boston: Little, Brown and Company, 1977).
4. The timing-of-events model, though not so labeled, was originally formulated by Bernice Neugarten. For several of her early papers, see B. L. Neugarten, ed., *Middle Age and Aging* (Chicago: University of Chicago Press, 1968).
5. Nancy Datan and Leon Ginsberg, eds., *Life Span Developmental Psychology: Normative Life Crises* (New York: Academic Press, 1975).
6. Jerome Kagan, *Infancy: Its Place in Human Development* (Cambridge, MA: Harvard University Press, 1978), p. 44.
7. Charlotte Buhler, "The General Structure of the Human Life Cycle," in C. Buhler and F. Massarik, eds., *The Course of Human Life* (New York: Springer, 1968), p. 14.
8. William James, *Principles of Psychology* (New York: Henry Holt and Co., 1890).
9. Piaget's publications were numerous and most have now been translated into English. In addition, there are several excellent overview volumes by others. For a brief but definitive presentation, see Jean Piaget, "Piaget's Theory," in P. Mussen, ed., *Carmichael's Manual of Child Psychology,* Vol. I, 3rd ed. (New York: Wiley, 1970).
10. Freud, like Piaget, produced a great number of scholarly papers as well as clinical descriptions. A general treatment of psychoanalytic theory as applied to the life course is given in Theodore Lidz, *The Person: His or Her Development throughout the Life Cycle,* 2nd ed. (New York: Basic Books, 1976).
11. Erik H. Erikson, "Autobiographic Notes on the Identity Crisis," *Daedalus,* 99 (Fall 1970), 730-59.
12. Erik H. Erikson, *Childhood and Society* (New York: Norton, 1950), pp. 217-34.
13. Daniel J. Levinson, *The Seasons of a Man's Life* (New York: Alfred Knopf, 1978).
14. Roger L. Gould, "The Phases of Adult Life: A Study in Developmental Psychology," *American Journal of Psychiatry,* 129 (1972), 521-31.
15. Roger L. Gould, *Transformations: Growth and Change in Adult Life* (New York: Simon & Schuster, 1978), p. 14.
16. These assumptions, here paraphrased from p. 39 of *Transformations,* are stated in slightly variant ways subsequently.
17. Gould, *Transformations,* p. 39.
18. But few adolescents appear to be as dependent on their parents as Gould assumes they are, based on his experience with adolescents requiring psychiatric help. See Chapter 5 for the evidence.
19. William Shakespeare, *As You Like It,* Act II, Scene 7.

20. The concept *role* denotes the formal expectations or norms that exist; *role behavior* includes the elaborations in expectation that occur when the role is enacted by an individual.

21. See, for example, Irving Rosow, "Status and Role Change through the Life Span," in R. Binstock and E. Shanas, eds., *Handbook of Aging and the Social Sciences* (New York: Van Nostrand, Reinhold Co., 1976), pp. 457–82.

22. J. A. Clausen, "Socialization as a Concept and as a Field of Study," in J. A. Clausen, ed., *Socialization and Society* (Boston: Little, Brown and Co., 1968), pp. 3–17.

23. This formulation was developed by Orville G. Brim, Jr., "Socialization through the Life Cycle," in O. G. Brim, Jr., and S. Wheeler, eds., *Socialization after Childhood: Two Essays* (New York: John Wiley & Sons, 1966), p. 25.

24. R. Hill and P. Mattesick, "Family Development Theory and Life Span Development," in P. B. Baltes and O. G. Brim, Jr., eds., *Life Span Development and Behavior*, Vol. 2 (New York: Academic Press, 1980).

25. An early but still cogent discussion of the concept of career is to be found in H. J. Becker and A. L. Strauss, "Careers, Personality and Adult Socialization," *American Journal of Sociology*, 62 (1956), 253–63.

26. As we shall see in Chapter 6, both institutional and individual characteristics shape career lines and the degree of continuity.

27. Rosow, "Role Change through the Life Span," pp. 463–67.

28. For example, Marjorie Fiske Lowenthal, M. Thurner, and D. Chiriboga, *Four Stages of Life: A Comparative Study of Women and Men Facing Transitions* (San Francisco: Jossey-Bass, 1975); Linda K. George, *Role Transitions in Later Life* (Monterey, CA: Brooks/Cole Publishing Co., 1980); David A. Karp and C. Yoels, *Experiencing the Life Cycle: A Social Psychology of Aging* (Springfield, IL: Charles C Thomas, 1982).

29. Marjorie Fiske Lowenthal, "Intentionality: Toward a Framework for the Study of Adaptation in Adulthood," *Aging and Human Development*, 2 (1971), 79–95.

30. Abraham Maslow, *Motivation and Personality* (New York: Harper, 1954).

31. Robert Dubin, "Central Life Interests: Self Integrity in a Complex World," *Pacific Sociological Review*, 22 (1979), 405–25.

32. For a good discussion of the concept and review of the status of research, see G. R. Elliott and C. Eisdorfer, eds., *Stress and Human Health: Analysis and Implications of Research* (New York: Springer Publishing Co., 1982).

33. L. I. Pearlin and C. Schooler, "The Structure of Coping," *Journal of Health and Social Behavior*, 19 (1978), 2–21.

34. See Elliott and Eisdorfer, *Stress and Human Health*, Chapter 7.

35. Vaillant, *Adaptation to Life*.

36. Elliott and Eisdorfer, *Stress and Human Health*, pp. 159–73.

37. Orville G. Brim, Jr., "Life-Span Development on the Theory of Oneself: Implications for Child Development," in H. Reese, ed., *Advances in Child Development and Behavior*, Vol. 11 (New York: Academic Press, 1976).

38. See for example, D. L. Featherman, D. P. Hogan, and A. B. Sorenson, "Entry into Adulthood: Profiles of Young Men in the 1950s," in P. B. Baltes and O. G. Brim, Jr., eds., *Life Span Development and Behavior* (New York: Academic Press, 1984), pp. 160–202; also M. T. Hannan and N. B. Tuma, "Methods for Temporal Analysis," *Annual Review of Sociology*, 5 (1979), 303–28.

39. William McKinley Runyan, *Life Histories and Psychobiography: Explorations in Theory and Method* (New York: Oxford University Press, 1982).

40. A cogent discussion of the effects of placement in the society and of the mix of relationships and cultural norms in social settings is given by Urie Bronfenbrenner, *The Ecology of Human Development: Experiments by Nature and by Design* (Cambridge, MA: Harvard University Press, 1980).

CHAPTER 3
INFANCY
AND
EARLY CHILDHOOD

Behold the child, by nature's kindly law,
Pleased with a rattle; tickled with a straw.
— Alexander Pope

The more we learn about infancy and early childhood, the more we are likely to become fascinated with the almost unlimited possibilities that are built into the human organism. The development of the infant through the first two years has great intrinsic interest for most of us, male and female, whether we are parents, parents-to-be, or merely bystanders. But this is a book about the whole life course, not about infancy, and our aim in this chapter is limited to seeking to understand the nature of constitutional givens and those aspects of early development that make a difference for the adult life course. Rather than dwell in detail on the stages of physical and cognitive development, we will seek to understand the general principles that underlie such development and the influences that can enhance or retard normal development. We shall be interested in temperament and the underpinnings of personality, but we shall not be much concerned with the behavior problems of small children. The problems of infants and small children show little continuity with problems of the later years, nor do they predict the kind of life-style or plan of life that will shape the years of maturity.

What, then, are the relevant questions to be addressed here? We need an understanding of the following, at very least:

1. How do infants vary at birth by virtue of genetic potential, the circumstances of intrauterine life, and the experience of birth, and how do such variations influence the life chances of the infant and the course of its development?

2. What are the capacities of the infant and child at various ages and what are the basic processes of normal development—physical, cognitive, and social?

3. How do the acquisition of competence in language and the emergence of self-consciousness contribute to the child's purposive coping with the environment?

4. How do different societies seek to shape the infant's potentials toward adult ideals, and, specifically, how do such efforts and other aspects of the provision of infant and child care influence the development of constitutional potentials and the degree of continuity in various attributes of the individual over time?

5. What attributes of the infant and child appear to have the highest degree of continuity into the later childhood and adult years, and when do such attributes first appear in relatively stable form?

Some of these questions may at this point seem abstract or obscure. Clarification will come as we attempt to provide at least tentative answers to each of them.

THE HUMAN ORGANISM

When the author began graduate study, before World War II, sociologists and biologists often argued vehemently as to which was more important in its influences on behavior and on intelligence, nature (the genetic input), or nurture (the rearing of the infant and child). The arguments were both inconclusive and futile. As knowledge of genetics and of developmental processes has increased, we have come to see that hereditary potentials and environmental factors constantly interact, moderating or enhancing each other's effects.

Certain physical attributes—such as height, hair and eye color, and facial appearance—are very largely determined by our genes, while many behavioral patterns—such as the language we speak, the foods we eat, and the implements we use to eat them—are largely or entirely determined by our culture and our location in the social organization. But temperament, intelligence, and many other attributes are clearly products of interactive processes in which one cannot say unequivocally that either heredity or environment plays a more important role. If environmental variations are very great and the range of variation in a particular gene pool (that is, a population whose members interbreed) is relatively limited, we can expect greater environmental contributions to intelligence than if hereditary potentials varied much and the environment little.[1]

A few elementary propositions from human genetics should be sufficient to start us on our way.[2] We know now that the basic building material for all animal life is the DNA (deoxyribonucleic acid) molecule. The discovery of its double-helix structure led to one of the most widely publicized Nobel prizes. The molecules of DNA are strung together in 23 chromosomes, each containing many thousands of genes. Genes are thus tiny sections of the double helix, and they may be thought of as containing chemical codes for development.

The complexities of genetic transmission need not concern us here. What is important to recognize is the tremendous number of messages carried by the genes—literally billions—that will produce, singly or in particular combinations, attributes of each unique organism. Conception brings together two sets of chromosomes and their genes. Genes derived from mother and father match up through a complex interchange that differs for every pairing. Once conception has occurred, the genetic program is activated.

No two individuals will have the same genetic program unless they come into being as a consequence of a splitting of the fertilized ovum soon after conception, producing identical twins. Identical twins bear the same combination of genes and must therefore be of the same sex and, except for environmental influences, the same physique and inborn proclivities, whatever those may be. Nonidentical or fraternal twins result from near-simultaneous fertilization of two egg cells by two sperm cells and are thus no more similar, genetically, than are other full brothers and sisters. This circumstance gives us a major methodological tool for examining relative contributions of heredity and environment in particular circumstances, as we shall see.

Brothers and sisters do, of course, have many gene combinations in common, and therefore they tend to resemble each other. But they also have many gene combinations that differ, and they therefore may show variations in size, coloring, intellectual potential, and almost any other attribute one can name that depends largely on heredity.

What Heredity Contributes

We have referred to the program provided by heredity. Just how detailed is that program? A generation ago, the infant was seen primarily as a bundle of reflexes waiting to be conditioned. Now we know that the human infant is designed to perceive the environment and to process information in particular ways, beginning at birth. The script or program calls for a sequence of capacities to come into existence with the maturing of the nervous system over the first two years. There is now general agreement that the human infant has many innate capacities.[3] Among them are the capacity to perceive the primary colors as distinct entities (not merely gradations of wavelengths), to respond to different forms and shapes without prior learning, and to master the structure of a complex language—any language—within the first few years of life. These are built into human germ plasm, shared by all normal humans.

The genetic program determines most obviously such attributes as sex, eye, hair, and skin color, and whether we tend to be large or small. It also influences to a large extent whether we shall tend to be fat or lean and to mature sexually at a relatively early or late age, but here environmental influences will also play a significant role. A small number of infants will be born with gene combinations or extra chromosomes that produce biological anomalies or mental deficiency. Many more who had serious genetic defects or developmental problems in the womb will have been spontaneously aborted.

Apart from the effects of gene combinations that produce malformation or pathology, there is a considerable range of variation in any but a highly inbred population. The crossing of racial and ethnic boundaries in tens of thousands of years of contacts between and among societies has blurred the relationships between physical attributes and adaptive capacities, assuming that such a relationship once existed. Thus eye color, skin color, and other physical features appear to have little to do with visual skills, adaptation to life in particular climates, or any other adaptive skills except as they have become bases for making social judgments that affect life chances.

Prenatal Development

For roughly 40 weeks after conception, the embryo and fetus develop within a fluid medium that provides both a constant temperature and a cushioning against shocks in the uterus of the mother. The bloodstreams of mother and child are in indirect contact through the cell walls of the placenta. This provides the child with oxygen and nutrients and permits the elimination of its waste products.

Embryonic growth—the period of the first two months—is rapid, considering the size of the cells with which it began, but at eight or nine weeks the embryo is still only about an inch long. At this stage the features of the head and face have begun to take shape; arms and legs have appeared. The internal organs are now also taking shape. In the embryonic period, the rudiments of the various organ systems have been laid down. In the fetal period, which extends from about the beginning of the third month until birth, these systems become well developed and begin to function.

The developing organism is especially vulnerable to harmful effects of drugs or of various traumata to and illnesses of the mother during the first three months. Before rubella ("German measles") was largely eradicated in the United States through vaccination, significant numbers of deaf, blind, and mentally retarded children were born to mothers who had experienced the disease during the first three months of pregnancy. Roughly one in eight mothers who had rubella during this period gave birth to a defective child.

Diet. The fetus's food supply comes from the mother's bloodstream, so it is not surprising that the mother's diet has a direct effect on the development and health of the fetus. A deficient diet, common among the poor, increases the probability of miscarriage, complications of pregnancy, stillbirths, and premature birth, and also the frequency of illness in the infant through the first six months of life.[4]

Cigarette smoking, heavy alcohol use, and use of various other drugs by the mother frequently impair the development of the child and its well-being at birth. Radiation and X ray of the mother's pelvic region may also lead to anomalies, both physical and mental. Thus environmental effects on the genetic material with which the infant starts life begin well before birth.

The Impact of Birth

Birth itself is a source of threat to the organism that has previously been so well protected within its mother's body. Many infants are born before they have come to full term (roughly 37–40 weeks). Because it is often difficult to date conception, prematurity is usually assessed on the basis of birth weight. An infant under 2500 grams (about 5½ pounds) is regarded as premature, since this birth weight would normally be attained by 37 weeks. Slight prematurity is not serious, but the infant who is more than 8 weeks premature will be less well able to begin and maintain breathing, and it will have a less well-developed sucking reflex, a less efficient digestive system, and a diminished ability to maintain control of body temperature. It must therefore receive special care: oxygen, perhaps intravenous feeding, and incubation. Prematures are subject to much higher death rates and to impaired early development, with severity of impairment inversely proportionate to birth weight.

But prematurity is not the only complication of birth. Development has proceeded most rapidly in the head, which constituted almost half the length of the fetus at the beginning of the third month and still accounts for one fourth the length of the newborn infant. Birth entails great pressures on the head of the fetus as it passes through the birth canal and the pelvic girdle. Delivery using forceps to assist the infant's emergence may also threaten hemorrhaging in the brain. Fortunately, the infant's skull is remarkably resilient, but some degree of bleeding may occur and may impair oxygen intake to the brain. The most severe threat comes from deprivation of oxygen as a consequence of failure to breathe soon after delivery.

In the uterus, the fetus received oxygen from its mother through the umbilical cord. At birth it must begin to take in oxygen on its own, and quickly. Lack of oxygen causes damage and ultimately death to nerve cells. In a difficult birth or in the instance of markedly delayed breathing, the infant may suffer from anoxia, or oxygen deprivation. If prolonged, anoxia will cause severe brain damage or even death. Such damage will often be manifest in defective motor processes such as partial paralyses and tremors (so-called cerebral palsy).

Longitudinal studies of children who suffered varying degrees of anoxia and brain injury at birth give a basis for assessing long-term consequences. Roughly 2 percent of live births in the United States involve severe insult to the infant organism.[5] A recent study reveals that the great majority of individuals so afflicted are impaired psychologically or physically at least into adolescence, with a high incidence of mental retardation. But among infants who suffered less severe trauma at birth, cognitive impairment tended to be limited to the preschool years if the child was raised in a middle-class home.[6] In working-class families, where there is more pressure on resources and in general less verbal interaction between mother and child, children who had suffered from comparable degrees of anoxia and birth trauma continued in the school years to show some deficits in performance relative to their working-class peers who had had normal birth experience.

MATURATION OF THE INFANT
AND YOUNG CHILD

At birth the nervous system is not yet fully developed, but the human infant normally has the use of all the senses except taste. It can see, hear, and smell, and it is sensitive to pain and to change in position. It is capable of a large number of reflex actions, from sucking, grasping, and crying, to tracking a moving light and flexing its arms and legs. It is in touch with what goes on immediately about it.

The developmental psychologist Jerome Kagan has noted, nevertheless, that the infant probably takes in stimuli one at a time, rather than responding more or less simultaneously to all the stimuli that impinge upon it. What might otherwise seem a chaos of stimulation may be filtered by the attentional process to let through one perception at a time. What the infant does with those perceptions in the first months depends on the state of development of the nervous system. No amount of stimulation in the early weeks will permit the child to speak or even to retain a memory trace for a person or object.

The early weeks are a time of coordination of reflex actions. Although the infant can track a light in the early days, convergence of the two eyes to give accurate binocular fixation on a moving object does not occur until about seven or eight weeks, and accurate distance focusing takes a month or two longer.

In the early weeks, the infant's bodily movements become coordinated in response to caretakers and in adjusting position generally. The one-month-old infant can grasp and manipulate objects placed in its hand, but an object placed nearby will not elicit a reaching out for another two to three months. Even then, the reaching is likely to be so poorly coordinated that the object will elude the infant's grasp. But by four months, the hand will begin to respond to the message that the eyes convey as to where the hand and the object are, relative to each other, and soon thereafter the infant can begin systematically to manipulate objects that he could previously only see or hear.

Cognitive Development

As noted in the previous chapter, we owe to Piaget the basic conceptualization that has come to dominate psychological theorizing about the cognitive development of infant and child. The infant, according to Piaget, is constantly engaged in trying to make sense of his world. He does so initially by acting upon that world, organizing perceptions and manipulating them, developing *schemas* or mental images and coordinations. New ideas and objects are incorporated into existing schemas by a process Piaget called assimilation. As new experiences become assimilated, existing schemas are modified to accommodate the new information. But such accommodation depends primarily on the state of readiness of the central nervous system and the accumulation of experiences rather than on what others do to or for the infant.

The first year and a half constitutes the sensorimotor stage of development. Mental processes are developed through the physical experiencing of people and objects in the process of interaction. In the first two or three months the infant is not yet a purposive explorer of experience, but by four months he appears to act in ways that will produce changes in the external environment. He kicks and watches the results of his kicking. He shakes objects to produce interesting effects. By one year of age the infant begins to show an interest in exploring the effects of his own acts and the qualities of objects around him much more systematically.

Developmental psychologists who have been building on Piaget's formulations have learned a great deal about the first years. Perhaps the most basic key to understanding the infant and conducting research of infant development has been the recognition that "change is the central quality governing the alerting and maintenance of attention in the newborn and very young infants."[7] From an early age, infants attend to movement and to alterations in what they perceive—contour, color, sound.

By 10 weeks of age infants have the capacity to recognize an object or event that they had experienced the previous day. That is, they respond differently to the presentation of a particular stimulus—say a colored ball—than they had initially responded. This does not mean that the infant has a memory that permits it to retrieve a representation of the past. Retrieval memory will not come for another six to eight months, but some trace is left, some schema or perceptual organization that permits recognition of a previously presented sequence of objects or movements.

The 10-week-old infant does not look to find a ball that had intrigued her but that has suddenly been hidden or has otherwise disappeared from view. The ball no longer exists for her. But at eight or nine months, when retrieval memory exists, objects come to have permanence, and seeking after hidden objects becomes a playful possibility.

The child's manipulation of objects early takes on repetitive patterns that are pleasing to it. From the wiggling of a foot or the shaking of a rattle to the stacking of blocks and the rolling of a ball, the earliest play is sensorimotor activity, lacking symbolic content. The objects at hand may differ from one society to another, but what the child does with them is remarkably similar.

Attachment.   Attachment to the infant's primary caretaker—most often her mother—might be expected to occur almost from the beginning. Certainly there are indications that the infant knows when she is in the hands of her usual caretaker. But evidence of strong attachment, of distress when the caretaker leaves the infant, and of fear reduction and contentment in the presence of the caretaker, is another behavior dependent on maturation of cognitive capacities. It is not until somewhere around the eighth month that most infants show strong signs of apprehension when their primary caretaker leaves them with a stranger.[8] Attachment—to mother, father, an older sibling, or a nurse—appears to occur slightly earlier than fear of strangers, but the two are undoubtedly linked in their origins to the infant's attainment of a new ability to make mental connections. The six-month-old shows no fear of a stranger whether the mother is present or not; the 10-month-old becomes apprehensive if left alone with a stranger.

The importance of attachment and of separation anxiety—distress when the primary caretaker is absent—was first recognized when infants and young children were removed from families resident in the larger British cities that endured almost constant bombing during the second year of World War II. Sent to nurseries in the countryside, where they would be spared the horror of air attack, many infants and young children failed to respond to the loving care they received. They cried and were inconsolable. But those under six months of age were much less upset than those who were between six and about 24 months old. Moreover, the distress of many of these young children was so acute as to suggest the danger of long-term emotional consequences.[9]

Subsequently, research by Harlow and his students on the nature of mothering by Macaque monkeys and the consequences of their being deprived of maternal care gave further clues as to the importance of attachment for primates generally.[10] All primates are profoundly social beings, and their normal development requires both nurturant care and interaction with others from an early age. We shall return to further consideration of the importance of attachment later in the chapter.

The Second Year.   In the second year physical and mental development attain a uniquely human level. As the lower body and legs strengthen and begin to catch up with the development of head and torso, the infant stands and walks. Soon he becomes an explorer who must be closely watched or tethered as he gets into and onto everything. Now he can make many more things happen—noise from banging pots together, interesting effects of gravity as books are toppled from shelves onto the floor, new vistas achieved by climbing on chairs standing near windows.

The year-old infant begins to engage in symbolic play, letting the materials at hand represent other objects, such as using a hairbrush as a telephone or mud as food for a doll. By two, such play may be much elaborated and language will embellish the fantasies that are played out. Imitation of caretakers and others will become a frequent organizer of action. If small children are brought together, however, they may play in parallel but they do not engage in interactive play. At two, the child is still not able to take the perspective of another or to fit his actions appropriately to those of his associate. That ability to do so emerges gradually as a consequence of opportunities for interaction with adults and with peers.[11]

A substantial vocabulary and the rudiments of a sense of self will usually be evident by two, and the term *infant* (which means "without speech") will no longer seem appropriate. Because language and the sense of self are such crucial aspects of human development, they deserve more detailed consideration.

LANGUAGE AND THE ATTAINMENT
OF SELFHOOD

Human society is based on communication, employing language. No other creature possesses the capacity for an elaborated language. Without language it is not possible to learn more than a tiny fraction of what one needs to know to become a full participant in society. Before sign languages were developed, for example, persons born deaf were destined to be regarded as idiots. No matter how great their intellectual potential at birth, there was no way that potential could be realized.

The child does not have to be taught a language; given normal development in other respects and membership in any group where a language is spoken, the child will begin before one year of age to pick up meanings and soon thereafter to use words to communicate. Although learning theorists have attempted to explain the acquisition of language through imitation and conditioning, the rapidity with which the young child masters the structure and vocabulary of a language cannot possibly be accounted for by theories that require the shaping of behavior through conditioning or differential reward for correct usage. It is now widely agreed that humans have a built-in readiness to learn and use language.[12]

Early Language Development

Whether spoken to or not, the infant will begin to babble by the age of six months. Babbling is another way of making things happen, of producing sounds that are as fascinating to experience as the motions that can be produced by waving arms and legs. Certain sounds are more easily produced than others, but infants ultimately try out a repertoire of vocalizations that may approximate the range used in all languages. Well before they have attained meaningful speech, however, the sounds they utter have begun to approximate those of the language to which they have been exposed. However, deaf children, who hear neither their own babbling nor the language of others, gradually stop babbling by the end of the first year.

The first words spoken are generally names for persons, objects, or acts.[13] The child initially uses a single word to stand for a whole sentence or idea, an idea that can usually be understood because of the context in which it is uttered. Within a few more months two words are being combined to make "telegraphic" sentences or questions: "Drink milk"; "Where Mommy?"

Rules for making plurals, for using prepositions, and for using auxiliary verbs are all learned within a matter of two or three years after the beginnings of speech. There appears to be a high degree of constancy in the order in which rules of a particular language are learned, though many will not be totally mastered for some time. Parental coaching or correcting the child's grammatical lapses seems to make little difference in the rate of learning or the correctness of usage, perhaps because grammatical correctness is not the primary consideration of either parent or child most of the time. What the child is trying to say in terms of ongoing interaction is more often the focus of concern.

Social Class Differences. Even though parental coaching does not seem to make an appreciable difference in the child's use of language, social-class (and ethnic group) differences in vocabulary and in verbal facility begin to appear almost from the first words spoken. Middle-class children tend to have larger vocabularies—to know more words—at any given age level beyond a year.[14] It does not appear that ability to learn new words is associated with other cognitive skills, yet the vocabulary score on a standard intelligence test tends to be highly correlated with total IQ score. Thus middle-class children have an early edge over working-class children in dealing with the kind of test that best predicts later school success.

Some degree of genetic difference between the classes cannot be ruled out, but studies of working-class children adopted into middle-class homes indicate that the home environment has a considerable effect on verbal facility. Such children adopted at an early age tend to have essentially the same verbal facility as the biological children of middle-class parents. Language is elaborated to a greater extent and the child is more likely to be encouraged to talk about her feelings and experiences in a middle-class home. In a society where verbal skills are highly valued, the consequences of such early exposure are considerable.

Types of Speech. Much of the child's early use of language is an accompaniment to activity, seemingly not so much for the purpose of communicating to others as to comment on himself, to himself. In one of his early works, Piaget distinguished between two categories of speech, egocentric and social.[15]

> When a child utters phrases belonging to the first group he does not bother to know to whom he is speaking nor whether he is being listened to. He talks either for himself or for the pleasure of associating anyone who happens to be there with the activity of the moment.

Egocentric speech may take several forms—simple repetition of words or phrases, a running monologue in which the child appears to be speaking to himself or thinking aloud, or what Piaget called a "collective monologue," in which the child's commentary is a response to the presence of others but does not take their perspective into account.

In social speech the child takes into account the perspective of another person. While Piaget viewed egocentric and social speech as successive developmental stages, it is now generally agreed that both occur in early childhood but that egocentric speech represents the child's developing thought, serving for self-guidance and self-instruction.[16] Egocentric speech may not reflect a failure to take into account the perspective of others, but because it is addressed to self, it does not require the elaboration that would be needed in speech addressed to others.

Language adds a new dimension to cognition. The child can label objects and experiences, can repeat and rehearse injunctions or restrictions that his parents have placed upon him. Language helps in problem solving, though certain cognitive skills that are still to be mastered do not seem to be primarily dependent on language. But increasingly, the child's reflective thought will entail the use of internal or covert speech, while the child's interactions with others are mediated through language.

Language and play both serve to permit the development of the human's unique psychological organization based on a sense of self, an ability to view one's own behavior from the perspective of others.

The Self and Self-Awareness.   Language (not necessarily speech) seems to be an essential feature of fully developed self-awareness. In the first year the infant experiences her own body, but there is little evidence that she has any sense of being an entity. A child can become an object to herself only after she has begun to master symbolic meanings—to recognize in the speech and actions of others what the others intend, want, or are doing. Particularly as others act toward the child, and as their actions place restraints on the child's actions or express strong sentiments toward her, the child can rehearse those actions or utterances and apply them to herself. A parental "don't" may be echoed by the child later as she inhibits a forbidden act that was in process—for example, as she was about to run into the street.

The sense of self is also enhanced as the child engages in dramatic role playing, one feeding her doll as she has been fed, another giving a lecture to his toy dog as his father has spoken to the family dog. By making believe that he or she is someone else, the child learns to take the perspective of that other person. In this way the child can further rehearse or relive interactions involving himself. The perspective will often be distorted, and it will be some years before the child is able to envision with fair accuracy how things seem from a very different position than his own, but once the child has a sense of self he also has a much better sense of others.

We owe to the social philosopher George Herbert Mead our understanding of how the sense of self emerges through the grasp of symbolic meanings, the process of role taking in early childhood, and, ultimately, through what Mead calls the perspective of the "generalized other."[17] His example of the generalized other is again an instance of play, but this time in a complex game where each player has a different task and thus a somewhat different perspective, yet each must be able to share the perspective of others. In baseball, for example, the pitcher, batter, catcher, and fielder all have different tasks and objectives, but each must know what the others will (or should) do in a given instance, say a long fly ball or a wild pitch when there is a runner on third. The cognitive complexity of such a game is not mastered in the preschool years, but as simpler collective interactions are mastered, the child comes to have a sense of self and others that permits the complex accommodations that are the essence of social life.

WHAT SOCIETY EXPECTS OF PARENTS
AND OF INFANTS

Every human is born into a family that is part of a society, an organized group of persons of all ages who share a culture or set of designs for living. Among the beliefs that make up the core of the culture are those that relate to birth and death, to the nature of human nature and of the human infant, and to the differences between males and females.[18] These vary over time, as anyone who has studied the history of Western civilization or the vagaries of child rearing practices in the last hundred years well knows. In modern, industrial society many diverse beliefs exist side by side—some new, some traditional, some based on systematic theory, some based on current fads. Nevertheless, a broad consensus seems to characterize the majority of middle-class persons and families, even in our own heterogeneous society.

All societies tend to have dominant views or values as to the ways infants and children should be treated and the forms of behavior expected of boys and girls at different ages. In rural Mexico and in much of Latin America that has a Mayan heritage, for example, it is believed that stimulation of the infant will lead to excitement and ultimately to fear, which may have grave physical consequences. Therefore infants are restricted and shielded from stimulating experiences. By contrast, many North American parents try to provide such stimulation for their infants and young children in order to make them more competent and independent.

If human nature is seen as essentially evil, as it was in Puritan society, children are likely to be harshly dealt with to curb their evil tendencies and "break their will," just as one might break a wild bronco. If, on the other hand, children are seen as "good and beautiful in their potential, as flowers opening to the sun" of loving care, they will be nurtured and encouraged in quite different ways. Each society will manage to convey to each new generation the message of what is expected and how the expected is most likely to come about. The message will be delivered in many ways. It will be delivered in expressions of praise for persons who exemplify the cultural model and in expressions of blame and ridicule for those who fail most abjectly to meet expectations. Initially, it is the parents whose behavior toward the infant is most shaped by such forces. Later, cultural norms will impinge more directly on the child.

A generation ago students of child development were preoccupied with modes and timing of feeding, weaning, and toilet training, all of which vary greatly from culture to culture. Now we are reasonably sure that these are relatively trivial elements in the child's experience.[19] But the relationships parents have with their children are not trivial, nor are their interactions with the infant and the consistency of their responses to it. Are parents for the most part rewarding or are they punishing of the small child's efforts to explore and experience? Do they attend to the child's needs immediately and shield it from unpleasant feelings, or do they seek to develop in it early on some sense of self-control and discipline? Does it matter whether the infant is attended to primarily by its mother or by other relatives or in some other arrangement such as a day nursery or even a boarding facility? Under what circumstances does the mode of caretaking make a difference in the infant's cognitive development, its temperament, its ability to relate closely to others? Recent research on the developing infant and child addresses such questions and emphasizes that parent-child relationships and influences are reciprocal, not a one-way street.

Parents and Infants

In most societies, parents are the primary caretakers of infants. Parents (mothers, for the most part) initially provide primarily for the infant's physical needs and shield her from harmful exposures. But very early, parents begin to make demands on the infant. They may feed her on a fixed schedule or they may feed her at the first sign of fussing. They may let her sleep whenever she falls asleep or they may want to have her sleeping scheduled to have her awake at particular times. And, sooner or later, they attempt to impose their wishes and expectations.

But the infant is no slouch at imposing new demands upon the parents. If parents are said to socialize infants and children, it is equally true that infants and children socialize their parents and often rather forcefully induct them into the parental role. As Harriet Rheingold has noted, the parents' own patterns of eating and sleeping and their whole round of normal activities are likely to be profoundly modified by their first child.[20]

Above all, most parents want to keep their infants happy. The infant's cry is extremely wearing for a parent (or almost any adult) to listen to. Indeed, physical abuse of an infant is perhaps most often a response to unchecked crying, an impulsive act by a desperate parent whose psychological resources are limited. But if the infant's cry is painful to hear, its smile is a rich reward, likely to elicit smiles from parents and assorted bystanders. Rheingold suggests that the smile is a kind of challenge, demanding parental response in kind. There is, then, in most societies a lively two-way process of interaction and influence. Parental patterns that are ineffective need to be modified, just as behaviors of the older child that are offensive to the parent need to be modified if there is to be a satisfying relationship for all parties.

In most societies fathers are interested in and emotionally invested in their offspring but not active in child care. The infant and small child is almost always with or near its mother or other caretaker (often mother's sister or an older sibling). In many societies, it is only when boys become old enough to emulate men that most fathers become closely involved with their sons.

In less technologically developed societies, the infant's survival depends for some time on being nursed by his mother or some other woman. This both extends the definition of a woman's role and tends to insure primacy in child care. No such constraints need apply in modern industrial society, and a large majority of infants are not nursed at the breast but are bottle-fed. Yet the traditional role of mother as primary caretaker of infant and young child remains the dominant pattern. We shall leave for a later chapter detailed consideration of the social and the biological differences between the sexes.[21] In this chapter we shall rather be concerned with whether the mother's full involvement with the child's upbringing is of crucial importance.

Early Childhood Socialization

To become an effective member of the society into which he or she is born, the young child must master many different competences. The child, parents, peers, and others interact in ways that influence all participants and that give the child not only an exposition of what is expected and examples of desirable behavior, but also opportunities to try out the skills and master the controls that must be acquired. Early childhood socialization may be thought of as entailing a series of developmental tasks. Building on the earlier work of Havighurst, I have elsewhere noted that the child and the agents of socialization, most especially his parents, both have a part to play, though often they are only dimly aware of the nature of the process in whch they participate.[22] Table 3-1 reproduces the earlier summary of parental aims or activities on the one hand and the child's task or achievement on the other, in

Table 3-1   Types of Tasks of Early Childhood Socialization in the Family

PARENTAL AIM OR ACTIVITY	CHILD'S TASK OR ACHIEVEMENT
1. Provision of nurturance and physical care.	Acceptance of nurturance (development of trust).
2. Training and channeling of physiological needs in toilet training, weaning, provision of solid foods, etc.	Control of the expression of biological impulses; learning acceptable channels and times of gratification.
3. Teaching and skill-training in language, perceptual skills, physical skills, self-care skills in order to facilitate care, insure safety, etc.	Learning to recognize objects and cues; language learning; learning to walk, negotiate obstacles, dress, feed self, etc.
4. Orienting the child to his immediate world of kin, neighborhood, community, and society, and to his own feelings.	Developing a cognitive map of one's social world; learning to fit behavior to situational demands.
5. Transmitting cultural and subcultural goals and values and motivating the child to accept them for his own.	Developing a sense of right and wrong; developing goals and criteria for choices, investment of effort for the common good.
6. Promoting interpersonal skills, motives, and modes of feeling and behaving in relation to others.	Learning to take the perspective of another person; responding selectively to the expectations of others.
7. Guiding, correcting, helping the child to formulate his own goals, plan his own activities.	Achieving a measure of self-regulation and criteria for evaluating own performance.

the course of early childhood socialization in the family. As I wrote in elaboration of the summary table:

> We may note the following major responsibilities which parents must to some degree fulfill if the child is to survive and to achieve sufficient competence to be acceptable to his parents and to others:
>
> 1.   Provision of sustenance and nurturance for the infant.
> 2.   Training and channeling of physiological needs—for food, elimination, sleep, etc.—to suit the convenience of parents and (ultimately) to meet cultural standards.
> 3.   Teaching, skill training, and providing opportunities for practice of motor skills, language, cognitive skills, social skills, and technical skills in order to facilitate care, insure safety, and develop potentials for autonomous behavior.
> 4.   Orienting the child to his immediate world of kin, community, and society in a variety of social situations and settings.
> 5.   Transmitting cultural goals and values; motivating the child toward parental and societal goals.
> 6.   Promoting interpersonal skills, concern for and responsiveness to the feelings of others.
> 7.   Controlling the scope of the child's behaviors, limiting "transgressions," correcting errors, providing guidance and interpretations (and here we crosscut several of the above tasks).

Most of these responsibilities or tasks are further defined in any society by norms that specify how and when parents are to carry them out; that is, a mother is expected to be nurturant in a particular way, "good parents" invest time and effort and follow accepted techniques to make sure that their children learn particular skills, avoid particular kinds of transgressions by certain ages. In all societies there appear to exist ideals of "good child" and "good parent," even though there may be a great deal of latitude in many realms of parent-child interaction.

For each of these statements of parental aims and activities, we can offer a corollary task or achievement for the child. These are summarized in Table 1 [Table 3-1]. The parents' provision of nurturance, affection, and warmth should permit the child to develop a sense of trust and at very least to adapt his bodily movements to those of his caretaker. Failure to adapt, either because of biological deficits in the child or anxiety and tension in the caretaker, will cause a great deal of frustration for both infant and caretaker. Descriptions by psychiatric clinicians suggest that failure to achieve mutual gratification in the nurturing relationship is likely to be associated with a long train of emotional difficulties for the child.

Parental training aimed at the channeling of the child's physiological needs has as its counterpart the demand that the child control his biological impulses, expressing them only in acceptable modes and giving up unacceptable ones. As every parent knows, there can be a great deal of give-and-take and effort on the part of both parent and child before the child willingly accepts the solid foods offered him, gives up the breast or the bottle, and consistently uses the approved toilet arrangements. There MAY be much effort expended, but then again, there may not. Much depends on the vigor and skill with which parents pursue their aims and on the child's readiness. In many societies it appears that such matters do not tend to become important issues;

yet in all societies children do learn the necessary measures of control and channels of gratification.[23]

We have noted that the child's development of certain physical skills and of language will depend primarily on the opportunity to use maturing skills and on immersion in a language community. Nevertheless, stimulation and the provision of models for the child is important, and so is a measure of demand for performance. The mother who always dresses and feeds her child does not maximize the child's ability to dress and feed himself. A good many tasks can probably be learned by children much earlier than we permit them to learn; continued parental babying prevents both skill learning and the development of a sense of competence and autonomy. More important than performance of the tasks themselves will be the child's ability to exercise judgment in his own behalf. As he matures, he must learn to make decisions and to experience their consequences.

The tasks of childhood socialization and their accomplishment are clearly not one-step matters. They entail mastery of increasing complexity as the child's cognitive ability and physical development permit increasingly great demands for performance. They also entail increasing differentiation of perspectives, depending upon where one is located in the society and the ecology; for example, whether in an upper-middle-class professional family, the family of an Appalachian coal miner, or a single-parent family in an urban slum.

Play, Patterns, Culture, and Sex Differentiation

Almost all cultures provide boys and girls with different play materials and encourage sex differentiation. American tradition has been to disapprove most strongly of boys who choose cross-sex play activities and toys, and less strongly of girls who are "tomboys." Until very recently in Western society the earliest forms of symbolic play have been subtly and not so subtly shaped by providing models, materials, and encouragement to "act like a boy," "act like a girl," which is to say, "follow the traditional patterns of sex differentiation that have been recognized by our people."

Although preschool boys and girls play in somewhat different contexts and use different materials, the amount of time spent in social versus solitary play is very similar. In American preschool settings, boys spend more time in gross motor activities such as rough-and-tumble play and use more physical space, while girls more often engage in sedentary activities such as painting and crafts that use fine motor skills. Such differentiation is greatest in traditional schools and least in those schools that expose boys and girls to the same apparent expectations. In nursery schools and kindergartens in the People's Republic of China, boys and girls are given different toys to play with, but boys are given far more training in the use of fine motor skills than in America. Sex differences in China seem muted, despite separation of the sexes in many activities.[24]

Solitary play in which the child successively plays different roles or enacts the role of caretaker to a doll or mechanic to his broken car is an important step in moving toward more mature social interaction with others and at the same time acquiring the interests expected of members of the society. We shall be noting in later chapters how at each life stage, cultures shape (and sharpen) differences in the interests and activities of males and females.

THE IMPORTANCE OF INFANCY AND EARLY CHILDHOOD

The importance of the early months and years was a major premise of Freud, and life-course theorists who take psychoanalytic theory as their basic frame of reference stress the importance of love and consistent care in the first year of life. It will be recalled, for example, that Erikson sees infancy as the period in which the first developmental task, that of coming to trust others, is normally accomplished. If the infant is treated harshly and inconsistently, it will fail to achieve basic trust and will subsequently have difficulty not only in establishing close ties but also in the accomplishment of later tasks. Let us now examine existing evidence on this matter.

There are two general issues to be considered. One relates to the stability of early attributes such as temperament, intellective or cognitive power and skills, or physical well-being. The other relates to whether particular early experiences or circumstances tend to have a determining effect or even a significant influence on the personality and competence of the individual in later life. Both issues are extremely complex and difficult to resolve, but we have some evidence bearing on each.

The Stability of Early Temperament

At birth the human infant is in process of undergoing extraordinarily rapid transition and growth. It is not surprising, then, that there is little stability in the attributes of infants in the early weeks of life. Infants who appear very active one week may be less so the next. Irritability may give way to placidity and vice versa. Whatever innate differences exist, they are not evident at the start, even when infants are studied very intensively. By the time stabilities begin to be evident, they are a reflection of the interaction of infant and caretaker. Research has repeatedly shown that parents tend to behave differently toward irritable and placid infants, and infants may respond quite differently to similar parental behaviors.[25]

In any event, the assessment of stability requires that researchers study the same children over a period of time, using the same measures but safeguarding against bias. If one believes that there is a high degree of stability and knows how an infant or child scored in a previous assessment, there is danger that the investigator will see more continuity than exists. Moreover, longitudinal studies are extremely costly to carry out and require both long-term funding and dedicated researchers.

Results of the half dozen major longitudinal studies of personality and temperament carried out in the past 50 years are not entirely consistent but lead to the general conclusion that there are short-term stabilities in the first two or three years, but that these have little carry-over into later childhood. On the other hand, by age five there appears to be greater stability in certain attributes that show continuities into the later years.[26] Activity level, expressiveness versus withdrawal, dependency versus autonomy, and "difficult versus easy" temperament in the early years all show some degree of continuity into the adolescent and sometimes the adult years.[27] In general, continuity is quite substantial over short periods of years but drops off in the longer run.

Consequences
for Later Intellectual Development

Psychologists have devised a wide variety of tests to assess intellectual skills and capacities. They have been successful in developing tests that are highly predictive of success in academic pursuits, especially as such success rests on verbal or mathematical reasoning.[28] Few would argue that the tests measure innate capacity, but the genetic component in intelligence certainly accounts for a good deal of interpersonal variation *when comparing persons subject to comparably stimulating and rewarding environments and social conditions.* When life conditions and intellectual stimulation vary sharply, however, we simply do not have adequate means of assessing the relative contributions of heredity and environment.

Tests of intelligence that can be used with school children are of course administered through the use of language, and verbal facility is both required for testing and a major component in what is tested. With infants, observation of responses to a variety of stimulus situations—presentation of blocks or puzzles, demands on physical skills—yields a basis for comparing the infants on their manifest abilities. There is a fair measure of stability in the rankings of infants on such measures from one period to another during the first two years,[29] but these rankings are little related to later rankings on measures of verbal intelligence. This does not mean that there may not still be stabilities in some of the skills earlier assessed, but rather that new cognitive skills come into play with language and become preeminently important in performance of the reasoning tasks that are presented in tests of intelligence. Those tests predict the kind of performance skills that academic learning entails, but not necessarily other aspects of intelligence that make for success in dealing with people or with the dilemmas of everyday life.

What is perhaps most impressive about the kind of intelligence that is measured by tests administered after the age of five or six is how much stability it shows over a lifetime if there are not sharp changes in life circumstances. By the age of three a fair measure of stability becomes apparent; and by seven a reasonably good prediction can generally be made of measured intelligence at maturity. "Reasonably good" for most, that is, but changes may occur in either direction. A child moved from a grossly unstimulating environment such as a state hospital or an orphanage may gain as much as 20 IQ points if placed in an intellectually stimulating home, and persons who are not intellectually challenged may decline in IQ. Health, emotional state, and marked environmental change can all influence test scores.[30] In general, increased education tends to enhance IQ. IQ is influenced by family resources and cultural opportunities. Working-class children tend early on to score somewhat lower than middle-class children, and in general they drop further behind in the adult years because of lower educational attainment.

In summary, we can say that assessments of infant intelligence do not tell us much about later intelligence, but it is likely that the stimulation and challenging of the infant's curiosity and the encouragement and enhancement of verbal skills as infancy draws to a close have an influence on later cognitive development.

Early Parental Behavior
and Emotional Development

We do not have longitudinal studies of children who have been abused in childhood, although there have been follow-up studies of children subject to severe deprivation by virtue of war and displacement. There can be no doubt about the emotional distress of these children during the early years, but longer time consequences seem to depend on the subsequent love and support they receive. Thus homeless European children orphaned by World War II who were adopted by middle-class families in the United States at ages five months to 10 years were studied some years later by a team of investigators. Despite the children's showing severe anxiety, sleep disturbances, and excessive clinging to their new parents in the initial months and years, these symptoms vanished over the years and the children made normal school progress.[31]

On the other hand, there are many examples of the tragic consequences of child neglect and abuse in our prisons and psychiatric institutions. Those who practice wanton violence, who abuse those closest to them, who murder for the thrill of seeing another die, are frequently found to have been the unwanted offspring of parents who rejected and abused them.[32] Often they spent their early years in a succession of institutions and foster homes. Each disruption of existing relationships would appear to have made them less able to trust adults. Less dramatic but no less significant is the evidence from longitudinal research that offspring of parents who had been rated relatively less accepting and inconsistent in their treatment of the children were more likely in their middle years to be hostile, heavy drinkers and given to explosive rages.[33]

There is, then, both evidence of resilience on the part of young children and evidence that early experiences can make it extremely difficult for the young child to establish trusting relationships that will enable it to develop a secure and accepting sense of its own self-worth. Every rejection and instance of abusive treatment can be a message to the child that it is not worthy of respect and love. It requires long, consistent, unconditional love to undo the effects of such messages.

Beyond rejection and inconsistent care, how critical for the child's future is early parental behavior toward it? In the United States there was long a belief that nothing short of a mother's care could be depended on to produce a happy, effective child. Day care centers and nurseries have been regarded by some as inevitably damaging to the child. Careful research very definitely refutes such accusations. Extended day care, beginning before the age of six months, has proven to be as effective in furthering the child's cognitive and emotional development and well-being as care in the home by its mother.[34] Moreover, children who participate in well-staffed and well-run day care programs prove to be no less attached to or affectionate with their own mothers despite their spending more waking hours with their caretakers in the center than with their mothers.

In conclusion, infancy and early childhood see enormous changes as the helpless organism becomes a little person, equipped with language, a sense of self, and an ever-increasing set of skills and understandings. A certain amount of shaping of future potentialities occurs right from the start, but the small child is still a bundle of almost infinite capacities for development and change. If a sound, undamaged organism receives reasonably consistent, loving care, the primary shapers of the child's future are likely to be the resources that caretakers have available to them and can bring to bear. These in turn depend very largely on where within the larger society and its strata and cultural groups the family is located. For beyond early childhood the family is no longer the primary locale for learning. The individual must be launched on a larger sea, and both the tranquillity and the ultimate goals of the successively longer voyages from home port will depend on the outfitting that has preceded launching, the learning experiences of early ventures, and the supports or maintenance work that is constantly required. But above all, the developing person will be assuming ever-increasing responsibility for deciding what he or she will do and be.

NOTES

1. Theodosius Dobzhansky's *Mankind Evolving* (New Haven, CN: Yale University Press, 1962) still affords one of the most cogent analyses of the interactions of biology and culture.

2. Developments in the science of human genetics continue at a dizzying pace. A good basic treatment is provided in A. P. Mange and E. J. Mange, *Genetics: Human Aspects* (Philadelphia: Saunders College Publishing Co., 1980).

3. For an excellent overview, see Jerome Kagan, Richard Kearsley, and Philip Zelazo, *Infancy: Its Place in Human Development* (Cambridge, MA: Harvard University Press, 1978).

4. For references to research on the effects of diet and of premature birth, see Paul Mussen et al., *Child Development and Personality*, 6th ed. (New York: Harper & Row, 1984), pp. 61-63.

5. This proportion may be increasing as a consequence of the effects of neonatal intensive care, which permits the survival of many neurologically damaged and otherwise vulnerable infants who would have died just a decade ago.

6. Emmy E. Werner and R. S. Smith, *Kauai's Children Come of Age* (Honolulu: University of Hawaii Press, 1977).

7. Jerome Kagan, *Psychological Research on the Human Infant: An Evaluative Summary* (New York: William T. Grant Foundation, 1982).

8. The systematic study of attachment owes much to Mary Ainsworth, beginning with her *Infancy in Uganda* (Baltimore: Johns Hopkins University Press, 1967).

9. The wartime experience of young children separated from their parents was the long-time focus of the research and theorizing of John Bowlby. See his *Attachment and Loss,* vol. 2, *Separation, Anxiety and Anger* (New York: Basic Books, 1973).

10. Harry F. Harlow and Margaret K. Harlow, "The Affectional Systems," in A. M. Schrier, H. F. Harlow, and F. Stollnitz, *Behavior of Nonhuman Primates* (New York: Academic Press, 1965).

11. On the functions of play, see Jean Piaget, *Play, Dreams and Imitation in Childhood* (New York: Norton, 1951) and Jerome Singer, *The Child's World of Make Believe: Experimental Studies of Imaginative Play* (New York: Academic Press, 1973).

12. See Mussen et al., *Child Development and Personality,* 6th ed., pp. 180–217.

13. An excellent description and analysis of language learning is provided by Roger Brown, *A First Language* (Cambridge, MA: Harvard University Press, 1973).

14. Kagan, Kearsley, and Zelazo, *Infancy,* p. 151.

15. Jean Piaget, *Language and Thought of the Child,* 2nd ed. (London: Routledge, Kagan, and Paul, 1952), p. 9.

16. This perspective was convincingly developed by the Russian psychologist L. S. Vygotsky, *Thought and Language* (New York: Wiley, 1962).

17. George Herbert Mead, *Mind, Self and Society* (Chicago: University of Chicago Press, 1934).

18. For a fascinating examination of childhood in several societies, see Erik Erikson, *Childhood and Society* (New York: Norton, 1951). Perhaps the most ambitious cross-cultural study of child rearing is reported in Beatrice Whiting, ed., *Six Cultures: Studies of Child Rearing* (New York: Wiley, 1963). How society's demands vary by social structure is discussed in detail in Alex Inkeles, "Society, Social Structure and Child Socialization," in John A. Clausen, ed., *Socialization and Society* (Boston: Little, Brown and Co., 1968), pp. 73–129.

19. Excellent reviews of the vast literature on this topic are found in Howard Orlansky, "Infant Care and Personality," *Psychological Bulletin* 46 (1949), and Bettye M. Caldwell, "The Effects of Infant Care," in Martin Hoffman and Lois W. Hoffman, eds., *Review of Child Development Research,* vol. 1 (New York: Russell Sage Foundation, 1964).

20. Harriet Rheingold, in a delightful essay, characterizes the infant as socializer of his parents: "The Social and Socializing Infant," in David Goslin, ed., *Handbook of Socialization Theory and Research* (Chicago: Rand McNally, 1969).

21. For a good discussion, see Alice Rossi, "A Biological Perspective on Parenting," *Daedalus,* 106, no. 2 (Spring 1977), 1–32.

22. The full elaboration is given in J. A. Clausen, "Perspectives on Childhood Socialization," in J. A. Clausen, ed., *Socialization and Society,* pp. 130–81.

23. Ibid., pp. 139–41.

24. William Kessen, ed., *Childhood in China* (New Haven, CN: Yale University Press, 1975), pp. 110–11.

25. An influential study bearing on early temperament is that of A. Thomas and S. Chess, *Temperament and Development* (New York: Brunner-Maisel, 1977).

26. Howard Moss, "Longitudinal Studies of Childhood." Paper prepared for Behavioral Sciences Research Review Panel, National Institute of Mental Health, 1983.

27. Wanda Bronson, "Adult Derivatives of Emotional Expressiveness and Reactivity Control: Developmental Continuities from Childhood to Adulthood," *Child Development,* 38 (September 1967), 801–17.

28. For a good discussion of the state of knowledge on this topic, see Mussen et al., *Child Development and Personality,* 6th ed., Chapter 8.

29. There is, however, some evidence of discontinuities at ages when new cognitive skills come into operation, such as when infants are able to retrieve representations of past experiences (around eight months) and when language emerges (12–13 months). See Kagan, *Psychological Research on the Human Infant,* p. 6.

30. See Mussen et al., *Child Development and Personality,* 6th ed., pp. 274–98.

31. This research was reported in C. Rathburn, L. DiVirgilio, and S. Waldfogel, "The restitutive

process in children following radical separation from family and culture." *American Journal of Orthopsychiatry,* 28 (1958), 408-15.

32. Intensive research on violent children is reported in Fritz Redl and David Wineman, *Children Who Hate* (Glencoe, IL: The Free Press, 1951). See also R. Kaplan, V. J. Konecni, and R. W. Novaco, eds., *Aggression in Children and Youth* (The Hague: Martinus Nijhoff, 1984).

33. For example, Jack Block and Norma Haan describe one subgroup of their male study members—Type E: unsettled undercontrollers—that shows such tendencies. See their *Lives over Time* (Berkeley, CA: Bancroft Press, 1972), pp. 178-88.

34. See Kagan, Kearsley, and Zelazo, *Infancy,* pp. 260-93.

CHAPTER 4
LATER CHILDHOOD

The child is father to the man.
—William Wordsworth

At two, the average child is a toddler with a vocabulary of about 300 words. Unless she has been attending a day nursery, has a daytime sitter, or has been placed in an institution, she is likely to have been almost totally in the care of family. Before the child reaches three, she will in all likelihood attain half of her mature height. By four the average child's vocabulary will include 1000 words, and these will most often be used in sentences that follow the basic grammatical rules of the child's native language.[1]

Early childhood is thus a time of rapid physical, linguistic, and cognitive development. It is a time when the family is the basic agent of socialization and the child is being groomed to move outside the family, into nursery school or kindergarten, into the neighborhood, onto the playground or perhaps the streets, in American society. By five or six, boys and girls will be entering elementary school, and their behavior will now be subject to evaluation by others.

In this chapter we shall briefly consider the basic processes of physical and cognitive development from early childhood to puberty, the onset of adolescence, and then examine in more detail the roles of family and school in child socialization. From early childhood there are increasing demands from others that the child behave in accordance with established norms and standards. Children must learn those norms and standards and become increasingly responsible for their own behavior. Our primary interest is in the child's preparation for competent performance at each step along the developmental progression toward adulthood and the implications of early attainments or problems for adult attainment.

PHYSICAL DEVELOPMENT
IN THE PREADOLESCENT YEARS

Physical growth is most rapid in infancy and early childhood. The infant's "height" (length) at birth gives some indication of mature height, though differential maturation both in the early years and again at puberty can result in major resorting of children by height. Moreover, a deprived versus an abundant diet in the first three years can make as much as a two-inch difference in mature height.[2]

In general, however, a child who is taller than his or her peers by the start of kindergarten is likely to be taller at maturity, especially in the case of boys. To a very great extent, height is determined by heredity *if* individuals have comparable diets and are equally free of serious disease. Identical twins (i.e., those having identical genes) tend to be almost identical in height, whether reared together or apart, while other brothers and sisters show a much more moderate resemblance (represented by a correlation coefficient of roughly 0.5).[3] Most girls attain mature height before age 18, while boys may continue to add height for several years.

Whereas height is a very stable characteristic, weight tends to go up and down over time. There is no such thing as "mature weight," and most persons tend to gain weight into their middle years. In general, weight is related to height, but its relations to height over the life course are strongly influenced by body build— whether one is stocky and muscular, round and soft, or lean and tall.

Body build also influences strength and other physical capacities, and all of these attributes—height, weight, body proportions and capacities—influence appearance and the social stimulus value that an individual has for others. This in turn influences the self-image and self-esteem, especially in the years of childhood and adolescence. Therefore we shall want to examine more closely the ways in which physical attributes may make a difference.

Early Correlations of Body Build

By the early school years individuals will be changing much less rapidly in height and weight than they were in the first three years, but a group of first graders will show a wide range of variation. Boys will be a bit taller and heavier than girls, but differences among boys or girls will be far greater than differences between the sexes. Some children will be tall and solidly built, some tall and thin, some short and heavy, some short and thin, and all conceivable other combinations. There will be a tendency for many adults to assume that the larger children are older and that more should be expected of them. The larger, heavier boys and girls are likely to be somewhat stronger than their smaller peers, but they may also be a bit awkward and self-conscious about the way they stand out.

In a study of the social consequences of size, body build, and rate of maturing among members of the Institute of Human Development's longitudinal projects, I found that the taller boys were not only rated more submissive from the age of five or six to early adolescence, but were judged by psychologists as less given to showing off all during childhood and the early years of adolescence.[4]

Perhaps because the taller boys and girls seem at first to lack self-assurance, the most admired boys are not the tallest but those who are well built, muscular, and athletic. William Sheldon (whose career was devoted to the study of body build and its effects) called the well-built, muscular types *mesomorphs* (*meso*—middle + *morph*—form, shape). Mesomorphs are neither skinny nor fat in their childhood and early adult years but tend to be fairly broad of beam and muscular. Most professional athletes are mesomorphs.

Whether or not there is a biological connection between body build and temperament—and most psychologists and geneticists doubt that there is an important linkage in the genes—children learn very early that it is desirable to be a mesomorph. Several studies have found that by the early grades of school, boys respond to pictures of adult males representing endomorphs (plump, rounded bodies), mesomorphs, and ectomorphs (thin, somewhat sticklike bodies), quite differently.[5] Mesomorphs are stereotyped not only as athletes but as leaders, as more friendly, more courageous, most able to endure pain, and, in general, as ideal males. Endomorphs are stereotyped not only as self-indulgent but as lazy, lacking in courage, and least likely to be a leader or to be wanted as a friend. Ectomorphs are hardly any more favorably viewed than endomorphs in most aspects and are seen by older boys as most likely to have a "nervous breakdown." In American society we have quite clear stereotypes of body build which children learn early.

It is certainly true that mesomorphs are more likely to be athletes than are either extreme ectomorphs or extreme endomorphs, but these body types are not distinct, mutually exclusive entities. The endomorphic, mesomorphic, and ectomorphic dimensions are just that—component dimensions for characterizing body build. A person may be rated as to degree on each component, and most of us are mixed types—perhaps endomorphic-mesomorphs, or mesomorphic-ectomorphs. Moreover, what we do with our potentials can vary greatly, so all athletes need not be built like the idealized Apollo. And if we study the personality correlates of body build over the adolescent and adult years, we find that they do not at all support the stereotypes. The stereotypes are to a large extent social fictions apart from their contribution to physical performance and early evaluations.

On the other hand, we do find that mesomorphs are more likely to be named by their grade school and high school classmates as leaders, to be chosen as typically daring and aggressive, and to be popular in their preadolescent years.[6] What is most interesting is that mesomorphy has the greatest payoff for positive evaluation in the working class, where social reputation is enhanced by fighting ability and strength. Moreover, working-class mesomorphs are more likely to develop their potential for physical strength than are middle-class mesomorphs.[7] This is perhaps one reason why professional athletes are so largely drawn from working-class origins; strength is a readily identifiable resource to be developed, perhaps to the detriment of other, less easily identifiable potentials. Ectomorphs tend to be devalued in the working class, but much less so in the middle class, perhaps because academic performance counts for relatively more among middle-class children, and ectomorphs who are not athletically inclined may turn to academic exploits.

Body build thus makes some difference in physical abilities but far more difference because of its social meaning. In our longitudinal research it is not unusual to interview persons at age 50 who recall childhood as a time of low self-esteem and much unhappiness because they were fat or were skinny and ungainly and felt that they could not therefore be acceptable to others. Also, we all know of short men who, like Napoleon, seek to exert mastery over others. It is natural that persons should seek to compensate for what they view as their deficits, and often efforts at such compensation will motivate persons to unusual achievements.

Just prior to the onset of puberty, at around 10 to 12 for girls and 12 to 14 for boys, more rapid growth occurs and persists for several years. Girls may suddenly become taller than the boys with whom they have grown up. Other bodily changes gradually occur that move the boy or girl into adolescence. The timing of these changes has a major impact on the status of the individual, and we leave discussion of them till the next chapter.

COGNITIVE DEVELOPMENT
IN CHILDHOOD

There are a number of mental processes that enter into what we commonly refer to as "thinking," and what psychologists more often call "cognition." They are nicely summarized in a leading textbook on child development:

> Cognition refers to the processes involved in: (1) *perception*—the detection, organization, and interpretation of information from both the outside world and the internal environment, (2) *memory*—the storage and retrieval of the perceived information, (3) *reasoning*—the use of knowledge to make inferences and draw conclusions, (4) *reflection*—the evaluation of the quality of ideas and solutions, and (5) *insight*—the recognition of new relationships between two or more segments of knowledge.[8]

Each of these component processes is itself far from a single, simple ability or capacity in operation. We noted in the previous chapter the difference between *recognition memory* (the knowledge that one has experienced a stimulus or event in the past) and *retrieval memory* (the ability to bring forth information learned in the past for use in the present). The first is acquired in the early weeks of life, while the second begins to be evident in the second half of the first year. Similarly, the other basic processes that enter into our ability to think develop at different rates and build up gradually during childhood. Moreover, abilities to perceive, to remember, and to reason are not global or general in nature. A child may be able to perceive and recall stimuli of one kind and not another. For example, objects in simple scenes may be readily recalled by a six-year-old, while the same objects in more complex scenes may not be recognized as having been presented previously. Again, the child may be able to reason about the necessary arrangement of blocks to build a tower that will not fall down but not be able to reason about seemingly similar problems that he/she has not yet dealt with directly. Thus thinking or cognition entails both the maturing of certain component cognitive processes and the organization of experience to produce general abilities where there were previously situation-specific abilities.

It is not necessary that we understand the details of cognitive development, but there are a few basics that will help us to understand what goes on. As we have previously noted, we owe to Jean Piaget our general perspective on how the infant and child organizes its perceptual experience—what it sees, hears, feels—in *schema.*[9] A *schema* is a mental representation of some object, event, or perceptual-motor coordination. For example, a picture of an oval with a couple of dots at about the place where eyes would be in a human face interests an infant much more than a circle or a square. It appears that the infant has formed a *schema* for the human face, and this schema exists long before the infant recognizes specific individuals. We store experience in terms of schemata (plural of schema) that permit us to recognize the physical realities around us.

Schemata are like simplified blueprints. They represent in summary form the arrangements among the important elements in an object. We also build up much more detailed *images* to represent objects, persons, and events that are important to us. It is generally thought that young infants do not generate images, but only schemata. But by the time the infant acquires retrieval memory, we may suppose that it can generate images of its primary caretakers and of other persons and objects.

Symbols, we noted, come into being in the second year. Now an arbitrary meaning can be assigned to objects; the doll can be treated "as if" it were a baby to be cared for. With images and symbols comes the beginning of the ability to form *concepts* (for example, to group objects according to their attributes). Concepts are constructs that are crucial for reasoning. They are abstractions that represent important qualities or relationships among objects and events. Initially, such concepts may be crude and often invalid by adult criteria. "Doggie," for example, may be attached to any furry, four-legged animal smaller than a horse. The toddler may call any male about the age of his father "Daddy," sometimes to the consternation of the child's mother. But correction and guidance shape basic concepts toward cultural norms.

Thinking about complex matters involves using effective strategies for bringing to bear all of the abilities one possesses. It involves learning rules about concepts and relationships. The rules tell us what kinds of inferences may be made. Some rules, like those of logic, are highly formal. Others are intuitive or informal and may relate to imperfect relationships observable from experience, for example.

Perception

What we see depends partly on what we are looking for. Beyond infancy, the biggest change in the child's perceptual ability is that it learns how to search for information. Such a search requires ability to sustain attention. The child under five is easily distracted, but by seven most children have dramatically improved in the ability to focus attention and sustain it.[10]

What the child sees is also strongly influenced by cultural norms and values and even by the environment in which it grows up. For example, children in Western society grow up in "carpentered" housing, with walls perpendicular to each other, while in many societies dwellings are round (American Indian teepees, Eskimo igloos, African thatched huts). Those who grow up in carpentered environments or in tropical jungles appear to be much more susceptible to certain optical illusions (which influence distance and size judgments) than those who live on prairies or open savannahs (who are susceptible to a different kind of optical illusion).[11]

As the child gains experience of the world around it, knowledge becomes organized and synthesized. Expectations are built up and the child is able to interpret clues as to what is going on. It does not appear that older children perceive more, but they are able to be much more efficient, selective, and accurate in organizing their perceptions—what they see, hear, feel, or otherwise experience.

Memory

Memory involves registering or "coding" what is perceived by the senses, maintaining it briefly in consciousness (short-term memory, as for a phone number), transferring information from short-term to long-term memory, and being able to bring back the information into consciousness (retrieval). The young child probably registers representations almost as well as an adult though it cannot, of course, encode and interpret what it sees or hears as well as an adult can. Ability to recognize and to recall depends in part on ability to organize what one perceives. Memory is enhanced by rehearsal and by association with other information.

We noted that ability to focus and sustain attention shows a marked increase between the ages of five and seven. Around seven there is usually a sharp increase in the ability of American children to recall strings of numbers or words. This seems to be the result of learning strategies for organizing information to aid memory. These strategies are not learned until a later age by children growing up in areas where schooling is absent or of poor quality, as in much of the developing world.

Memory, like perception, thus improves as a result of maturation, of experience, and of learned strategies and principles of organization. Memory depends on motivation, on interest in learning and remembering. A boy who cannot remember the rules of grammar may remember the scores of baseball games or the yards gained by football stars. Anxiety and fear of failure interfere with ability to remember. These relationships can accentuate the problems of children from backgrounds where cognitive strategies are not developed through intellectual stimulation. They may be less motivated to learn what schools teach and more impaired by virtue of fear of failure.

Reasoning

Reasoning entails learning to classify and to compare bits of information, using rules of inference. The child must be able to keep the elements of a problem in memory, must have enough experience or knowledge of the problematic situation to understand the problem and must have attained a maturational stage of development that will permit the mental operations required. During early childhood, the child can use symbols and draw inferences from her own perspective, but she cannot take the view of another child or adult. For example, she cannot imagine how a village would look if one were behind a mountain flanking the village. Up to roughly seven years of age, the child's thinking tends to be, in Piaget's terms, *preoperational*. The preoperational child cannot comprehend relative relationships and reversals but thinks in absolutes. For example, my grandson, who spent his first year in France, said when he was four years old that he didn't want to return to France because he didn't want to be a baby again.

Somewhere between six and eight years of age, most children growing up in urbanized Western societies obtain the stage Piaget called *concrete operations*. In this stage they have mastered the rules of grouping objects and drawing logical inferences about them. For example, they learn the meanings of "bigger than," "smaller than," "equal to," and the relationships among classes of objects. They learn that when a liquid is poured from a wide glass into a narrow one, the level of the liquid will be higher, but the amount will be the same. This principle, known as *conservation*, cannot be adequately grasped by the preoperational child, according to Piaget, because the child is not yet able to comprehend that the liquid can be poured back into the original container, reversing the effect.

At the stage of concrete operations, the child can reason (formulate explanations, test hypotheses) about the properties of real objects and persons but not yet about abstractions or hypothetical situations. The level of reasoning that can handle abstractions and hypothetical situations, searching for hypotheses in seeking to solve such problems, is called *formal operations*. Not everyone attains this stage, which Piaget characterized as starting anywhere from twelve on.

Piaget's formulations have led to a tremendous body of research evidence that gives general support to his theory of cognitive development but also reveals many respects in which features of his formulation are in need of modification. Early manipulation for gaining schemata may not be as important as Piaget thought, and individual (and cultural) differences appear to be substantial. He based his theory on a few children (including his own), and he was perhaps not fully aware of the effects of different modes of questioning on the child's comprehension and ability to demonstrate its abilities. The ages for attainment of certain cognitive skills, dem-

onstrated with familiar objects, may be much earlier than Piaget thought. Nevertheless, the major developmental sequence does appear to be a valid formulation.
Between the ages of three or four and seven or eight there are profound changes
in the child's ability to think problems through.

While the early stages of cognitive development seem to depend on maturation and the accumulation of experience that comes only with time, attainment of
later stages depends much more on the kind of stimulation and intellectual challenge that the child receives, as well as on native intellectual capacity. Children in
developing countries, where diet may be seriously deficient and schooling either
minimal or absent, do not develop concrete operations as early as do children in the
developed nations. There are probably even greater differences in the proportions
attaining the stage of formal operations and the ages at which this is accomplished.

Reflection and Insight

To think effectively, one must be able to evaluate premises and inferences
and to consider alternative possibilities. This requires a pause for reflection, an in-
hibition of the impulse to act on the first hunch one has. In the early years of
school (and often later as well), children who are impulsive make faster decisions
when faced with test situations, but they make many more errors than children
who reflect on their initial hunch. How errors are responded to in a given culture
will to some extent shape the child's response style. For example, Japanese children
are consistently taught to try to avoid errors, and they are found to be slower and
more accurate than American children when administered comparable tests.

Finally, insights into relationships frequently require that one be able to ask
"what would happen if" some particular action were taken. If a small boy wants
to climb a tree whose lowest branch is out of reach, he may see a box he could
carry to the tree which would permit him to reach the branch. Assuming that the
boy is not simply copying the action of another, seeing the box as a potential aid
is a significant insight. It requires the ability to makes a series of inferences relevant
to achieving a goal. The quality of insights in tackling problems increases greatly
in the school years as the child's knowledge base increases and as logical rules and
strategies are rehearsed and mastered.

Moral Development

It may seem strange to discuss moral development under the general heading
of cognitive development, but to a large extent a child's recognition of moral principles rests on that child's general reasoning ability. This is not to say that bright,
intellectually advanced children are more moral than less-bright ones; reasoning
correctly about moral issues does not guarantee moral behavior and in fact is only
slightly related to it.

The research of Kohlberg on moral reasoning in the child started with Piaget's
theories. Kohlberg then devised a test that asked the child how she would deal with

each of a series of descriptions of persons faced with moral dilemmas.[12] The small child sees moral rules as absolutes and has great difficulty in considering issues that entail conflicting rules. Kohlberg postulates a series of developmental stages beginning with the idea that one should behave according to moral rules in order to escape punishment, moves through stages based on the maintenance of legitimate expectations in social life, and finally to the enunciation of ideals and logical principles as a basis for moral behavior. We shall discuss this topic at greater length in the next chapter.

EARLY SOCIALIZATION IN THE FAMILY

In the previous chapter we noted that the process of socialization requires parental teaching, guidance, and demands upon the child for increasingly competent performance and self-regulation. The small child is totally dependent upon its caretakers. They provide for all of the child's needs, and their approval is all-important to the child. Nevertheless, the infant and small child must learn ways of making his/her needs known and maximizing gratifications. Initially, securing these gratifications is not likely to require much in the way of self-restraint, though a measure of frustration is inevitable as weaning, toilet training, and demands for cooperation in eating and dressing are imposed. Moreover, even in the second year the child will often assert him/herself in ways that are difficult or unpleasant for parents to cope with. It does not take long for child and parents to develop expectations and typical patterns of response.[13]

If early temper tantrums by the child—throwing himself on the floor and screaming when he is thwarted in his demands—bring consternation and rapid surrender on the part of the parents, the child will have a powerful technique for controlling the parents subsequently. If parents are harshly punishing of the child's efforts to assert himself, on the other hand, they may produce a fearful, unhappy child. We now know a good deal about the antecedents of competence in children and adults, thanks to several longitudinal studies that have followed the same individuals from early childhood.

The efforts of parents to carry out their part in preparing the child for competent performance are shaped by a number of different influences. As noted in Chapter 3, the culture provides guidelines as to what ought to be expected of a child of a given age and how a parent ought to behave toward the child. The parents' own childhood experiences and the ways in which each of them was raised also provide models, whether positive or negative. Some see their own parents as having been wise and helpful; others say, "I swore I wouldn't make the same mistakes with my kids that my parents made with me."

Size of family, the age and sex of brothers and sisters, and the number of adult caretakers in the family all have a bearing on the child's development. In societies where several adult women may minister to the child's needs, attachment to the biological mother is less intense, children tend to be kept under greater control, and physical punishment is less often administered than where only the mother cares for the child.[14]

In societies that are becoming modernized and industrialized, formal schooling tends to modify parental attitudes and child care by calling into question many traditional practices. Those adults who do not receive formal schooling but work in factories also appear to become more "modern" in their attitudes and behavior.[15] Declining family size and changes in what is expected of children—no longer being seen as family workers from an early age but as potential students who will ultimately move into a different world—go along with parental participation in modern industrial organizations.

The occupational experiences of the parents in any society are likely to be important influences on what they regard as the most important qualities to be instilled in their children. And finally, but by no means least important, the personalities of the parents make a difference both in what they regard as important and how they manage themselves in attempting to guide and discipline the child. A parent who cannot abide minor frustrations without screaming or who lashes out in anger against the child is likely to produce children who in later life will have trouble in dealing with authority figures (and modern, bureaucratically organized society is run by authority figures). Each of these sources of influence on parental socialization deserves further consideration.

What Parents Want for Their Children

Assuming that children are wanted, they are likely to be loved. Most American parents want above all else that their children will be happy. Beyond this, there will be considerable variation in the priority listing of parental concerns and values. Most parents want their children to be competent, acceptable members of society, though many probably take for granted that they will become so.

The research of Melvin Kohn[16] over the past 25 years has focused on the values parents hold for their children—the attributes they want most to instill in the children. By asking fathers and mothers to consider a listing of desirable attributes (made up from earlier interviews with parents) and to pick out and rank the most important ones and the least important ones, Kohn and his colleagues discovered that the choices and rankings largely derive from an underlying dimension— conformity versus self-direction. Conformity is reflected in parental choices of good manners, neatness, and cleanliness, being a good student and obedience to parents. Self-direction, on the other hand, appears to be a general value underlying choice of considerateness of others, interest in how things happen, sound judgment, and self-control.

The earliest studies on parental values focused on differences between the social classes. Middle-class parents tend to favor self-direction for their children, while working-class parents more often report a concern for attributes that connote conformity. The differences are not enormous; some middle-class parents say they want obedient, neat children who are good students, and some working-class parents say they want considerate children who show self-control and good judgment. Indeed, it is probably the case that almost all parents would like to see their children have nearly all these attributes. The difference is in what seems *most* important. And, of course, a critical question is whether what parents in interviews say they regard as important is reflected in their behavior with their children.

That there are real differences in the way middle-class parents and working-class parents guide, encourage, and discipline their children has been well documented. Where punishment is involved, middle-class parents have been found to be more concerned with the intent of a child than with overt behavior.[17] Breaking a dish, for example, might lead to punishment for a working-class child, whether or not breakage was an accident, but punishment of a middle-class child might be expected only if the child broke the dish intentionally in a fit of anger.

The Social Classes in America

We use the terms *middle class* and *working class* rather loosely. There are not sharp boundaries between the classes, but rather a continuum from positions of highest prestige, life-style, and social power to those of lowest status. The best indicators of an individual's or family's position in the status hierarchy are education, occupational prestige, and (to a lesser degree) income. Families at the bottom of the hierarchy—the lower class—live most precariously. Possessed of the least education, the least occupational skills, they suffer the highest level of unemployment in hard times and experience an almost constant struggle to eke out a living. Minorities who experience serious discrimination are found in disappropriate numbers at the lower levels of status.

Middle-class parents tend to have more time to talk to and play with their children. They tend to be more concerned with and responsive to the child's feelings and more often seek to understand the child's needs for information and orientation to the world.[18] When the child starts school, for example, middle-class parents are likely to give the child a much fuller (and more positive) explanation of what to expect than are lower-class parents.[19] The lower-class parents are more likely to warn the child not to get into "trouble," in keeping with the high priority given to overt conformity.

Middle-class fathers tend to be more supportive of their children, especially their sons, than are working-class fathers, even if they are at home less because of longer work hours. And, in general, father-son relationships appear to be closer in the middle class, beyond early childhood.

In attempting to delineate what it is about social status that makes a difference for the rearing of children, Kohn has closely examined the relationships between occupational conditions and parental values. He finds that much of the difference in values between the classes derives from such job conditions as the substantive complexity of the work (the demands it makes upon the worker) and the closeness of supervision that a man experiences.[20] We shall discuss these features in Chapter 6.

Our interest here is not in the dynamics of the socialization process, but in the long-term consequences for the individual life course. In general, the higher the family status, the more likely the child is to have a head start in language usage, in intellectual stimulation, and in preparing for successful participation in the classroom. But social status is not everything, especially when we consider the great bulk of the population that occupies intermediate levels between the upper middle class and the lower class.

Authoritative Versus Permissive Parenting

Child-rearing practices have changed considerably in the United States over the past 50 years. Many immigrant groups brought to America the authoritarian patterns that were typical of their countries of birth. DeTocqueville, writing nearly 150 years ago, noted the easy relationship between fathers and sons in the American democracy as contrasted with the states of Western Europe. Well-to-do American parents were certainly more involved with the rearing of their children than were comparably comfortable parents in France and Britain. Even so, a strong measure of discipline seems to have been prevalent as compared with parenting today. Restrictions on children's activities and the use of physical punishment occurred widely.

In the 1930s, with the coming to power of fascism in parts of Europe, we became aware of the problems posed by authoritarian persons who viewed the world in terms of dominance and submission.[21] Moreover, the roots of authoritarianism appeared to be nurtured by parents who demanded obedience and forcibly obtained it. Then came the call for a greater measure of leeway and avoidance of unnecessary frustration of the child. For a while the cult of permissiveness held sway, at least in many upper-middle-class circles.

The child must, however, learn to control unacceptable impulses in public and must be able to understand and accept limits on his or her behavior. We now have very solid evidence that such learning is best insured by parents who are authoritative (neither authoritarian nor highly permissive) in setting standards for the child and insisting on adherence to those standards, while remaining warmly supportive. In a study that began with three-year-olds in nursery school, Diana Baumrind has traced out the consequences of different styles of parenting.[22]

Baumrind found that parents who were authoritative and yet supportive had children who tended to be more friendly, cooperative, and achievement-oriented than either authoritarian or permissive parents. Permissive parents and overprotective parents had children who were less independent and more immature in their behaviors, while authoritarian parents often produced anxious and less socially responsible children.

Baumrind found that parents who stressed individuality, self-expression, initiative, a questioning attitude, and who tolerated a certain amount of aggressiveness had children who were more competent and independent, provided that the parents were not lax and inconsistent in discipline or unwilling to make demands upon the child.

PEER RELATIONSHIPS

Parents provide nurturance, guidance, and a measure of demand coupled with discipline. Peers, on the other hand, provide the opportunity of learning to act cooperatively (and often competitively) with others. The importance of play with peers as a way of learning how to cope with the behavior of others does not appear to have been fully appreciated until the psychologist Harry Harlow conducted his experimental studies with rhesus monkeys.[23] Harlow raised some monkeys in isolation from others of their species, some with their mothers, and some with peers. No matter how carefully the isolated monkeys were treated, many died while quite young. And of those who survived, none was able to establish easy relationships with its own sex or with the opposite sex. If raised with peers, however, they learned the give and take of playful aggression, they learned the natural ways of approaching or being approached by the opposite sex through playful mounting of either sex, and they learned to gauge the strength and temperament of others whom they might or might not want to challenge in some respect.

Interaction with peers is a less crucial kind of socialization experience for humans than for monkeys, because humans can learn many things through the medium of language. Nevertheless, some degree of early experience with peers or siblings seems to facilitate cooperative and altruistic behavior. It may also reinforce aggressive tendencies, if the child who aggresses against others thereby gets his way. In nursery schools, for example, the aggressive child frequently becomes *more* aggressive over time.[24]

Children tend to model their behavior on older and admired peers. They are as likely to imitate the behavior of another child as that of an adult. Moreover, from older peers children learn elements of the culture of the younger generations that are just coming into being—games, slang, language, and practices—as well as elements disapproved of in conventional society but known by almost everyone. "Things my mother never taught me" are part of the secret and not-so-secret lore of childhood.

At the same time children learn to abide by rules. They learn what is "fair" and what is "cheating" in ways their parents are less well able to teach than are peers. The child who is concerned about others and helpful to them tends to become popular and wanted as a friend, whether or not this child is perceived as a leader. Recent research suggests that the child's status among peers is largely a consequence of social skills. Children who are neither positively nor negatively perceived by peers in one group may become positively or negatively valued in a new group, but those who acquired a negative reputation in one group tend to act in ways that bring rejection in new groups as well.[25]

During the childhood years, social skills are being learned cumulatively. Difficult or shy children at one age may acquire skills and confidence a little later on. Nevertheless, by age 10 or 12, the child's ability to form close and relatively enduring ties with another child already appears to have implications for adult friendships. In an examination of early friendships among boys in the Berkeley Guidance Study, some boys were found to have stable relationships with the same individuals for several years, while others had a succession of "spoiled friendships." The boys who at 10 or 12 had preserved stable friendships were much more likely at age 30 to be seen as warm and friendly persons than were those who in preadolescence experienced spoiled friendships.[26]

Initially, the peers with whom the child has most contact will be the children of neighbors or of relatives, who are likely to be relatively similar in social origins. Once the child starts to school, however, especially in urban public schools, the peer group is likely to have diverse backgrounds and to present greater challenges and opportunities for skill learning, coupled with greater threats to the child's sense of self-confidence if s/he is ill prepared for what school entails.

SCHOOL AND THE STUDENT ROLE

Many children attend nursery schools or day care programs, but for the majority, school begins at five with kindergarten or six with the first grade. We have already noted that children from middle-class families tend to receive a fuller and more positive orientation toward school than working-class children. In addition, there are substantial differences among ethnic groups in the value parents place on education and in their efforts to motivate their children to do well in school.

If we view the life course as a series of transitions entailing the taking on of new relationships and roles, the first great transition is entry into school. In the home, the small child is most often an object of special care, attention, and unconditional love. In the school each child is one of many who must fit into a scheduled round of curricular activities, some more demanding, some more entertaining. Whether explicitly graded or not, each child will be evaluated relative to peers and relative to the norms the teacher holds for boys and girls. Each year's promotion to the next grade constitutes a minor *rite of passage* leading up to that first major celebration of accomplishment, graduation.

We know far less than we need to know about how early experience in the classroom influences the child's later views of school and the prospect of later academic success. The evidence available suggests that early experiences of success in elementary school tend to be associated with higher achievement later in the same year; the children who do best early in the year are in general the ones who learn the most during the year.[27] Those who learn to read quickly have a powerful tool for mastering other subjects, while those slow to read are likely to drop behind in almost everything else.

School affords an opportunity for many other kinds of learning than reading and arithmetic. Friendships are formed, cooperative and competitive activities are organized, and the child is subject to discipline and regimentation quite different from conditions prevailing in the home. It has been suggested that at the lower levels of schooling we tend to regiment children in ways that discourage creativity, ways that are designed to prepare them to fit into relatively menial jobs in the industrial system.[28] Just as working-class families tend to stress conformity over initiative and self-direction, the early years of school are organized to serve the same ends. Except for a few elite schools, however, no developed society seems to have escaped this general pattern, and it is difficult to see how a markedly different approach might be developed to serve the diverse populations of modern cities.

Schools in the United States have long been regarded as the means by which any normal child can overcome the deficits of deprivation and low social status. Yet most studies of the effects of schooling suggest that the sociocultural level of the home and the parents' valuing of education account for a very large part of school performance. Some children from upper-middle-class homes may do poorly in school and some from lower-class backgrounds may do brilliantly, but they tend to be the exceptions.

In the era of heavy European immigration, our schools were to a great extent the basis for making "Americans" out of the members of many ethnic populations. Many immigrants were intent on their children getting an education in the United States, something not available in the country of origin. More recently, the idea of the American "melting pot" has been widely repudiated, and bilingual education for children of Hispanic-speaking parents has been urged as a means of preserving their heritage. But bilingual education has too often meant a failure to secure adequate command of the dominant language in which the work of the society is carried out. Those who do not learn English early in the school year tend to drop behind very quickly.

A striking example of how one Mexican-American family that settled in Sacramento, California, helped their children to master English—and the consequences of extraordinary scholarship on the part of one son—is presented in the autobiography of a young Mexican-American who loved language, *Hunger of Memory: The Education of Richard Rodriguez.*[29] Rodriguez's parents were of the stable working class. They sent their children to a parochial school in which there were few if any other Mexican-American children. Early on, the family spoke only Spanish at home, and the children had much difficulty with English in school. The teachers visited the home and suggested to the parents that it would help the children if the family were to speak English at home. When they did so, the children's progress improved markedly, despite the difficulty that the parents themselves had with English.

Parental appreciation of the importance of education and encouragement of their children's achievement in school may be almost as important as the knowledge the parents themselves possess. In any event, as we shall see, no life experience appears to have a greater influence on a person's attainments in life than their own ultimate educational attainments, coupled with their family background.

DEVELOPMENTAL TASKS AND STAGES IN CHILDHOOD

Up to this point we have considered development in terms of physical growth, increasing cognitive skills and capacities, and new social roles and the demands they entail. These tend to be interrelated, for, as earlier noted, certain performances require a given level of physical and cognitive maturation. The scheduling of various demands and controls on children in any society tends to be consonant with maturation, though some societies will push hard for early performance and others may not impose demands until well after the child has the capacity to perform.

The demands of the school years are an extension of the developmental tasks discussed in the previous chapter. Particularly in the realm of learning social and moral norms, values, and skills, the tasks of later childhood become more complex and more diverse. Demands for self-regulation increase steadily, and so does the opportunity to plan activities and pursue individual interests and goals.

In many developing societies children do not attend school but are drawn directly into the family's productive activities. In some societies boys tend herds of sheep or goats; in others they help their parents in the fields. Some may attend school for a total of a year or two, spread over many years. Girls are far less likely than boys to receive any formal education. Tasks such as herding or working in the fields during the childhood years shape intellectual development and personal responsibility in quite different ways than does formal schooling.[30]

In Chapter 2 we briefly considered Erikson's eight stages of man. Basic trust versus mistrust and autonomy versus shame and doubt were seen by Erikson as issues of infancy and early childhood. By the third or fourth year, Erikson's "play age," the child normally develops initiative in relating to its peers.[31] The male child, in particular, is intrusive, entering into new situations and activities. Oedipal feelings (rivalry with the father) are aroused, and there is, Erikson holds, the danger that initiative will be overwhelmed by guilt and result in lack of purpose. The small girl turns toward motherliness in her activities, for they are patterned on the mother.

In the school years, Erikson sees the child's prime developmental task as one of developing a sense of *industry.*[32] The danger is that he will develop a sense of *inadequacy,* either because of hopeless rivalry with the father in a continued Oedipal struggle or because of barriers and negative messages that the larger society provides. He must become industrious yet not overly conforming if he is to become maximally competent. Erikson does not address the development of girls at this period.

Erikson's stages relate to important tasks and possible dangers, but there is no evidence that any given level of attainment of one attribute must precede another attribute. The child must be able to trust others, and must have some degree of autonomy and initiative, but a very dependent child may become a highly autonomous adult. Moreover, children may achieve initiative and industriousness in many different ways, some much earlier than others.

Psychoanalytic treatment like that of Erikson tend to focus on psychodynamics and especially on the Oedipal relationship and its resolution. Undoubtedly this may be crucially important in some instances, but for most boys in American society we see little evidence of an acute Oedipal struggle. There are important differences in the ways in which boys and girls come to identify with their same-sex parents, and Freud's formulation of the Oedipus complex incorporated brilliant insights into the developmental process. Nevertheless, it was basically incorrect in proposing the mechanism of the Oedipus complex.

Both boys and girls are initially dependent upon their mothers and might therefore be expected to model themselves on their mothers. Boys must shift their focus to the father. It appears that they do so not because they are afraid that their fathers (perceived as their rivals for possession of the mother) will castrate them, as Freud suggested, but because their fathers provide accepting models and guidance toward manly pursuits. Much research attests to close identification of sons with fathers who are loving and warmly accepting; fathers who are feared far less often serve as role models.[33]

Girls have a very special relationship with their mothers, a relationship that entails close sharing and confiding. Nancy Chodorow has nicely delineated some of the developmental differences between boys and girls in *The Reproduction of Mothering*.[34] In the confines of our focus on the life course as a whole, we cannot go into greater detail here, but as we observe the childhood years, we must keep our eyes open to the many ways in which relationships, opportunities, and expectations for boys and girls tend to diverge.

Sex Differences in Childhood

We have already noted that the games and other activities in which boys and girls participate show differences at an early age. Several studies have examined the play of school-aged boys and girls. In a study of the play of fifth-grade children in and out of school, Janet Lever found that boys played outdoors more often than girls, they played more competitive games, and their games were more complex and lasted longer than those of girls. Most interesting, she found that boys quarreled a good deal more than girls in the course of games.[35] At the same time they managed to resolve their quarrels, so that even a violent dispute did not end the game. In contrast, among girls the eruption of disputes tended to end the game. The boys tended to be rule enforcers and rule elaborators; the girls tended to be tolerant of bending the rules but to be very wary of interpersonal tensions.

Lever argued that boys receive much more useful socialization experience from their games than do girls. But as Carol Gilligan points out, one reaches such a conclusion only if one accepts the male model of what is good—good perhaps for corporate success later on.[36] Concern for the preservation of close personal ties and the minimization of sources of tension has its payoff value for society, a payoff value that has only recently begun to be recognized by males in contemporary America. The competitive rat race may put a premium on asserting oneself and using all the rules and laws to one's own advantage. It does not tend to lead to rewarding, intimate relationships with peers and family.

During childhood, then, boys and girls are diverging in activities and in general orientations in accordance with the expectations of the culture and milieu in which they find themselves. Their orientations will also be shaped by the structure of the family, especially the number of older siblings of the same or opposite sex. A daughter who is the only child of a man with strong aspirations for achievement in his child may be tutored by her father into very different channels than a daughter with several older brothers. This is just one example of how social structural features may influence the course of development.

SOCIAL STRUCTURAL INFLUENCES ON DEVELOPMENT

There are many ways in which family circumstances (divorce, illness or death of a parent, father's unemployment) and social conditions may influence the child's developmental experiences. Marriages ended by divorce usually entail a period of turmoil and competition for the child's affection; there is much evidence that children suffer anxiety and diminished school performance in the year following the parental separation.[37] Yet longer-term research does not suggest that deficits found in the year following the breakup of the marriage persist, except perhaps for children who were under seven at the time.[38] Nor does research suggest that being reared by a single parent necessarily leads to problems.

Most students of psychological development have stressed the importance of a positive adult model for the young child to identify with and emulate. Boys raised by their mothers alone often lack such a model, at least within the home. The effects of father absence upon a boy's development appear to depend very much on the reason for the absence, the resources available to the mother, and the light in which the father, and men in general, are presented to the boy. An idealized dead father may serve as a very positive model, while a devalued former spouse may lead the boy to devalue himself. A mother harried by the necessity of earning a living and maintaining the home may feel guilty about her limited availability and therefore unable to demand mature behavior on the part of the son. But with the help of the child's grandmother or another woman, a single or divorced mother aware of the need for firm controls and for making demands for maturity upon her children can to a considerable extent offset the potential consequences of the father's absence. When a mother remarries, a warm and accepting stepfather can provide both emotional support for the mother and a model for her son. Without some such compensating measures, father absence is likely to lead to anxieties about masculinity and to deficits in cognitive development and school performance.[39]

Effects of Economic Depression

At some time or other, but most often in periods of widespread economic depression, families experience hard times. In the depth of the Great Depression of the 1930s, nearly one fourth of all adult males were out of work. Many others had markedly diminished incomes. Periodically, in times of economic recession or as a consequence of technological change and shifting markets, large numbers of men and women are unemployed or have markedly lower incomes. For men in particular, the work role tends to be a major source of their sense of identity and worth. Its loss or curtailment leads to feelings of frustration and, in time, despair. In families where the marital relationship is good, the morale of the husband and father can often be sustained by his wife's emotional support.[40] This is less true when there are preexisting tensions in the relationship. Under such circumstances, marital tensions increase and so do expressions of irritability with the children. Fathers tend to give inconsistent discipline, to act more on the basis of their own mood than on the basis of the children's behavior. And if a child is already "difficult"— prone to temper tantrums or to being quarrelsome and negativistic—the parents' behaviors are in turn more explosive and inconsistent.

The consequences of economic hard times for the children are thus mediated through the personalities and behaviors of the parents, especially through the father's irritability and arbitrary discipline. That those consequences have their ramifications in the children's later lives has been conclusively demonstrated by data from the Berkeley Guidance Study, examining the efforts of parental behavior in the early 1930s on the careers of the children up to age 40.[41] Males who were "difficult" and given to temper tantrums in childhood—attributes that were enhanced by fathers' income loss and arbitrary discipline—were much more likely to have unstable work careers than were other males. They were also more likely to have broken marriages. Females who had been "difficult" in childhood were more likely to marry men of relatively low economic status and to report that they were less "affectionate" than other women.

Cohort Effects

As noted in Chapter 1, members of each birth cohort (i.e., each group of people born in a given year) encounter a somewhat different world from that of their brothers and sisters, and often a vastly different world from that of their parents. Children born in the decade following the end of World War II contributed to a "baby boom" that was nearly double the size of the cohort born in the decade before the war, during the Great Depression. Many of the postwar babies experienced half sessions in crowded schools. Their families "exploded" into suburbs that had few facilities when they arrived. The children came on the scene just as television did, and it became a major factor in defining their interests and their leisure pursuits. Space will not permit us to discuss the effects of television on this and subsequent generations, but without question television has changed educational practices and goals as well as values and interests.[42]

Thus in the course of the childhood years, historical events may impinge upon the family and on other institutions to change the worlds of children, and such changes are not evenly distributed in the population. Social status, cultural norms, parental personalities, and the child's experiences in school and the peer group all serve as mediators of the effects of historical events and social changes. The school years do not in any sense *determine* later outcomes, but their influences are nevertheless measurably large and increasingly predictable, as we shall see when we examine the adult years.

NOTES

1. For a discussion of the phases of the child's mastery of language see Roger Brown, *A First Language* (Cambridge, MA: Harvard University Press, 1973) or P. Dale, *Language Development Structure and Function,* 2nd ed. (New York: Holt, Rinehart and Winston, 1976).

2. Data on developmental norms and and the influences upon them are summarized in Benjamin S. Bloom, *Stability and Change in Human Characteristics* (New York: Wiley, 1964). There are more recent studies, but they are in general consonant with the data summarized and the very thorough discussion by Bloom.

3. For readers not familiar with correlation coefficients, it may suffice to know that if two sets of measures are not at all related, the correlation coefficient will be 0.00, while if they are perfectly related, the coefficient will be 1.0.

4. The research is reported in John A. Clausen, "The Social Meaning of Differential Physical and Sexual Maturation," in Sigmund Dragastin and Glen H. Elder, eds., *Adolescence in the Life Cycle: Psychological Change and Social Context* (New York: Halsted Press, 1975).

5. Somatotypes are fully described in William H. Sheldon, *The Varieties of Human Physique* (New York: Harper Brothers, 1940). Research on the responses of children to somatotypes is reported by R. M. Lerner, "The Development of Stereotyped Expectancies of Body Build–Behavior Relations," *Child Development,* 40 (1969), 137-41.

6. Clausen, "The Social Meaning of Differential Physical and Sexual Maturation," p. 40.

7. Ibid., p. 31.

8. P. H. Mussen, J. J. Conger, and J. Kagan, *Child Development and Personality,* 5th ed. (New York: Harper and Row, 1979), pp. 233-34.

9. For the most general treatment see Jean Piaget, "Piaget's Theory" in P. Mussen, ed., *Carmichael's Manual of Child Psychology,* Vol. 1, 3rd ed. (New York: Wiley, 1970).

10. See Mussen, Conger, and Kagan, *Child Development,* 5th ed., pp. 245-51.

11. An overview of ways in which perceptual development is influenced by cultural and ecological elements is given in Chapter 8 of Emmy Werner, *Cross-Cultural Child Development* (Monterey, CA: Brooks/Cole Publishing Co., 1979).

12. Lawrence Kohlberg, *Stages in the Development of Moral Thought and Action* (New York: Holt, Rinehart & Winston, 1969).

13. For general discussions of the process of socialization see John A. Clausen, ed., *Socialization and Society* (Boston, MA: Little, Brown and Co., 1968) or David Goslin, ed., *Handbook of Socialization Theory and Research* (Chicago: Rand, McNally and Co., 1969).

14. For an overview, see Werner, *Cross-Cultural Child Development,* pp. 257-86.

15. Alex Inkeles and D. H. Smith, *Becoming Modern: Individual Change in Six Developing Countries* (Cambridge, MA: Harvard University Press, 1974).

16. This research is reported in two books, Melvin L. Kohn, *Class and Conformity: A Study in Values* (New York: The Dorsey Press, 1969) and Melvin L. Kohn and Carmi Schooler, *Work and Personality: An Inquiry into the Impact of Social Stratification* (Norwood, NJ: Ablex Publishing Corp., 1983).

17. Kohn, *Class and Conformity,* Chapter 6.

18. For a general discussion, see Alan Kerckhoff, *Socialization and Social Class* (Englewood Cliffs, NJ: Prentice-Hall, Inc., 1972).

19. Robert D. Hess and Virginia Shipman, "Maternal Attitude and the Role of the Pupil: Some Social Class Comparisons," in A. H. Passom, ed., *Fifth Work Conference on Curriculum and Teaching in Depressed Lives* (New York: Columbia University Teachers College, 1967).

20. Kohn, *Class and Conformity,* Chapter 10. The extent to which parents succeed in transmitting their values to their children has received much study in recent years. For several attempts to formulate the process in theoretical terms, see the chapters by Kohn, by Smith, and by Stryker and Serpe in Alan Kerckhoff, ed., *Research in Sociology of Education and Socialization: Personal Changes over the Life Course,* vol. 4 (Greenwich, CN: JAI Press, Inc., 1983).

21. T. W. Adorno et al., *The Authoritarian Personality* (New York: Harper & Brothers, 1950).

22. Diana Baumrind, "Socialization and Instrumental Competence in Young Children," *Young Children,* 26 (1970), 104–19.

23. Harry F. Harlow and Margaret Harlow, "The Affectional Systems," in A. M. Schrier, H. F. Harlow, and F. Stollnitz, eds., *Behavior of Nonhuman Primates,* vol. 2 (New York: Academic Press, 1965).

24. Peter Renshaw and Steven Asher, "Social Competence and Peer Status," in Kenneth H. Rubin and Hildy S. Ross, eds., *Peer Relationships and Social Skills in Childhood* (New York: Springer-Verlag, 1982).

25. Ibid.

26. Henry Maas, "Preadolescent Peer Relations and Adult Intimacy," *Psychiatry,* 31 (1968), 161–72.

27. Doris R. Entwisle and Leslie A. Hayduk, *Early Schooling* (Baltimore: Johns Hopkins Press, 1982).

28. S. Bowles and H. Gintes, *Schooling in Capitalist America: Educational Reform and the Contradictions of Economic Life* (New York: Basic Books, 1976).

29. Richard Rodriguez, *Hunger of Memory: The Education of Richard Rodriguez* (Boston, MA: D. R. Grodine, 1982).

30. For an example drawn from research in a Lebanese village before Lebanon became a battleground, see Judith Williams, *The Youth of Haouch-el-Harimi–a Lebanese Village* (Cambridge, MA: Harvard University Press, 1968).

31. Erik Erikson, *Childhood and Society* (New York: Norton, 1951), pp. 224–26.

32. Ibid., pp. 226–27.

33. One of the best descriptions of the process of identification remains the frequently reprinted paper by Urie Bronfenbrenner, "Freudian Theories of Identification and their Derivations," *Child Development,* 31 (1960), 15–40.

34. Nancy Chodorow, *The Reproduction of Mothering* (Berkeley, CA: University of California Press, 1978).

35. Janet Lever, "Sex Differences in the Complexity of Children's Games and Play," *American Sociological Review,* 43 (1978), 471–83.

36. Carol Gilligan, *In a Different Voice: Psychological Theory and Women's Development* (Cambridge, MA: Harvard University Press, 1982).

37. Mavis Hetherington, "Children and Divorce" in R. W. Henderson, ed., *Parent-Child Interaction: Theory, Research and Prospects* (New York: Academic Press, 1981).

38. Frank Furstenberg has followed up, after five years, children whose parents had been divorced prior to 1976, the year of an initial survey of a cross section of children aged 7–11. Frank F. Furstenberg, Jr. and Paul D. Allison, "How Divorce Affects Children: Variations by Age and Sex." Unpublished manuscript, Department of Sociology, University of Pennsylvania.

39. For a general overview, see David B. Lynn, *The Father: His Role in Child Development* (Monterey, CA: Brooks/Cole Publishing Co., 1974).

40. See Sydney Cobb, "Social Support as a Moderator of Stress," *Psychosomatic Medicine,* 38 (1976), 300–314.

41. Glen H. Elder, Jr., Jeffrey K. Liker, and Catherine Cross, "Parent-Child Behavior in Hard Times and the Life Course: A Multi-Generational Perspective," in Paul B. Baltes and Orville G. Brim, Jr., eds., *Life-Span Development and Behavior,* vol. 6 (New York: Academic Press, 1984).

42. David Pearl, L. Bouthelet, and J. Lazar, eds., *Television and Behavior: Ten Years of Scientific Progress and Implication for the Eighties,* D. H. H. S. Publication No. (ADM) (Rockville, MD: National Institute of Mental Health, 1982), 82–1196.

CHAPTER 5
ADOLESCENCE
AND
YOUTH

Youth's a stuff will not endure.
Shakespeare, Twelfth Night

Youth is wholly experimental.
Robert Louis Stevenson, Letter
to a Young Gentleman

It is a time of seeking: a seeking inward to find who one is; a searching out-
ward to locate one's place in life; a longing for another with whom to satisfy
cravings for intimacy and fulfillment. It is a time of turbulent awakening to
love and beauty but also of days darkened by loneliness and despair. It is a
time of carefree wandering of the spirit through realms of fantasy and in pursuit of idealistic visions, but also of disillusionment and disgust with the
world and self.[1]

Thus does Theodore Lidz describe adolescence, and these same themes per-
vade recent literature as well as providing grist for the mills of the researcher into
adolescence. Adolescence in Western society is a time of self-exploration and self-
expression, yet it is also a period when social and cultural influences play a major
role in shaping the person to be. Moreover, the sorting processes that go on in adolescence—self-sorting and social sorting—tend to determine potentialities for the rest
of the life course.

The characterization of adolescence as a time of turmoil and philosophical
searching dates back to the "discovery"—less than 100 years ago—of this period
intervening between childhood and adulthood. Some elements in the typical experience of American adolescents have changed markedly in the past 60 years, perhaps
none more sharply than patterns of sexual behavior, but we still see turmoil and

stress. We see them now, however, not as inevitable features of adolescence but as features of adolescence in modern industrial society. For in the 1920s a young woman anthropologist, Margaret Mead, went to Samoa and studied the development of girls ranging in age from 9 to 19 in a small village there.[2]

In their prepubertal years, the girls of Samoa cared for the babies of their mothers, their aunts, and their older sisters, and they learned some of the basic skills they would need after marriage. But after puberty they were in no hurry to marry or to move quickly to full adult status. In Margaret Mead's words:

> The girls' minds were perplexed by no conflicts, troubled by no philosophical queries, beset by no remote ambitions. To live as a girl with many lovers as long as possible and then to marry in one's own village, near one's own relatives, and to have many children, these were uniform and satisfying ambitions.[3]

Coming of age in Samoa is no longer as tranquil as it was. The undermining of the values and of the intricate formal system of interpersonal relationships that characterized the Samoan culture has brought strains between adolescents and their parents. Adolescent suicide is now a widespread phenomenon among Polynesian peoples. In both the United States and Samoa, the adolescent experience has been transformed by historical change. New generations and cohorts come of age in different worlds.

Here we shall be primarily concerned with adolescence in the United States, with institutional settings and developmental demands that are very different from those of Samoa or those of the United States a century ago. Cultures and epochs present different types of opportunities and settings for behavior; they define in quite distinctive ways the appropriate behaviors for prepubertal and adolescent males and females, and they impose demands that may accentuate or moderate the adaptations to physical and sexual maturing that constitute a major facet of the adolescent experience.

Adolescence is a biological stage and a period of major social transition. It has given rise in Western society to distinctive social forms and norms often called "the adolescent culture." Yet until the late nineteenth century, the concept of adolescence hardly existed. On farms and in towns, children over seven tended to be gradually absorbed into the world of adult work, assisting their parents or serving as apprentices. In the nineteenth century, when elementary education became widespread in Western society, many children went as far as the sixth or even the eighth grade, but very few remained in school beyond the age of 14.[4] Early adolescence still brought adult work roles for most of the population.

High school education began to be available to a substantial portion of the population only at the end of the nineteenth century. In the 1890s, my parents, children of German immigrants, both went to work at age 12 to help support their families, as did their brothers and sisters. Neither parent had known that public high schools existed, despite their living in New York City. And few did exist. Even in 1900, students comprised less than 10 percent of the total 14-to-16-year-old population.[5]

Adolescence as a social category is largely a product of the extension of schooling beyond the primary grades. The demands of increasing urbanization and technological development for a more highly educated work force led to the expansion of educational opportunities and the deferring of entry into the labor force until well after the onset of puberty. Age itself then came to have much greater consequence for the scheduling of the transition from childhood to adult status.

It is easier to date the onset of adolescence at sexual puberty than to specify its upper limit. The completion of height growth does not yet represent full maturity, but in most respects the late adolescent is physically and intellectually close to full potential. Motherhood early in adolescence entails more risks to mother and child than will motherhood a few years later, but by 13 or 14 most girls can conceive. Boys are also quite capable of fathering offspring early in adolescence. In most societies, however, marriage and parenthood are deferred until considerably later than midadolescence. In Western society, especially in the United States, there tends to be a long period, now called "youth," when many young adults attend college or engage in athletic or recreational activities or travel to foreign countries rather than making firm commitments to work or marriage. For some adolescents at least, the period seems to offer a moratorium from the pressures to assume full adult status, even as it did for Margaret Mead's Samoan girls.

Nevertheless, the developmental tasks of adolescence are many; for all but the highly affluent, they have considerable urgency. In a few years the child, dependent

Table 5-1   Change and Adaptation in Adolescence

A. *Physical changes* (due to hormonal action)
    Development of primary and secondary sexual characteristics
    Rapid growth and weight increase

B. *Psychological tasks posed by physical changes*
    Coming to terms with changing appearance
    Coming to terms with sexual feelings
    Handling emotional lability related to hormonal action
    Adapting to differential development vis-à-vis peers

C. *Social changes*
    Entrance into adolescent society—high school culture
    New emphases in cross-sex relationships
    Increased demand for mature behavior, responsibility
    Legal authorizations: driving, drinking, voting
    Choice of further education, work, or marriage

D. *Personality development and social character*
    Coming to know self, formulate identity
    Contemplation of life goals, values
    Development of specialized interests, skills
    Trying out tentative scripts, social roles
    Modulating demands of self and others
    Establishment of intimacy with opposite sex
    Preparation for occupation and for marriage

on parents for physical and emotional support, must become an adult, having a sense of identity, competent to fill significant roles within the institutional framework of the society, able to relate meaningfully and responsibly to members of both sexes. Table 5-1 summarizes some of the major changes and adaptations called for in the adolescent years.[6] Within much less than a decade, the individual must become capable of making choices that will to a large extent shape the rest of the life course. Some will make poor choices or will drift into roles they did not really choose—teenage mother or unemployed school dropout. Others will remain students well into their twenties or even their thirties. But all will to some degree be expected to take responsibility for their own lives.

PHYSICAL GROWTH AFTER PUBERTY

The onset of puberty was itself affected by historical change. The improved diet of the general population following the Industrial Revolution seems largely responsible for the finding that both boys and girls have tended to mature sexually and to attain their full stature at earlier ages over successive generations during at least the past century. Nevertheless, there is considerable variation in the ages at which primary and secondary sex characteristics appear, beginning at anywhere from 8 to 14 for girls and 10 to 15 for boys.[7] Full maturing usually takes from three to five years.

For girls, the first signs of puberty are likely to be breast development and pubic hair, with menstruation usually beginning a year or so later. For boys, pubic hair growth and testes development tend to mark pubertal onset, followed by penis growth and accelerated growth in height. Earlier acceleration of growth in girls moves most girls ahead of boys their age in height and weight from ages 10 or 11 to 14 or 15. The average boy in the United States attains 98 percent of his mature height by age 17.5; the average girl reaches this point at 15.5.

We noted in the previous chapter that height and body build can strongly influence the social reputation of boys and girls. Even stronger influences attach to early or late sexual maturing. For both boys and girls, early maturing means greater height, weight, and strength, so that the early maturer has a great advantage over later-maturing peers in athletics and in attractiveness to the opposite sex.[8] The latter attribute has particular significance for girls, because it exposes them to pressures for dating and sexual favors from much older boys and men.

In addition to effects on performance capacities and social reputations and expectations, there are both direct and indirect influences of early maturing upon self-image and self-esteem. The adolescent must cope with a rapidly changing body and with hormonal and other physiological changes that bring new urges and heightened emotions. If physical maturing comes early, there is less time for preparation and for developing an understanding of the social consequences of these changes.[9] If it comes late, there may be, especially for boys, gnawing anxiety about attainment of full male status and the persistent experience of being treated like a younger child.[10]

The sexually mature early adolescent is neither intellectually nor socially any more mature than a prepubescent child of comparable years, yet physical maturing leads to new demands from others as well as changed self-perceptions. At the very least, greater independence and the beginnings of systematic planning for the adult years are expected of the adolescent, especially by middle adolescence. At the same time, the lure of peer activities and the awakening of sexual interests beckon from a different direction.

Psychoanalytically oriented students of adolescence emphasize the surge of instinctual sexual energy that occurs after puberty.[11] *Id* impulses threaten to overwhelm the *ego,* leading to a battle between impulsive demands for self-gratification and repressive defenses against yielding to such demands. Psychological adaptation to one's attainment of sexual maturity often, perhaps usually, takes far longer than the physiological processes that are involved. New relationships, whether with the same or the opposite sex, become invested with intense emotion. Intimacy takes on a new meaning as deeper thoughts are shared, not naively, as in the case of children, but with a sense of mutual communion.

It is not surprising, then, that adolescence has been of special interest to psychiatrists and psychologists as well as to biologists and social scientists. The adolescent has been characterized as a battleground for warring emotions and impulses, and much research suggests that the transitions occurring through adolescence in Western society are among the most difficult in the life course. When the physiological transition takes place early and at the same time as entrance into a new school, as it often does for the junior high school entrant, it is likely to be doubly stressful.

Social Correlates of Early and Late Maturing

The longitudinal studies carried out at the University of California followed groups of participants who entered adolescence in the 1930s and early 1940s. This research found early-maturing boys to be more poised, relaxed, and good-natured than their late-maturing peers. Moreover, the later maturers tended, both in junior high school and in senior high, to be seen by observers as acting younger than they were. They were less popular with their peers, seldom occupied positions of leadership, and more often expressed hostile feelings to their peers than did early maturers.[12]

Early maturers were not only more easygoing than later maturers, but were also seen as more conventional and less expressive. Late maturers often felt that their parents restrained their activities, while early-maturing boys felt that their parents were accepting of their steps toward maturity. And just as mesomorphy was closely associated with high peer status among preadolescents from the working class, early maturing of adolescent boys was especially significant among working-class boys.

Similar patterns appear to hold for adolescents who have been studied more recently, using cruder measures of rate of maturing but for much larger study samples. Early-maturing boys appear to be most satisfied with their muscular development and to have more positive self-esteem.[13] The positive consequences of muscular development are found primarily among seventh graders in junior high school (as against those in elementary schools with eight grades), suggesting that it is especially in the context of association with older boys that early maturing seems most important.

Sex Differences. For girls, the consequences of early maturing are more complex. Athletic performance has traditionally been less important for girls than for boys, though this tradition seems to be rapidly passing. But for most girls, appearance and sociability have a higher priority value than does athletic performance. It has been suggested that the rapid change in a girl's appearance at puberty, as her figure fills out, coupled with the social expectations for dating that are felt once the girl has entered junior high, makes the early maturer more vulnerable.[14] There is a qualitative difference between the figure of a prepubescent girl and that of the physically mature young woman, but only a quantitative difference between the prepubescent boy and the man he will become.

It is among the early-maturing girls in the seventh grade of junior high, especially those who date, that recent research by Simmons and her associates find the greatest evidence of stress and turmoil. These girls were much more likely to score low on achievement tests and to acknowledge themselves to be school behavior problems than their nonpubertal peers.[15] They were also more likely to drop out of school by the tenth grade. In the context of junior high school dating, then, early maturing appears to entail considerable costs to many girls. Not the least of these are the costs of unplanned pregnancies, which we shall discuss later in the chapter.

Longer-Term Consequences. How persistent are the consequences of early versus late maturing? Surprisingly persistent, in that they influence not only school performance but also the general orientations of males and females to their peers and to the adult world. At age 30, early-maturing males from the Oakland Growth Study scored higher on psychological scales for dominance, conformity, and good impression.[16] The early maturers remained somewhat more conventional and more often pursued careers in business, while the late maturers more often found their careers in the professions and the arts.

If early maturing initially posed problems for girls, the long-run consequences appear to be more positive, at least among middle-class girls.[17] On the other hand, early-maturing girls who dated early, especially working-class girls, tended to get less education and to marry earlier than their late-maturing peers.

COGNITIVE DEVELOPMENT
IN ADOLESCENCE

By the age of 11 or 12, the average middle-class child exposed to reasonably good schooling becomes capable of the beginnings of that ultimate stage of cognitive functioning which Piaget called "formal operations." The younger child made logical inferences on the basis of concrete operations—that is, based on observable phenomena. In *formal operations,* a more abstract kind of theorizing and of drawing inferences becomes possible. The thinking process is itself something that can be thought about. Hypotheses based on nonobservables can be entertained, and alternative explanations can be examined to explain puzzling events.[18]

In early adolescence the realm of the subjective becomes much more real. The adolescent is often exquisitely sensitive and self-conscious. If these attributes are reflections of the stresses involved in coming to terms with physical changes and new social roles, they are also the source of motivations to understand one's experiences in the world one occupies. Adolescence is par excellence a time of poetic expression and philosophical questioning.

Moral Reasoning

The moral reasoning of the young child tends to be based on fear of punishment or of disapproval, and that of the older child to be based on feeling obligated to conform to authority or to the common good, according to the research of Kohlberg.[19] But that of the adolescent who has attained formal operations may entail an appreciation of moral principles that have universality of application, such as the Golden Rule of treating others as one would wish to be treated. The adolescent is often highly idealistic and may be derided by more "realistic" and cynical adults.

Kohlberg's formulation of stages of moral reasoning proposes, as we have noted in previous chapters, a progression from concern with avoiding punishment through conventional "law-and-order" morality, to a concept of universal morality based on ethical principles.[20] These stages are dependent on cognitive development, with ethical principles clearly entailing formal operations. Only a relatively small proportion of the population reaches Kohlberg's final stage of principled morality as measured by the set of moral dilemmas on which he bases his classification. But that set of items itself poses more problems than the general ideas that gave rise to it.

Morality in practice is somewhat different from morality as assessed in a formal test situation. Norma Haan, studying adolescents who were confronted with moral dilemmas in the course of group activities, found that interpersonal solutions that worked for groups were only weakly related to moral reasoning as displayed in interviews with the individual group members.[21] Having to deal with the consequences of one's decisions in the here and now demonstrates that logic, intellectual skill, and "principles" will not suffice to produce moral outcomes in the real world.

Yet another problem with the formalistic logical approach of Kohlberg is pointed out by his former associate Carol Gilligan.[22] Girls and women place a much higher value on maintaining relationships and positive emotional climates than do boys and men. Males are more concerned with instrumental results, with achieving success, even at the cost of alienating others. And Kohlberg's moral dilemmas put an emphasis on abstract principles rather than on the maintenance of social solidarity and the preservation of close ties. As so often happens when tests are developed by males, there is a built-in bias in favor of the male perspective. As Gilligan so well observes, women speak "in a different voice."

The Development of Intellectual Interests

Particularly in the latter part of adolescence, the depth of learning experiences may greatly increase. Motivation to learn may lead the bright high school student to become a true scholar, even if not necessarily a conventionally good student in classwork. One thinks of Darwin, who showed little interest or ability in most of his schoolwork but collected minerals and insects as a child. He had no clear goals through adolescence, but he avidly observed nature.[23] Perhaps even more one thinks of Einstein, who was regarded as a dull student throughout his school years. He began to wonder about the world as a small child when his father first showed him a compass, but it was at the age of 12 that a new world was opened up for him through his introduction to Euclidean plane geometry. For the next four years he familiarized himself with the elements of mathematics, including the principles of differential and integral calculus, an experience that he termed "truly fascinating."[24]

The cognitive ability of the adolescent is less trained than it will later be, but it is no less powerful, given the motivation to learn. That motivation depends, however, on social contexts and stimulating influences. One of the dilemmas of our time is that the context of "the adolescent society" in the contemporary United States is not strongly supportive of motivation to learn.

THE SOCIETY AND CULTURE
OF ADOLESCENCE AND YOUTH

Cultures, conceived as patterned behaviors based on norms and values, are built up in response to the conditions of life in particular environments. The culture of the Sioux Indians, for example, centered on the exploitation of the great natural resource found on the Great Plains of America, the buffalo:

> When the buffalo died, the Sioux died, ethnically and spiritually. The buffalo's body had provided not only food and material for clothing, covering and shelter, but such utilities as bags and boats, strings for bows and for sewing, cups and spoons. Medicine and ornaments were made of buffalo parts; his droppings, sun-dried, served as fuel in winter.[25]

The typical environment for most adolescents, in which they interact primarily with one another, is the school. As high school attendance became the expected way of life for the great majority of 14-to-18-year-olds, it is hardly surprising that the high school became a kind of small society with a unique culture (or better, subculture, since high schools are, after all, a part of the larger Western culture).

The features of the adolescent society were first sketched out by James Coleman in his book *The Adolescent Society,* which reported on a study of clique formation and social status in the high schools of an American city in the 1950s.[26] Coleman noted the importance of high school athletics, cars, clothes, and dating for the members of the leading sets in the schools studied. The high school scene was dominated not by the quest for knowledge but by the quest for fun and status. In part, this was an extension downward from the subculture of college youth, but it was of course far more widespread. Nevertheless, it may be more appropriate to speak of the youth culture than of the adolescent culture, for the patterns certainly persist in most private colleges as well as in high schools.

There are a number of elements to this culture, as Coleman and others have pointed out.[27] It is characterized by a *looking inward*. Young people look to one another for their primary cues to behavior and their satisfactions. They tend to evolve their own fads and fashions in music and entertainment and in dress. The more adolescents have been segregated from participation in the adult world of work, the more they have become sensitive to one another in their tastes and interests.

Their *psychic bonds* are also to each other. Whereas dating was originally a part of courtship ritual, in the high school it became a means of finding intimacy. And to reduce the uncertainties in the competitive market of the "dating and rating" system that was first described as a phenomenon of college life, "going steady" became a familiar pattern. For many adolescents, really close ties tend to be confined to other adolescents. Others continue to find emotional support and satisfaction in family relationships, but by early adolescence participation with the family in its leisure activities tends to drop off even when there are no serious tensions.

Often, of course, there are tensions between the adolescent and his or her family. For running through the adolescent society as described by Coleman and others is a strong current that stresses *autonomy* from adult restrictions. Like minority group members chafing under the dominance of the majority, adolescents tend to admire those who buck the system. A degree of alienation from the larger society, which seems dominated by adults who derogate the activities of adolescents, became increasingly apparent during the 1960s and 1970s, when marijuana and other drug use became pervasive in many schools.

Another element of youth culture, perhaps less evident today than it was in the 1970s, has been *concern for the underdog* and for fair treatment of persons subject to the authority of others. In part, such an orientation may be antiestablishment, but it is also a reflection of idealism and the belief that certain principles are not to be compromised in the name of being "realistic." Youth are, in a sense, underdogs, and they know how this feels.

Finally, as formulated by the Panel on Youth of the President's Scientific Advisory Committee, youth are interested in change, in seeing social institutions modified. They are interested in changing especially the rigid, faceless bureaucratic features of modern society, though they may have little idea of what alternative patterns of social life might feasibly take the place of bureaucracy.

Coleman's description of the adolescent society focused on American high schools and on the social life of the leading cliques in such schools. It tended to ignore or play down the importance of family ties and influences and also the importance of planning for the future on the part of adolescents. Moreover, while large segments of the high school population, in addition to "leading crowds," share an interest and involvement in athletics, dress, cars, and dating, most adolescents have not been so engrossed with the adolescent culture as to become alienated from their parents and the larger society.

Parents' values clearly count heavily for most adolescents in the United States and in other countries where research has been carried out. Kandel and Lesser, in a study comparing parental and peer influences on adolescents in the United States and in Denmark, found that peer influence was relatively stronger in the United States, but nevertheless most U.S. adolescents reported that they felt emotionally close to their parents and relied heavily on their parents for guidance and advice.[28] American adolescents relied more often on mothers, while Danish adolescents tended to rely almost equally on mother and father.

Of special interest is Kandel and Lesser's finding that Danish adolescents are much more independent of parental rules (at a median age of 16) than are American adolescents. The explanation appears to be that in Denmark much stricter parental control is exerted during childhood, so that a greater degree of self-discipline and personal responsibility is attained early, permitting greater independence. The generally more permissive American parents appear to have less responsible and less independent offspring. And in both countries Kandel and Lesser found that adolescent offspring who had permissive parents were most involved in peer society and least likely to talk over problems with their parents.

SEXUAL EXPRESSION IN ADOLESCENCE

Kinsey's early research on sexual behavior revealed that in the period immediately following World War II, only about one fourth of males had sexual intercourse prior to age 16.[29] Predominantly, these were working-class males. Less than 10 percent of males whose education went beyond high school had had intercourse prior to age 16. The comparable figures for women were much lower, though for both sexes premarital sexual experience in later adolescence was substantially higher than that prior to age 16. Those women who had later premarital sexual experience tended to marry the men with whom they had the experience.

In the 1980s, on the other hand, at all class levels many adolescents are sexually active by age 16.[30] The gap between onset of puberty and onset of sexual activity has narrowed, while that between onset of sexual activity and marriage has widened appreciably. As a consequence, the risk of premarital pregnancy has risen sharply, despite the presumed availability of effective contraceptive procedures. The result has been a great increase both in abortions and in children born out of wedlock. And for the lives of the adolescent mothers who keep their infants, the consequences tend to be enduring ones, for the expectable life course is now on a different track.

An important element in the causal sequence of a woman's life course is the orientation she receives in the family, early in adolescence, toward her sexuality.

Most mothers and daughters find it difficult to talk about sex, and studies of communication in the family find that it is often limited to explaining menstruation. When mothers and daughters are interviewed separately, they frequently disagree as to whether they have ever had a discussion of sex behavior and contraception. Mothers may have made oblique references to birth control, references whose meaning totally eluded their daughters.[31] Fathers and sons are equally unlikely to discuss the significant aspects of adolescent sexuality, but the consequences are in general less drastic for boys than for girls.

The use of contraception by a girl entails planfully thinking of herself as sexually active and seeking information on potentially available means of contraception. Most girls will be loath to talk directly to their mothers about being sexually active and will be more likely to seek information from peers who are close friends or from sources with which they can preserve their anonymity. As a consequence, there is a lot of risk taking in early (and even later) sexual behavior, and such risk taking is most likely to lead to pregnancy among those girls who are least well informed about sex and reproduction.[32] Although adequate longitudinal data are not available, it appears that the general orientations regarding conduct and personal responsibility that a girl receives in the family may be more important in their influence on sexual expression and contraceptive use than the specific discussion of sexuality and birth control in the family.

Premarital Pregnancies

The consequences of premarital pregnancy in Christian and in Moslem societies have historically been tragic for girls and women. Perhaps no other theme in literature recurs as often as the story of the innocent girl seduced and abandoned by a scoundrel, though in the modern era motivations have become somewhat more complex and the outcome for the woman less grim.

A generation ago, premarital pregnancy was far more likely to be concealed if at all possible and to be terminated in an abortion or in giving up the infant for adoption. Because abortions were illegal, there are only crude estimates of the number that took place, but the frequency was high enough to make a travesty of the law. In our longitudinal research, a number of women interviewed in their sixties acknowledged that they had abortions while in high school (in the 1930s). Others married early, especially those whose pregnancies resulted from a steady relationship. Almost all completed high school, though this may reflect the probability that those who did not complete high school dropped out of the study.

Today, in addition to the tremendous increase in the frequency of adolescent pregnancies, a major problem is that so many of the girls drop out of high school years before graduation. If they keep their child, as many now do, they most often continue to live with their parents. This arrangement may permit the new mother to continue going to school, while those girls who either marry or establish independent households almost always leave school. Adolescent mothers in couple-headed households can usually count on their mothers to look after the child while they attend school, but if the adolescent's mother is herself the head of a single-parent family, this is less often feasible.

Early childbearing, in or out of marriage, tends to define the later career or at least to limit educational attainment and thus preclude any sort of professional career. Moreover, when someone else cares for the child, this may impair the mother's own relationship to her infant, and at the same time reinforce the adolescent mother's own dependency. The result can be continuing problems into the adult years.[33]

EDUCATIONAL ATTAINMENT
AND OCCUPATIONAL CHOICE

By the high school years, most adolescents have some idea of their strengths and their weaknesses, how they stand in popularity with their peers, and how they measure up in various skills and activities. Self-esteem and self-confidence are built on a base that is created by parental love and by meeting parental demands for responsible performance. School performance and school acceptance or rejection lead to further differentiation among children and adolescents in general self-esteem and in coming to sense special potentialities. Such attributes lead in turn to thinking about where one might fit in the adult world.

Few options are closed off early in adolescence, but by the end of this period the choices that have been made—or failure to make definite choices—are likely to have enduring consequences. Early school leaving for marriage or a job will most often put a low ceiling on occupational attainment. Precocity in the use of cigarettes, alcohol, or other drugs may also entail problems later on, though the consequences may be less enduring than those of dropping out of school.

Some boys and girls start high school with the expectation that it is simply another stage in the sequence of educational experiences that will take them to college and perhaps to graduate study so that they can enter professions. Others enter high school as representing just another four years of not-very-exciting-school. And for still others, school, when they attend, is just something to be gotten behind them as soon as is legally possible. Although most high schools offer alternative tracks for those who see themselves as approaching the end of the educational line and those who plan to go to college, American students generally have a good deal more flexibility available to them than do students elsewhere in the world. They can take elective courses, they can shift tracks, and they can attend many colleges simply by getting reasonably good grades in a not-very-demanding set of courses.

Because educational attainment is so important a determinant of later occupational status, or, for women who choose marriage as their primary career, so strong an influence on when they will marry and whom they will marry, it is important to identify the circumstances and the attributes that contribute to educational attainment.

Educational Attainment

Few topics of sociological research have been as systematically studied during the past decade as educational and occupational attainment. Inequality is a fact of life in all complex societies, regardless of political system. And in all societies, those who have more wealth and power tend to transmit their wealth and power to their children. It would seem ideal that a person's attainment should be directly proportional to that person's capacity of ability to perform, but the development of abilities depends as much on a person's position in society as on innate capacity.

At the start of senior high school there are a substantial number of attributes, behaviors, and attitudes that predict subsequent educational attainment. The most basic—that is, in terms of causal influence—are the socioeconomic level of the student's family and intellectual ability as measured by standard tests. The family's status and the individual's ability influence classroom grades, aspirations for college attendance, self-confidence in ability to do schoolwork, as well as occupational plans and general attitudes toward school. But even when family status and intellectual ability are controlled, superior classroom performance, college plans, positive school attitudes, absence of delinquent behaviors, and taking a college preparatory program—all as assessed in the ninth grade—are predictive of high subsequent educational attainment for both sexes.[34] As we shall see in the next chapter, additional years of educational attainment tend to translate directly into high occupational attainment for men and, to a lesser degree, women.[35]

The more highly educated parents are, the more likely they are to be able to pass on to their children some of the fruits of their own educational and occupational attainment. We noted that middle-class parents are able to provide their small children with more intellectual stimulation and a more positive orientation to school and to learning than working-class parents can. Parents who have themselves attended college can guide their offspring toward academic sequences that are appropriate to the children's interests. They can help enrich the high school experience of their adolescent children through discussion of topics under study in school. And, of course, they can help their children financially to attend college, so that the children take more or less for granted that they will do so.

The adolescent's ability to do well in high school is dependent not only on intellectual capacity but on the extent to which that capacity has been developed in the home and in early schooling; it depends also on the adolescent's general attitude toward school and his or her motivation toward academic achievement.[36] Motivation is particularly important in the working class, where many parents have little appreciation of the difference college attendance can make. The working-class youngster who wants to go to college must be sufficiently determined to overcome financial and informational deficits. For such lower-status youth, teachers tend to be very important influences on college aspirations and plans. In general, it appears that the indirect effects of the family's social status has as much to do with a youth's educational attainment as does that youth's own level of demonstrated ability.

Once in college, both parental social status and ability again make a difference in predicting graduation. In a longitudinal study of Wisconsin High School graduates of the class of 1957, Sewell and Shah found that 22 percent of the males and 15 percent of the females subsequently graduated from college.[37] The effects of measured ability (primarily intelligence) were striking: 42 percent of the boys and 29 percent of the girls who had ranked in the top third of their high school class in a junior year test of ability subsequently graduated from college. Only 4 percent of the boys and less than 3 percent of the girls who had scored in the *bottom* third of the same test subsequently graduated from college. But with ability held constant, the effects of parental status remain substantial. Considering the brightest third, 65 percent of the males and 62 percent of the females graduated among those whose parents had both attended at least one year of college; but only 28 percent of the males and 15 percent of the females graduated among those equally bright high school graduates whose parents had not themselves graduated from high school.

Half a century ago, high school graduation was considered essential for high occupational success. Today, college graduation is for most men and women a prerequisite to high occupational status unless they can step into a family business or have exceptional talents that are much in demand.[38]

Most adolescents in the United States now complete high school, although "completion" often means only that one has been moved along to graduation almost regardless of what has been learned. Beyond age 18, the proportion of youth in school or college drops off sharply. College enrollments increased enormously through the 1960s and 1970s, but roughly half of all males are in the labor force by age 19. In good times most will find jobs of some sort, but in times of recession many will remain unemployed. Especially poignant is the plight of minority youth who lack basic academic skills; inability to find work leads in time to the erosion of motivation and to turning toward illegal activities as the only alternative course available to them.[39]

A segment of the adolescent population that has only recently come to public attention consists of minority (largely black) youth who seek to make it big as professional athletes. The enormous salaries paid to a very few outstanding basketball, football, and baseball players serve to make the superstar athlete a far more attractive role model than the white-collar worker who achieves a relatively modest income after years of struggle to get an education. Unfortunately, the lure of millions of dollars and of public adulation as a superstar is for the overwhelming majority— at least 999 per thousand—a snare and a delusion. Academic skills become devalued and athletic skills become almost the sole preoccupation of many children and older youth, yet it is the academic skills that will afford them access to decent jobs in the real world. High schools and colleges too often exploit the black athlete for their own immediate competitive programs, and when the athlete has completed his eligibility, he is almost always destined to find that there are thousands who have his skills competing for a few places in well-paying professional sports. And all too often, when he reaches this dismal realization, he also realizes that he learned almost nothing of value in the course of the phony academic curriculum that was made up for him by the college that recruited him for his athletic talents.

Ability to master the basic skills of reading and arithmetic and to express oneself clearly in spoken or written English is as critical to success in business and industry as it is to college. A recent assessment of the kind of secondary education regarded by employers as most helpful in preparing noncollege youth for the labor market stresses that it is precisely these basic skills and not vocational training that will produce workers capable of the lifelong learning that a changing workplace requires.[40]

Students who during the high school years form a clear notion of their educational objectives will have an appreciable advantage over their peers who are uncertain as to where they are going. For example, the girl who seeks to become an electrical engineer may have eight or nine years of education ahead of her at the start of high school, but she can be certain that she will need all the math courses that are given in the high school if she is to move directly into the standard curriculum when she enters engineering school. Boys who have technical interests and who have found math relatively easy are likely to enroll in algebra, geometry, and trigonometry almost as a matter of course in better secondary schools, but most girls will be less interested in math or may even be dissuaded by counselors from taking math courses that have traditionally been the turf of males. Mathematics has been called "the invisible filter" that keeps many women from entering certain professional career lines.[41]

For young women, the alternatives to college attendance are likely to be almost-immediate marriage or a short-term job, then marriage. The more a girl has dated in high school, the earlier she is likely to marry. Those young women who go on to college not only have an opportunity to prepare themselves for careers but also have a wide range of continuing contact with men who will occupy high occupational statuses. A major problem for such young women, however, has been that until the last decade or so, relatively few of those who acquired the knowledge that would prepare them for careers at high occupational levels have found opportunities to utilize their knowledge and skills.[42] Among those who opted for marriage and who entered the labor force later, there was until recently little relationship between their educational attainment and their subsequent occupational status. As we shall see shortly, this situation is changing, and for both men and women educational attainment clearly ranks as a major determinant of subsequent life-style and life chances.

Political Orientations

The growing concern of the adolescent with the nature of the social order in which he lives—the restrictions it places upon individuals, the injustices it permits—leads many adolescents to develop an interest in political issues. Youth have almost always been regarded as more radical than their elders; they have less of a stake in the status quo, fewer commitments to the past, and more concern with the future.

Yet most adolescents are not radicals by any means. In the 1960s, when student rebellions swept American college campuses, they were led by a relatively small group of intellectually engaged leaders who were initially protesting mindless bureaucratic restrictions by university authorities.[43] Subsequently, the Vietnam War became a major case of student unrest and opposition to governmental policy, but even then only a minority of adolescents took any active part in demonstrations. The young were clearly more opposed to the war than their elders, however, and their opposition was not merely a result of their being the ones called upon to serve. Those most opposed were not working-class youth and minorities, who were drafted in much higher proportion than middle-class youth, but were more often college students who were appalled at the racist, colonial mentality that was so manifest in the wanton destruction visited upon Vietnam. The bombing and machine-gunning of civilians whose culture we neither understood nor respected seemed to them a mockery of the values the United States ought to manifest in its foreign relations.

Research on the antecedents of student activism in the 1960s revealed that most activists were not rebelling against the views of their parents, but had parents who were nonauthoritarian, believed in civil rights, and above all wanted their children to have an independent, questioning orientation toward the world around them.[44] It was only the severely alienated youth—the dissidents—whose actions seemed motivated by rebellion against conservative and often authoritarian parents.[45]

By and large, adolescents tend to follow the political preferences of their parents, but they are less politically active than they will later become.[46] Although 18-year-olds are entitled to vote in national elections, fewer adolescents and young adults actually vote than members of any other age group up to age 70 at least. Perhaps the reason for many is related to their not yet having a clear stake in the governmental processes that keep the society in some sort of order.

Along with a marked rise in activism among college students, the 1960s saw the development of countercultures or alternative life-styles among older adolescents.[47] Substantial numbers of youth dropped out of conventional society and lived in communes or group residences, often in rural or semirural settings. Conventional jobs in the world of commerce and industry were out; crafts and chores and rap sessions were in. The hippies or flower children of the 1960s symbolized alienation from certain prevailing emphases of the larger culture, while at the same time emphasizing some other themes that had long been highly valued: love and friendship, peaceful coexistence, self-expression, and the simple life. What was most profoundly threatening to many older adults, however, was the widespread use of mind-expanding or psychedelic drugs.

The legacy of the sixties has been much greater sexual freedom on the part of adolescents and a substantial increase in the proportion of older adolescents and young adult couples who live together without marrying. Most of those who dropped out have returned to conventional pursuits, but some still make a living in the arts or crafts. By and large our society has accommodated to alternative life-styles by becoming more tolerant of variations on conventional themes. What was billed as the battle of the generations was in part a response to particular historical circumstances by a cohort of youth that was far larger than any other in history, the generation of the post-World War II baby boom.[48] Perhaps the very size of that cohort explained the intensity of the shock when so many young people failed to accept the existing moral order. Be that as it may, the residual effects have been registered in very real changes in the society, but scarcely a ripple of the intergenerational turmoil remains.

IDENTITY: THE SELF IN ADOLESCENCE

Adolescence and early adulthood demand a great increase in autonomy and self-determination. The self originally came into being as a consequence of the child's ability to internalize the responses of others to his or her own behavior. Self-feelings in childhood become stabilized to a degree by the patterned responses of others—parents, teachers, peers. Our sense of who we are rests on how we think others see us, for it inevitably influences how we see ourselves. Perceived strengths and weaknesses include things others may not know about or may not value as we do, but they otherwise largely reflect what we have been praised or criticized for by others. Identity also depends on our sense of whom we belong with; it encompasses those who are most important to us. Ultimately, identity will come more and more to be centered on the values we are committed to, the activities that engage us most fully, and the persons who are most dear to us. By late adolescence and early adulthood, values and activities are likely to have become stabilized and our identity much more sharply defined.

Erikson has proposed that the development of identity is the prime task of the adolescent years.[49] Through trying out fantasies and exercising talents during a period when they can still depend on others to provide material and emotional support, adolescents get the chance to know themselves better. Erikson speaks of adolescence as affording a moratorium, a period of freedom from responsibility, and for many it does.

The process of achieving a clear sense of who one is, so that one can then plan systematically for a fruitful life through the adult years, would ideally require that a person experience a wide range of contacts with others in diverse situations. As Erikson analyzes the process, the desired outcome is to maintain flexibility until one is quite sure of what one wants for oneself. To decide who we are (or should be) on the basis of what others want for us, before we know for ourselves what we want, would be to foreclose possibilities. Premature identity foreclosure leads to rigidities and to ultimate dissatisfaction and alienation.

The alternative extreme, that of failing to achieve a clear sense of who one is or who one wants to be, seems often to result from an inability to choose among or to integrate the various social roles the person occupies. Erikson calls this problematic outcome "role diffusion." Many professional actors seem to suffer from role diffusion; they are, for a time, the roles they occupy; in real life they feel a great sense of confusion in knowing who they are and in relating stably to others.[50] For many adolescents and young adults role diffusion is a temporary state, but for some it becomes a lifelong problem.

Erikson's writing on adolescence is full of sensitive insights and gives us a better understanding of the source of some of the turmoil that adolescence entails. There are points at which one might disagree with him, however. He writes of "premature identity foreclosure," for example, as if early choices were almost inevitably the consequence of doing what others want for us. Most persons commit themselves to particular goals or courses before they have explored all the possibilities available to them, but many will have a reasonably clear notion of the most critical elements of what they want for themselves—the values they stand for, the activities that give them a solid sense of satisfaction, and the kind of people they would like to associate with. Very few of us get to try out more than a very small segment of the possibilities that exist for us in the realm of careers or leisure activities or expressive arts. The person who early in life finds activities that are deeply satisfying is likely to build more stable life patterns than one who does not. Identity may be prematurely foreclosed if major talents are denied expression, but an early recognition of what one believes in and what one wants in life appears more often than not to lead to satisfaction and fulfillment in the later years.

It is often through intimate relationships, whether with the same or the opposite sex, that we come to express and to know our own deepest feelings, and through their acceptance by another, we affirm them ourselves. Identity clearly does not emerge as fully formed; indeed, it is never *fully* formed, is always subject to some degree of change as our competences, the sources of our emotional highs, and our network of significant others change over the life course. But identity is much more clearly limned when it is reflected back from the mirror of a loved one's responses to our most intimately revealing acts. Because no other relationship entails such complete abandonment of pretense and protective defenses as does that between sexual lovers (and by lover I mean something much more than mere sexual partner), it is here that many young people come to feel confident that they know who they are. The capacity for intimacy requires an awareness of potential vulnerability and an ability to risk the abandonment of defenses, hence it does not emerge early in life.[51]

Other Aspects of Personality

By adolescence, temperament and character have been to a large extent shaped and to a degree stabilized. Attitudes and personal style may change markedly in the adult years, but increasingly the choices that are made by the adolescent and young adult will serve to further reinforce tendencies that have become apparent by late adolescence. Good work habits, dependability, and intellectual curiosity will usually have payoff value, at least for middle-class males. Their absence will often produce tensions and pressures for conformity. These, in turn, may produce either a degree of change or alienation and more problematic responses.

Some problematic adolescents will find themselves a few years down the road, while others will continue to be problems to themselves and to others through most of their lives.

Important facets of personality are shaped by the culture itself. We see the world through lenses provided by our culture and by our position in society. This is dramatically evident in the findings of a large-scale study of "modernity" conducted by Alex Inkeles.[52] Research teams interviewed nearly 6000 young men in six developing nations to assess their resemblance in attitudes, values, and behaviors to men in the modern industrial world. Inkeles describes "psychosocial modernity" as including the following central elements:

> (1) Openness to new experience, both with people and with new ways of doing things such as attempting to control births; (2) the assertion of increasing independence from the authority of traditional figures like parents and priests and a shift of allegiance to leaders of government, public affairs, trade unions, cooperatives, and the like; (3) belief in the efficacy of science and medicine, and a general abandonment of passivity and fatalism in the face of life's difficulties; and (4) ambition for oneself and one's children to achieve high occupational and educational goals. Men who manifest these characteristics (5) like people to be on time and show an interest in carefully planning their affairs in advance. It is also part of this syndrome to (6) show strong interest and take an active part in civic and community affairs and local politics; and (7) to strive energetically to keep up with the news, and within this effort to prefer news of national and international import over items dealing with sports, religion, or purely local affairs.[53]

Within the developing nations, scores on the measure of modernity, as defined above, were to a large extent dependent on years of schooling, whether a man worked in an urban industrial setting or a traditional one, features of the occupation, and the state of the mass media. These aspects of life experience accounted for a substantial part of the variations among nations in modernity, but there remained a good deal that could only be explained in terms of the unique cultural values and the economic systems (themselves parts of culture) of the countries.

Only as we examine lives across nations and cultures do we come to recognize how much of what we call personality is shaped by the understandings that we share with those around us, just as we share a language, a preferred diet, or particular pastimes. Culture and society afford much of the content that makes us as persons comprehensible to our peers and often incomprehensible to those from vastly different backgrounds.

THE TRANSITION FROM ADOLESCENCE TO ADULTHOOD

The transition from adolescence to adulthood involves a number of phases or aspects that have come increasingly closer together. A century ago, school leaving was almost always the first of these steps, followed by entry into a job or helping out at home, then marriage perhaps a decade later, and finally by the couple's establishing its own independent household.[54] Occasionally a boy or, less often, a girl would return to school after having worked for a time, and the later grades of elementary school might contain a wide age range, from 12 to late adolescence, prior to the enactment of child labor laws. Since marriage came somewhat later than it now does, and many couples lived with parents or with other families before they could manage a household of their own, the transition from a dependent in the parental home to a fully autonomous adult was accomplished slowly, with strong bonds to the parental family usually lasting into the middle twenties.

Today the transition has been collapsed into a very few years for most persons. Moreover, the sequence has been altered for many by the extension of schooling and earlier marriage. Work and school roles and even marriage, work, and school roles may be combined. And so depiction of the life course chronologically is no longer feasible except for broad periods.

"Splitting Off"

Most children leave the parental home between the ages of 18 and 25, with daughters moving out an average of about one year earlier than sons. For those who go away to college, it is often difficult to know whether the offspring still regard the parental dwelling as their primary base of operation or whether it is merely a place they visit occasionally during vacation periods. In any event, most college students will be more dependent on their parents financially than emotionally. Although psychoanalytically inclined scholars stress the importance of becoming emotionally independent of parents as a major task, systematic research suggests that most youth are eager to be on their own, even when they have good relationships with their parents.

In Chapter 2 we noted that Gould presents as the "major false assumption to be challenged: 'I'll always belong to my parents and believe in their world.'"[55] Undoubtedly there are adolescents who have great ambivalence about their ability to be on their own, but they appear to be decidedly in the minority. In a study of the transition to college away from home, a team of psychiatric researchers at the National Institute of Mental Health found that "for most of the students there was a certain anticipated pleasure about separation from parents."[56] Moreover, the great majority "handled the challenge with ease," having been prepared by earlier experiences in summer camp, independent travel, or summer jobs. Many parents had gradually loosened the reins and had previously given responsibility to their children.

For those adolescents who do not attend college, a sizeable majority do not leave home until they marry, but the last decade has seen a large increase in independent living. A study conducted several years ago revealed that among those who left before age 25, roughly a fourth of young women and a somewhat larger proportion of young men did so to live on their own or in a nonfamily group.[57] Proportions today would undoubtedly be higher. Splitting off, especially to establish a household as a single person, entails economic pressures much greater than those experienced in the parental home, and a small proportion of unmarried off-spring and those offspring who have separated or divorced return to live with their parents.

Stages in Adolescence

As we have seen, adolescence is a time of physical and social transitions, some of which make for considerable demands on the person. The scheduling of these demands is to a large extent dependent on physical development and, in Western societies, on the educational system. The adolescent may opt out of school at the earliest possible time or may be committed to higher educational goals. Insofar as any stages may be discerned, they are stages that depend on rate of maturing, on school transitions marked by rites of passage, and on choices or commitments made by the person. The choices are themselves influenced by physiology, by social class, and by family and peer relationships. They are not irrevocable, but making, or failing to make, choices and commitments is likely to have consequences that will extend far into the middle years.

Into the Adult Years

We have seen that in modern industrial societies adolescence is a period of preparation, a period when the child who has alternated between school and play or peer activities must begin to develop a plan for life. The two worlds which the adolescent will soon occupy—that of the procreative family and the world of work—will dominate the basic script for the rest of life. But the plot is to be written by the person who enacts it (albeit with much help from others).

We begin in childhood to know who we are, and somewhere in adolescence our conceptions of ourselves are likely to be greatly enriched by our first close heterosexual relationships as well as by our increasing mastery of the knowledge and skills we shall need later on. Yet our sense of who we are as adults will be further shaped by what we become, occupationally, and by the persons with whom we share, in intimate detail, our inner lives. We shift, therefore, from following a chronological account of the life course to an examination of these two most important adult roles and the various ways in which they are developed and interwoven. Because most men and women are employed for pay before they marry, we turn next to the world of work and the variety of occupational careers.

NOTES

1. Theodore Lidz, *The Person: His and Her Development Throughout the Life,* rev. ed. (New York: Basic Books, 1976), p. 306.
2. Margaret Mead, *Coming of Age in Samoa: A Psychological Study of Primitive Youth for Western Civilization* (New York: William Morrow & Co., 1928).
3. Ibid., p. 157.

4. *Youth, Transition to Adulthood*, Report of the Panel on Youth of the President's Science Advisory Committee (Chicago: University of Chicago Press, 1974), p. 12.

5. *Ibid.*, p. 26.

6. Robert J. Havighurst first formulated the concept of developmental tasks and proposed a somewhat similar set of tasks in *Developmental Tasks and Education*, 3rd ed. (New York: David McKay, 1972).

7. James M. Tanner, "Sequence, Tempo and Individual Variation in the Growth and Development of Boys and Girls Aged Twelve to Sixteen," *Daedalus*, 100 (Fall 1971), 907-30.

8. John A. Clausen, "The Social Meaning of Differential Physical and Sexual Maturation," in S. E. Dragastin and G. H. Elder, eds., *Adolescence in the Life Cycle* (New York: Wiley, 1976), pp. 25-47.

9. Harvey Peskin has analyzed the consequences of early maturing from a psychoanalytic perspective in "Pubertal Onset and Ego Functioning," *Journal of Abnormal Psychology*, 72 (1967), 1-15.

10. Tanner, "Sequence, Tempo and Individual Variation," pp. 926-27.

11. See, for example, Anna Freud, "Adolescence as a Developmental Disturbance," in G. Kaplan and L. Lebovici, eds., *Adolescence: Psychological Perspectives* (New York: Basic Books, 1969), and Peter Blos, *On Adolescence: A Psychoanalytic Interpretation* (New York: Free Press, 1962).

12. Clausen, "The Social Meaning of Differential Physical and Sexual Maturation," pp. 42-43.

13. D. A. Blyth et al., "The Effects of Physical Development on Self-image and Satisfaction with Body-image for Early Adolescent Males," in R. G. Simmons, ed., *Research in Community and Mental Health, Vol. 2* (Greenwich, CT: JAI Press, 1981).

14. R. G. Simmons et al., "Entry into Early Adolescence: The Impact of School Structure, Puberty and Early Dating on Self-esteem," *American Sociological Review*, 44 (1979), 948-67.

15. R. G. Simmons, D. A. Blyth, and K. L. McKinney, "The Social and Psychological Effects of Puberty on White Females," in J. Brooks-Gunn and A. C. Petersen, eds., *Girls at Puberty: Biological and Psychosocial Perspectives* (New York: Plenum Press, 1983).

16. Mary Cover Jones, "Psychological Correlates of Somatic Development," *Child Development*, 36 (1965), 899-911.

17. Harvey Peskin, "Influence of Developmental Schedule of Puberty on Learning and Ego Development," *Journal of Youth and Adolescence*, 2 (1973), 243-56.

18. For a good discussion of the concept of formal operations and the recent status of Piaget's formulations, see Daniel P. Keating, "Thinking Processes in Adolescence," in Joseph Adelson, ed., *Handbook of Adolescent Psychology* (New York: Wiley, 1980), pp. 211-46.

19. Lawrence Kohlberg, *Stages in the Development of Moral Thought and Action* (New York: Holt, Rinehart and Winston, 1969).

20. Ibid.

21. Norma Haan, "Two Moralities in Action Contexts: Relationships to Thought, Ego Regulation, and Development," *Journal of Personality and Social Psychology*, 36 (1978), 286-305.

22. Carol Gilligan, *In a Different Voice: Psychological Theory and Women's Development* (Cambridge, MA: Harvard University Press, 1982).

23. Charles Darwin, *The Autobiography of Charles Darwin and Selected Letters*, ed. Francis Darwin (New York: Dover Publications, Inc., 1958).

24. Albert Einstein, *Autobiographical Notes*, trans. and ed. Paul A. Schilpp (Chicago: Open Court Publishing Co., 1979).

25. Clark Wissler, "Depression and Revolt," quoted in Erik Erikson, *Childhood and Society* (New York: W. W. Norton & Co., 1959), p. 100.

26. James Coleman, *The Adolescent Society: The Social Life of the Teenager and Its Impact on Education* (Glencoe, IL: The Free Press of Glencoe, 1961).

27. This summary parallels the discussion of youth culture in *Youth, Transition to Adulthood*, pp. 112-25.

28. Denise Kandel and Gerald Lesser, *Youth in Two Worlds* (San Francisco: Jossey-Bass, Inc., 1972).

29. Alfred Kinsey, Wardell Pomeroy, and Clyde Martin, *Sexual Behavior in the Human Male* (Philadelphia: W. B. Saunders Co., 1948).

30. Ethnic and religious differences in attitudes toward sexual freedom are still substantial, and the social and psychological consequences of deviating from group norms can still be considerable. For recent research on adolescent sexuality among college students, see Karl King, J. O. Balswick, and J. E. Robinson, "The Continuing Sexual Revolution among College Females," *Journal of Marriage and the Family*, 39 (1977), 455-59.

31. Frank Furstenberg, Jr. et al., "Family Communication and Teenagers' Contraceptive Use," *Family Planning Perspectives*, 16 (1984), 163-70.

32. Kristin Luker, *Taking Chances: Abortion and the Decision Not to Contracept* (Berkeley, CA: University of California Press, 1975).

33. Frank Furstenberg, Jr., "Burdens and Benefits: The Impact of Early Childbearing on the Family," *Journal of Social Issues*, 36 (1980), 64-87.

34. Several excellent studies have consistently documented these findings for males. For one, see Karl Alexander and Bruce Ekland, "School Experience and Status Attainment," in *Adolescence in the Life Cycle*. For a discussion of some of the respects in which the educational attainment process of girls differs from that of boys, see M. M. Marini, "The Transition to Adulthood: Sex Differences in Educational Attainment and Age at Marriage," *American Sociological Review*, 43 (1978), 483-509.

35. J. G. Bachman, P. M. O'Malley, and Jerome Johnston, *Adolescence to Adulthood: Change and Stability in the Lives of Young Men* (Ann Arbor, MI: Institute for Social Research, 1978).

36. Glen H. Elder, "Achievement Motivation and Intelligence in Occupational Mobility: A Longitudinal Analysis," *Sociometry*, 31 (1968), 327-54.

37. William A. Sewell and Vimal P. Shah, "Socioeconomic Status, Intelligence and the Attainment of Higher Education," *Sociology of Education*, 40 (1967), 1-23.

38. Robert M. Hauser and David Featherman, *The Process of Stratification* (New York: Academic Press, 1977).

39. For a cogent analysis, see J. T. Gibbs, "Black Adolescents and Youth: An Endangered Species," *American Journal of Orthopsychiatry*, 54 (1984), 6-20.

40. Panel on Secondary School Education for the Changing Workplace, *High Schools and the Changing Workplace: The Employers' View* (Washington, D.C.: National Academy Press, 1984).

41. Lucy Sells, "Mathematics, The Invisible Filter," unpublished paper, Berkeley, CA, 1975.

42. Dissatisfaction with women's traditional lot has been most acute among highly educated women, and perhaps nothing has given greater impetus to the women's movement than the increase in the proportion securing higher education.

43. See, for example, Kenneth Keniston, *Young Radicals: Notes on Committed Youth* (New York: Harcourt, Brace and World, 1968). Appendix B deals with the sources of student dissent. Also, S. M. Lipset and S. S. Wolin, eds., *The Berkeley Student Revolt: Facts and Interpretations* (Garden City, NY: Doubleday Anchor, 1965).

44. J. H. Block, N. Haan, and M. B. Smith, "Socialization Correlates of Student Activism," *Journal of Social Issues*, 25 (1969), 143-77.

45. Ibid., pp. 173-74.

46. M. K. Jennings and Richard Niemi, *The Political Character of Adolescence: The Influence of Families and Schools* (Princeton, NJ: Princeton University Press, 1974).

47. Bennett Berger, "Ecstatic Youth, 1966-68," in *Looking for America: Essays on Youth, Suburbia and Other American Obsessions* (Englewood Cliffs, NJ: Prentice-Hall, Inc., 1971), pp. 119-40.

48. *Youth, Transition to Adulthood,* pp. 46–49.

49. Erik Erikson, "Identity and the Life Cycle: Selected Papers," *Psychological Issues,* 1 (1959).

50. An unpublished study based on intensive interviews of many leading actors, conducted some decades ago by William Henry, found that few felt that they knew who they really were as persons.

51. This account differs somewhat from the view of Erikson and other psychoanalytic formulations, but my thinking was stimulated especially by a paper by George W. Goethals, "The Evolution on Sexual and Genital Intimacy: A Comparison of the Views of Erik H. Erikson and Harry Stack Sullivan," *Journal of the American Academy of Psychoanalysis,* 4 (1976), 529–44.

52. Alex Inkeles, "Making Men Modern," *American Journal of Sociology,* 75 (1969), 208–25.

53. Alex Inkeles, "National Differences in Individual Modernity," *Comparative Studies in Sociology,* 1 (1978), 49.

54. John Modell, Frank Furstenberg, Jr., and Theodore Hershberg, "Social Change and Transitions to Adulthood in Historical Perspective," *Journal of Family History,* 1 (1976), 7–32.

55. Roger Gould, *Transformations* (New York: Simon and Schuster, 1978), p. 43.

56. E. B. Murphey et al., "Development of Autonomy and Parent-Child Interaction in Late Adolescence," *American Journal of Orthopsychiatry,* 33 (1963), 643–52.

57. Daniel Hill and Martha Hill, "Older Children and Splitting Off," in G. J. Duncan and J. N. Morgan, eds., *Five Thousand American Families: Patterns of Economic Progress,* vol. IV (Ann Arbor, MI: Institute for Social Research, 1976), pp. 117–54.

CHAPTER 6
THE ADULT YEARS: OCCUPATIONAL CAREERS

*It's very important that I'm a doctor.
I sometimes wonder, "What was I like
before I was a doctor?" because you're
always playing this role. . . .*
*Study Member,
Berkeley Longitudinal Studies*

From the early years of childhood, boys and girls form images of what they might be when they grow up. Boys used to think primarily of jobs and girls of being wives and mothers. The sexes still differ to a degree in the relative priorities given to work and family, and perhaps they always will. Nevertheless, enough women are now oriented to having careers, with or without marriage and children, to suggest that a woman's expectable life course is more likely than not to entail an occupational involvement that is substantial and enduring.[1]

In highly differentiated modern societies, the demands for specialized skills and abilities lead to a great variety of occupational options for members of each generation. Large industries and commercial organizations and, largest of all organizations, governments, operate through bureaucratic structures that provide many layers of jobs and levels of supervision. Within such organizations a person can spend a whole working lifetime. Most persons, however, experience a number of employers in the course of their occupational lives. Some follow a single line of work; others change not only employers but type of work, seeking to find something that gives satisfaction in the doing and adequate financial return. What they seek and what return they feel they should receive will depend on expectations built up in their families of origin and in the course of their education. We shall use the term *career* in its general meaning of "progress or course of action of a person through life, or through some phase of life"[2] to cover both orderly, progressive careers and those job histories that entail discontinuity and change.

General Features of Occupational Careers

Occupational careers vary widely in terms of the number of jobs held, the circumstances that make for success or failure, the succession of responsibilities on the one hand and rewards on the other, and the extent to which they become incorporated into the identity of the worker. We shall therefore discuss initially some of the most salient features of careers and then give a few examples of different types of careers.

Prestige. Some occupations require much greater talents, training, or executive ability than others. In general, the rewards that a job brings, in money, power, and prestige, are related to the levels of ability, training, and experience that are required for success. The prestige ranking of occupations has been the dimension most frequently used by social scientists for classifying jobs.[3] Toward the top of the prestige hierarchy are holders of high political offices, judges, physicians, and other major professionals and corporate board members, as well as the higher executives of major businesses. Toward the middle of the scale come bookkeepers, lower administrative staff members, skilled workers, and foremen, while toward the bottom come watchmen, waiters, workers in fast-food chains, and street sweepers. Salaries tend to vary with prestige, but only to a degree; scientists and top governmental officials and office holders tend to earn much less than physicians and business executives, but they are rewarded by perquisites other than monetary ones.

Career Patterns. Careers vary in the degree to which they represent an orderly progression of responsibility and reward within a single occupational field, as against shifting fields and possibly even some backtracking in pay and responsibility. Some scholars would use the term *career* only where there is a high degree of coherence and order—where each job change is a step up the ladder of success.[4] The ideal case is, of course, a lifelong career in government or in the military, advancing through the ranks from a college-graduate intern to a division chief in a government bureau or from an ensign to an admiral in the navy. Most work histories are not orderly, but perhaps a third are orderly over at least half the work life. The more orderly the work history, the stronger the involvement and participation of the person in the various organizations of the community.[5]

The larger the organization and the more layers of personnel in the administrative hierarchy, the more likely an employee is to have an orderly career within the organization. Smaller organizations offer less opportunity for advancement and less security; therefore large organizations are seen as preferred places to work. Following career disruption by service in the army in World War II, for example, more than four fifths of the men who had previously worked for companies employing 50 or more workers returned to their former employers, while less than three fifths of those who had worked a comparable length of time for smaller companies prior to the war returned to their former employers.[6] Small companies are more often the training ground for new workers who subsequently shift into larger companies, especially those with thousands of employees.

Stability of employment has multiple meanings. Many workers experience periodic layoffs or episodes of unemployment as a consequence of business conditions or the bankruptcy of an employer. Others give up their jobs because of dissatisfaction, inability to locate adequate housing, or other problems. Often, of course, people change jobs because they learn of something more attractive—either a higher salary or wage in comparable work for another employer, or a shift in type of work. This aspect of stability reflects both the orderliness of the career and the worker's *occupational mobility* or change in status over the career. Change of employer or change in the type of work done, with no change of level, is called *horizontal mobility*; if the new job is at a different level of prestige, we speak of *vertical mobility,* up or down. Thus we can ask of any career, does it reflect significant movement up or down from the status level of the person's family at the start of the career (intergenerational mobility) or from the status level of the person's first responsible job (intragenerational mobility)?

Career Stages.   Yet another feature of careers is the extent to which they entail a sequence of stages. Such stages will again be easy to discern in bureaucratic organizations, though stages there will for the most part be simply reflections of greater seniority and responsibility. But other types of occupations have stages, too. We may think in general of the sequence of preparation (if any) for the occupation, trial work experiences, and the stable stage that follows commitment to a particular field.[7] For some occupations, commitment is almost a precondition of entering the field, especially if long training and tested competence is required, as in medicine. In others, commitment will come only after alternative possibilities have been eliminated from consideration.[8]

In some fields, the stages of a career will be marked by very substantial changes in what one does, with or without a change of job setting.[9] Scientists become administrators; local politicians achieve national eminence; struggling entrepreneurs and lower-level managers become major executives of large corporations.

Job Complexity.   An obviously important feature of any occupation is the nature of the tasks the job entails and especially the complexity of the cognitive or intellectual demands the job makes. Some jobs are relatively routine, involving only a few simple operations; they may be demanding only in the sense that operations must be carried out at a pace determined by someone else. Other jobs are substantively complex, demanding the assessment of evidence, highly skilled operations, or the supervision and coordination of the efforts of others. Melvin Kohn and his co-workers have studied the correlates of high substantive complexity in the work of men and of women.[10] Complex work not only makes demands on its practitioners; it tends to shape the way they see the world and the values they hold dear, and it enhances their intellectual flexibility. Routine work, especially when closely super-vised, on the other hand, provides low intellectual stimulus and often goes with rather rigid, authoritarian attitudes. In general, those who work primarily with ideas or data have the most complex jobs, but work with people can also be substantively complex, and so can work with things, as when it entails an artist working in his medium or a highly skilled technician. Complex, demanding occupations are usually selected by persons who have high intellectual capacity and flexibility, and these attributes tend then to be further enhanced by the nature of the demands upon the worker. Thus selection and further socialization go hand in hand.

Effects of Social Change. Finally, it is important to recognize that the kinds of careers that are available depend upon the larger social and technological organi-zation. Prestige, mobility, and stability derive from a larger context. The changing menu of occupations available for selection, largely brought about by technological advances, has resulted in great cohort differences in work histories over the past century and more. At the beginning of the current century 37 percent of the work force was found on farms. By 1947 only 14 percent remained on farms, and by 1970 the figure had dropped to 5 percent.[11] Employment in manufacturing as a percentage of all employment increased in the early 1900s but has declined since World War II, giving rise to the characterization of our society as "postindustrial." Service occupations and the professions have increased from comprising roughly one fifth of all employment 100 years ago to comprising three fifths in the 1980s.

Throughout the past century there has been an increase in jobs demanding knowledge and skill and a decrease in the jobs demanding brawn. In 1900, laborers and domestics made up more than a third of the persons employed; by 1970 they comprised less than 10 percent. Along with the changing structure of the work force, there was a sharp decline in hours worked and a great increase in real income. In 1870 an average worker (who wore a blue collar) entered the work force at 14 and left when he died at age 61.[12] He or she worked ten hours a day, six days a week, for low wages that changed little over the course of the career. Periodically he or she was laid off and had to exist on whatever the charity of others might provide.

In the 1980s the average worker (who figuratively wears a white collar) enters the work force at around age 20 and works until retirement at age 65. He or she works eight hours a day, five days a week, for earnings that are, over the lifetime, roughly 300 percent higher, in real income, than earnings received over the lifetime a century ago. The average worker today receives far more benefits such as medi-cal and unemployment insurance and paid vacations than did the worker in 1870, and the gap in prestige between the average worker and the elite has markedly narrowed.

The worker a century ago was most concerned with survival. The worker to-day can afford to be concerned with job conditions and benefits. Perhaps in no other realm of experience are the effects of changing social structure on the individual life course so clearly evident as they are when we examine occupational careers over successive cohorts of workers.

With these concepts and considerations in mind, we turn to a closer look at the origins of careers in the choices made late in the adolescent or early in the adult years.

OCCUPATIONAL CHOICE

How and when is choice of an occupation made? Even casual observation and questioning of adolescents and young adults will indicate great variation among them. Men and women who become physicians have usually decided on their goal by their college years; they will complete, on the average, another eight or nine years of education and training before they actually enter the profession of medicine.[13] Late entry into the labor market will be typical of almost all professions, but early choice is not necessarily entailed; those who become lawyers, for example, tend to make the decision for law at a much later point than those who become physicians.[14]

Early entrants to the labor market will, of course, be those who leave school first. They include not only those youngsters who are poor students, but also those who have no resources or opportunities for higher education, those who must work to help support their families, and those who do not know what they want to do but want some experience of "the real world." There will also be a few who know what they want and who don't need any further formal education to achieve their goal.

Most adolescents, we noted, will have made some assessment of their strengths and weaknesses and will have given some thought to the possibilities that exist for them in the world of work. They will have been asked innumerable times by their parents and others what they want to be. Children will have heard adults talk about their jobs, especially their own family members. They will know that jobs entail frustrations, that there are "stupid" or "mean" or "incompetent" bosses and co-workers who complicate the work lives of their parents or siblings.[15]

Occupational Choice
and the Labor Market

The complex division of labor in modern societies produces a great variety of occupational tasks, which require specialized understanding and skills to perform them competently. There is, then, a need for institutional mechanisms to see that persons are prepared for and/or selected for appropriate jobs. There are mechanisms that inform and motivate young persons toward particular goals through the socialization process, and there are mechanisms that sift and sort potential entrants, mechanisms of the labor market itself.[16]

In the last analysis, the jobs to which each new cohort of entrants into the labor market can realistically aspire must be those that are available in the market. While the market for professions such as law or medicine may be considerably expansible, ultimately the saturation point is reached, though new specialties within the profession may still emerge. More generally, new occupations are constantly created as old ones become obsolete. The assembly line worker is replaced by a robot in building cars, but new jobs open up in the field of computer technology, without which robots could not be controlled.

The level of employment itself varies depending on economic conditions. In periods of major recession or depression, more than a tenth of the work force may be unemployed. The figure will be much higher for workers in manufacturing industries and in construction, industries in which blue-collar workers predominate. And when general unemployment is high, younger entrants to the labor force will be especially likely to be unemployed. During the recession of 1981-1982, a fourth of white teenagers seeking work and half of the black teenagers seeking work were unable to find it.[17] Under such conditions "occupational choice" has little meaning for the average high school graduate and even less for that fourth of all adolescents who do not complete high school.

Theories of Occupational Choice

Occupational aspirations do not, however, rest primarily on the state of the labor market, though they may be dampened by economic conditions. They are gradually built up as a consequence of parental commentaries and urgings, the development of life interests, getting to know attractive representatives of particular occupations, and other socialization experiences. For some, aspirations will be little more than idle dreams; for others they will be goals to pursue. A number of social scientists—psychologists, sociologists, economists—have studied the process of occupational choice.[18] We shall not try to summarize their individual theories but rather to draw upon the body of theory and research that has been amassed over the last 30 to 40 years.

There is general agreement that occupational choice cannot be viewed as a single decision, but rather as a series of decisions made over a number of years, often 10 years or more. The child's first verbalizations of occupational preference tend to be based on fantasies built up around images of particular occupations or persons in those occupations, and these fantasies have little bearing on subsequent choice. By early adolescence, however, most children become aware of the general qualifications that are required for particular occupations and some of the rewards that these occupations have to offer.

Youth who enroll in college will have a longer time to decide on an occupation, though for some the choice of a college major will already be a tentative commitment to a particular career (as in engineering, architecture, or social welfare). For youth who do not enroll in college, the choice of an occupation is more largely dictated by local labor market conditions and by personal ties, except for those who have had specialized vocational training that prepares them for available jobs. Several theorists have stressed that stable choice of an occupation entails adaptation to the realities that are encountered in the course of early employment experience. Before they have had any job experience, most youth are unaware of the various aspects of life that will be to a large extent contingent on the work they do. The specific job itself is likely to be of primary concern, but the quality of the work environment, the monitoring of the pace of work and the closeness of supervision, the cultural and intellectual interests of co-workers, the way an employee is expected to dress, and the kind of schedule that one has to meet cannot be fully appreciated until these facets of a particular occupational line have been experienced. Therefore, early job choice will be a trial-and-error learning experience for many, especially manual workers.

In his book *The Seasons of a Man's Life,* Daniel Levinson emphasized the importance of the "Dream." [19] He suggested that the Dream represents for many young men "an imagined possibility, more formed than a pure fantasy, yet less articulated than a fully thought out plan." Some young people have a clear dream that rather early becomes articulated in a plan of action; others have a succession of dreams that never go much beyond the fantasy level, remaining imagined possibilities that for the most part lie dormant. New visions and opportunities constantly materialize, and a dream may emerge only as one begins to get a sense of what is possible in a given occupational role. But as Ginsberg has noted, and this is very much in accord with our own research: "If the individual is able to conceptualize what he wants to be in the future, he acquires a major organizing principle which can give direction and provide continuity to what would otherwise be random and unrelated action." [20]

In the last analysis, entry into an occupation will entail both developmental stages and a more or less systematic weighing of rewards against costs, and abilities against the requirements of a given occupation. Some fields are highly competitive, and only a small proportion of aspirants can hope for success. To make a good living through the use of one's artistic talents, whether as painter, actor, or musician, those talents must be superior to those of other potential artists *and* one must have enough self-confidence to persevere in art. The talented musician who is afraid to risk not being able to make a living in music and who turns instead to becoming a school teacher might have been a great artist. No one will ever know. Thus strength of motivation to pursue one's dream is as important as the talent itself. Or, to put it another way, wanting a particular career badly enough may not bring it into reality, but it will help to do so.

Major Influences on Occupational Choice

Parental Occupations. Occupational choice is directly and strongly influenced by parental occupations beyond the indirect influence of family status or educational attainment. Particularly among professionals, high business executives, and proprietors of businesses, sons are more likely to follow their father's occupation or a closely related one than to enter any other field of endeavor.[20] Daughters are especially likely to have serious career plans if their mothers have had occupational careers. Family traditions of careers in medicine, law, or the ministry are less frequently found today than in the past, but they still can be found. Family businesses still flourish, though more and more are swallowed up by large corporations.

At the other end of the occupational hierarchy, many sons still follow fathers into local mines and many sons and daughters follow parents into manufacturing plants, especially in communities dominated by a single industry. A fascinating account of the recruitment of workers by kin in a large textile plant in such a community is given in Tamara Hareven's *Family Time and Industrial Time.*[22] Over a period of more than 50 years, kin groups made up the largest component of the work force of the giant mill that supported the local economy of Manchester, New Hampshire, until the Great Depression of the 1930s.

Personality.   Through vocational testing and counseling, most high school students now get a chance to make a systematic assessment of what they are interested in and, to a lesser extent, what the world of work has to offer them. Occupational researchers have classified jobs in various ways to try to see how well different kinds of interests and personality orientations may be matched to particular occupations. One such set of classifications, developed by Holland, has been used in recent studies that seek to examine job choices and job shifts in the early years in terms of the fit between personality and the most salient features of the job.[23]

Holland classifies occupations into six groups, in terms of the personality types judged most likely to have particular vocational preferences. The personality types and the occupations going with them are the *realistic* (valuing the objective, the concrete, oriented to the present); the *investigative* (analytical, rational, abstract, interested in problem solving); the *social* (typified by social skills and a need for interaction, nurturant); the *conventional* (espousing values sanctioned by custom, practical, correct, conservative); the *enterprising* (adventurous, persuasive, dominant, and self-confident); and finally the *artistic* (expressive of feelings, intuitions, and imaginations, valuing the subjective and the original). Holland sees the *realistic* person as preferring manual activities, and many blue-collar jobs would fall under this heading. So also would such occupations as surveyor, locomotive engineer, tree surgeon, and draftsman. The *investigative* model would obviously cover most professional occupations, except for a few that fall under the *social* rubric. The latter would also include teachers, counselors, judges, public relations workers, and the like. Occupations appealing to *conventional* persons would be bank tellers, post office clerks, and many other jobs that are highly respectable but not otherwise distinguished in terms of personality. It is somewhat easier to recognize the vocational choices of *enterprising* persons in the fields of sales, business management, and politics. Finally, the *artistic* model includes not only the various types of artist—musicians, writers, sculptors, etc.—but also clothing and furniture designers, music and other art critics.

Holland's hypothesis is that in general, people will be most satisfied if they select a career that seems appropriate for their personalities. If they select such occupations, they are much more likely to be satisfied than if they get into a field that calls for a different personality orientation. Several studies suggest that persons do tend to be most satisfied in occupations that reflect their personality orientations. Moreover, over the course of the early years of the career, individuals tend to gravitate to a significant degree out of inappropriate and into appropriate occupations when both personality orientations and occupational features are considered.[29]

Thus we expect greater stability and more orderliness in the career of a person who enters a field consonant with his or her personality than when the initial choice seems inconsonant. However, it should be noted that personality types and the requirements of occupations are overlapping, so one could hardly expect more than modest tendencies toward matching. Indeed, many occupations allow the worker some leeway in defining his role, which then can incorporate elements that will make it maximally rewarding. A pediatrician had better have some liking for children, but his primary source of satisfaction need not come from social aspects of the role. Or again, the creative scientist is likely to have a good deal of the artist as well as the intellectual in him.

Educational Attainment.   An eight-year follow-up of a national cross section of male students who had entered the tenth grade in 1966 revealed interesting differences in the types of jobs held in 1974 in relation to educational attainment.[25] Dropouts and high school graduates who went no further with their education held similar types of jobs and received comparable wages, except that twice as many dropouts were unemployed. This unemployment differential remained even when family socioeconomic level and intellectual ability were taken into consideration. College graduates held much higher-status jobs than did those with lower educational attainment, but there were only small differences between the job levels of those with some college and those with only a high school diploma.

At age 23, nearly three fourths of the dropouts and and of those whose formal education ended with high school graduation were employed in blue-collar jobs as craftsmen, operatives, or laborers, as against only 17 percent of those who graduated from college.[26] By contrast, more than three fourths of the college graduates were employed in professional, managerial, or clerical or sales jobs. Early employment in a field does not, of course, mean that a person will stay in that field. Many high school graduates may be expected subsequently to get additional education, and some will ultimately become college graduates. For the large majority of those whose schooling ended with only a high school diploma, however, their initial occupational experience will offer little opportunity for advancement or for challenging work.

In short, this study strongly supports the generalization that college graduation has become almost a necessity for high occupational attainment in the United States. As noted in the previous chapter, college graduation is itself very largely the expression or manifestation of a cluster of family and individual attributes, attitudes, and values that could be assessed at the time of entry into high school, but completing college adds a substantial benefit in its own right. It becomes the pathway through which family and personal resources exert their maximum impact.

Personality and Careers

Apart from the desirability of matching personal interests and orientations with salient features of the occupation, there is another respect in which personality is related to the career line as a whole. Longitudinal research demonstrates that aspects of personality assessed in junior high school, at the very start of adolescence, give strong clues as to the probability of career success and upward mobility on the one hand and disorderly, downwardly mobile careers on the other. Being seen as productive, dependable, ambitious, not rebellious, not self-indulgent, and, above all, as valuing intellectual matters when assessed in junior high school proves to differentiate professional and managerial workers from clerical and manual workers at ages 40 and 50 to a very substantial degree.[27]

Personality change does, of course, occur, and some men who were problematic adolescents become much more effective and better adapted socially in their adult years. Nevertheless, the dependable, intellectually involved adolescent tends to be successful in his occupation later on. Before that, he attains a higher level of education, so we cannot say that personality itself explains the adult outcome.

Regardless of academic attainment, some men and women tend to be self-defeating in their relationships with others, often by being unable to accept criticism or supervision. This attribute, assessed in the middle years, distinguishes the men with problematic careers to a much greater extent than it did in the junior high years, suggesting that while some men changed for the better in the adult years, others changed for the worse. Moreover, as Kohn and Schooler have so clearly demonstrated, personalities are shaped by occupational experience as well as influencing choice of occupation and making for success or failure.[28] The social roles in which the job involves a person, the intellectual and interpersonal demands it makes, the closeness of supervision received, all influence the priorities that the person establishes in other domains of life.

CAREER LINES: SOME EXAMPLES

Because of the great differences between blue-collar and white-collar careers, we shall examine them separately, while recognizing that many workers will experience a mixture of the two in the course of their work lives. This will be especially true of men and women who alternate between various types of manufacturing or service work and lower-level clerical or sales jobs that require little technical knowledge. Changes of employer and of type of work are especially frequent in the early years for manual and clerical workers. Complete job histories are difficult to compile retrospectively, but the average worker is likely to have had about 10 different jobs in the course of a work life. There will also be those who work for a time as mechanics or chefs or repairmen or in sales, and who at some point are able to establish their own businesses. We shall here have to confine discussion to careers within organizations and professions.

Blue-Collar Careers

For the youth who does not have a chance to go to college, or does not choose to go, occupational choice tends to become the search for a job that will either use some skill already possessed or will pay reasonably well. Some youth at all class levels will already be working part-time while in high school and many will be working part-time or even full-time while enrolled in college, as we noted in Chapter 5. The jobs that they occupy will not in general be ones that they will pursue after graduation, though some will develop into longer-term employment. And over a third of those who enter the labor force for more than a year after leaving full-time schooling will again return to school within the next decade. But as we have noted, a majority of those who do not continue school beyond the high school diploma will find blue-collar jobs in manufacturing, construction, or in service industries.

For the older adolescent (16-19) without a special skill, the search for a job most often involves asking friends who are already employed, applying directly to employers, asking relatives about jobs, or answering ads in local newspapers.[29] In 1975, roughly a third of the young applicants, male and female, finally got their job through direct application to an employer. Young males more frequently located their jobs through friends than did young females (21 percent versus 15 percent), while females more often found work through a newspaper ad than did males (12 percent versus 6 percent). This does not, of course, tell us anything about how long they looked for a job before getting one, or whether the job they took was what they had been looking for. Much depends upon the condition of the labor market at a particular time. We do know that most young people take the first job they are offered. For working-class youth in particular, job preferences have to be tailored to what is available, and career plans are themselves likely to be scaled down to fit opportunities on the local scene.

The wage worker in modern industrial society is often portrayed as alienated from his job, and the job as a fragmented, mechanical operation. Some men do indeed see their jobs largely in negative terms, but they are not in the majority. Despite the eloquence with which many of Stud Terkel's respondents in *Working* denounce the jobs they hold, most workers find much that is rewarding both in the work itself and in relations on the job.[30] Bad-mouthing one's job gives a more colorful account than describing its satisfactions, or perhaps colorful characters like to give scathing reports of their hassles on the job. There is little question but that workers on assembly lines tend to be alienated; they tend to be least satisfied, but they are only a relatively small fraction of blue-collar workers today. This may help to explain why popular accounts fail to square with systematic studies of worker satisfaction such as Blauner's *Alienation and Freedom.*[31] Blauner found, to his surprise, that workers in most manufacturing industries felt that their jobs were mostly or nearly always interesting, were essential, and were not too simple. Half felt they could try out their own ideas on the job. Three fourths said they would not want to change to another job at the same level of pay. But less than half felt their jobs would lead to promotion or that they would have security on retirement. Attitudes were strongly related to skill level and to industry. Skilled workers were generally highly satisfied. Workers in industries demanding extremely routinized operations and those where the workers had relatively little control over the pace of the work were least satisfied. Thus occupational context can markedly influence career satisfaction, and satisfaction influences stability.

In a study of working-class families, Lillian Rubin found that by age 30 about half the husbands had settled into jobs at which they had worked for five years or more.[32] The other half were already dropping behind in that they were late in acquiring seniority that would protect them from layoffs. Again, she found that those with a measure of autonomy and a chance to use their skills were challenged and rewarded, while those in closely supervised jobs were generally negative.

The white-collar worker can usually hope for advancement well into his forties and even fifties. The blue-collar worker cannot. By forty a man is likely to be very much locked into his skilled blue-collar job. In our longitudinal research, almost all of those who were skilled workers and foremen at age 38 were in the same jobs when we interviewed them at age 48. None expected advancement. None worked more than 40 hours a week except when overtime was required (though our white-collar workers of the same age averaged over 50 hours per week). Pay had been going up gradually with age and experience, but at a much lower rate for blue-collar workers than for managers and professionals.

Blue-collar workers are seldom fully absorbed in their work. It is seldom a central life interest, to use Robert Dubin's term.[33] They see the job as important, and some even see their identity as tied somewhat to what they do at work, but they get their major satisfactions elsewhere. They do not carry on-the-job worries home except as they experience interpersonal tensions or fear unemployment. Peak satisfaction may come when one first acquires one's skills and a steady job, but most older blue-collar workers say they are content with their jobs. Retirement means the total end of the job involvement for most men; given fair economic security, blue-collar workers are likely to look forward to the prospect.

Careers in the Professions

The motivations for entering any profession may be diverse, and the setting in which the profession is practiced will often vary depending on which values or goals are dominant. One person may decide to become a physician because of the high prestige and income afforded to physicians in private practice (often as manifest in a relative or other role model), another because of an interest in research on the causes of illness, a third in order to provide medical service to the indigent, and a fourth in order to develop and implement policy relating to public health and medical care in governmental service. Each will hold a somewhat different image of medicine, its objectives, and its rewards, and the career lines they follow will be likely to diverge before they have finished their education. All will have to take certain premedical courses in order to secure entrance into a medical school and will have to complete the basic curriculum of the medical school and a period of internship. The quality of the school and of the hospital in which the internship is served will affect subsequent career opportunities, especially for the physician who seeks a career in research and teaching. And here paths begin to diverge more sharply.[34]

Some physicians seeking to enter private practice will do so directly after their internship, perhaps by first joining a group practice. Many will, however, first take a residency in some specialized field of medicine, such as pediatrics or surgery. Once residency training has been completed and specialty exams (boards) passed, the task for the practitioner is to join a group practice or to set up his own office and arrange for hospital affiliations. Good hospital connections will help to produce referrals for the specialist and will help the physician to become known to his colleagues in the community.

The physician primarily interested in building a prosperous and prestigious practice will participate in community organizations. Being seen as a solid citizen and highly stable member of the community is important. It takes time to develop a reputation as a good physician, so one whose practice is going well does not often shift to another area. Doctors who have in some sense "messed up," on the other hand, are more likely to shift communities and perhaps go to another state, especially if they have been involved in several malpractice suits.

The successful solo practitioner may decide to take in a younger associate; within a group practice the mature physician will become a full partner. Keeping up with new developments will be important, and the office will acquire a good deal of expensive equipment, but the basic practice of medicine will not change much in the demands posed.

The research physician will want a university setting with well-equipped laboratories. He or she may take a Ph.D. in physiology or in biochemistry rather than residency training. Pay is likely to be modest (for a physician) and advancement slow. Teaching and research will often go hand in hand with a small practice on the side, but academic advance will depend on the quality of publications. The academic research physician may in time become the chairman of his or her department or may head a large research laboratory. Promising younger researchers and a few older ones who make outstanding research contributions may dream of a Nobel Prize before they retire. For the younger ones, having a sponsor or mentor who was an eminent scientist will help both their aspirations and their advancement.

The outstanding scientist will receive bids from other universities and research institutions. Some researchers will give up their dreams of glory as scientists to become administrators. Seniors are likely to serve as mentors to younger colleagues, advising them in both medical and research matters.

Careers of physicians in government are likely to show high stability relative to other occupations, but less than private practitioners or physicians holding university posts. Changes in setting are likely as appropriate positions are located. An initial appointment may be taken for training and experience as much as for the long-term opportunities it affords. Additional training may be sought along the way, perhaps a degree in public health or in public administration. Salaries and the prestige accorded by others will be lower for the public health physician than that accorded to the private practitioner or the academic physician, but the demands of the job may be less pressing and rewards will come in the knowledge of an important contribution to the well-being of the larger society. Ultimately, high status in a government bureaucracy may afford significant impact on policy.

Professionals, and especially physicians, tend to see themselves very largely in terms of their occupational roles. They tend to invest themselves very fully in their work; for many, the job serves as a greater source of satisfaction than any other activity. Leisure activities may be slighted, and their families will frequently feel neglected. In this respect, the professional will tend to resemble the business executive; their occupations often afford their central life interests.

Other professions than medicine will have a different set of stages or career contingencies, but all will tend to entail lifelong commitments to the profession except for the few who encounter serious setbacks or who have extraordinary talents that lead them out of the field for which they were trained.

Careers in Management.   A successful career in business may afford an even higher payoff in monetary rewards than do the professions, but only if one makes it to the higher levels of management. A substantial segment of the middle-class population is employed in business and an appreciable proportion has some managerial responsibilities. The successful executive is seen by vocational counselors as a doer, with a strong drive to get ahead. Social skills and drive count for at least as much as intellectual skills, both as a basis for recruitment and as a basis for getting ahead.

Aspiring executives are usually recruited directly from colleges and universities by the larger corporations. The more prestigious business schools offer their graduates—possessed of an M.B.A.—a "ticket to the top," according to the financial pages. They usually have a substantial choice of jobs that pay more than the salaries of assistant professors in the universities from which they have graduated. For those who do not go to business schools, a solid academic record helps one's placement, but having distinguished oneself in extracurricular activities, especially athletics, is likely to have even greater payoff. Most important is the consideration of whether or not the potential recruit will be a loyal, uncontroversial member of the team.

Several decades have passed since the publication of William Whyte's *The Organization Man,* but studies of business executives published since then generally support Whyte's assessment that the modern organization man is not a ruthless entrepreneur, but a group member who values belongingness above all else.[35] As Rosabeth Kanter points out in *Men and Women of the Corporation,* there are many uncertainties in the operation of a large corporation, and a substantial amount of trust has to be placed not only in those who execute decisions at the top but all along the line.[36] A sense of security (perhaps false) is enhanced when those who are in the same boat have similar backgrounds. As several students of the modern business executive have commented, they tend to reproduce themselves in their own image and to be somewhat leery of anyone who deviates from that image.

The young manager has to become intimately acquainted with his company and specific types of operation within it: product development, manufacturing, sales, accounting. In the early stages of a career, there are many opportunities for advancement, both because there are enough layers above to require constant replenishment from below and because new conditions often call for new positions. Having significant responsibility for some facet of a program or of an operation and achieving clear-cut success can bring quick recognition. Getting to be known by those who hold power can also bring rapid advancement. Kin relationships are likely to be very important in the upper layers of management, especially for corporations that started as family businesses, even if several generations ago.

The young manager (and for that matter the older one as well) is expected to put the job before all else. Promotions in large corporations frequently involve moves, and families that may have enjoyed life in a particular community will find that their preferences are less important than the corporation's decision. On the other hand, promotion may be turned down to stay in the same community, and not infrequently community and family ties will be a basis for leaving a corporation.

Applicants for technical and managerial jobs are more likely than lesser-skilled persons to use formal channels such as employment services and counseling services in seeking jobs that will match their abilities and interests, but personal ties play an important role in job seeking even at the professional-technical level. Having a large network of acquaintances who can put one in touch with potential employers brings superior results to having a tightly knit circle of mutual acquaintances. In Granovetter's words, "the strength of weak ties" is clearly manifest in the process of finding a job.[37]

While most corporations appoint executives from within, occasionally they reach out to recruit persons of demonstrated expertise, even young ones. Still, many—perhaps most—corporate executives will have spent the major part of their work life in the organization. Although salary increases may be relatively moderate during the twenties, considerable opportunities may lie ahead. In his late thirties, the manager may for the first time become head of a division or even of a plant. Job pressures may become heavier, but salary mounts very substantially with increased responsibility. The successful executive has a much easier time helping his children go to college than does the man of comparable education and seniority in academic and governmental positions.

Within large corporations, there are variations in the types of skills and personality tendencies that seem to make for greatest success at various levels. An intriguing analysis of types of personalities found in high-technology corporations is provided by Michael Maccoby in *The Gamesman.*[38] There are still a few "jungle fighters" around in highly competitive industries, but at the middle-management level Maccoby agrees with Whyte and Kanter that the most prevalent type is the "company man," that loyal, responsible, conforming member of the team. At lower organizational levels one often finds the "craftsman," concerned most with the quality of the product. Such persons are often considered as being unsuited to the highest levels of management. At those highest levels, the "gamesman" frequently plays out his complex strategy; he seeks to be a winner, involving every ounce of effort to keep the team mobilized and the game plan working. Such types are "ideal types," in the sense that they are built up by selecting facets of personality and organizational functioning that tend to be found together but seldom in such pure form. They give considerable insight, however, into the processes by which careers in business are shaped.

Some men succeed beyond their wildest dreams; others do not quite make it to the level they had hoped to attain. Interestingly, those who change jobs in their middle years are more likely to be the successful ones who have moved up substantially from the status of their fathers and their own earlier status, while less-successful men remain locked into a job that they know will be the end of the line.[39] Ultimately, each person has to come to terms with the costs of high attainment, balancing them against the aspects of life that have to be slighted in order to achieve that high attainment. We shall turn to this topic in discussing the later middle years.

Women's Careers.   Although women have been entering the labor force in increasingly large numbers in the last few decades, the proportion who have continuous occupational careers is still relatively small. Early in the century, the pattern was for girls to leave school and go to work at about the same age as boys—14, on the average—but for them to leave paid employment when they married, usually in their mid-twenties.[40] As years of schooling increased, labor-force entry came later, but until the 1960s marriage tended to occur at earlier ages, so the length of time worked before marriage was markedly curtailed. In recent years, however, the average age of marriage has again risen; moreover, many women continue to work until they have children. At this point, most women take at least a few years off from paid employment. The length of their stay at home will most often depend on the adequacy of the family income and the relative rewards they receive from motherhood and from following an occupation outside the home.

Even today, most women do not regard their occupations as comparable in importance to their family involvement. The job is rather an "add-on," a source of social contacts, of extra income and of added self-confidence, especially while children are young. Currently in the United States, roughly 85 percent of all women of childbearing age become mothers, and for most the maternal role becomes the central feature of life for many years.[41] But once the children are in school, many women find that they want a solid involvement outside the home, and they return to the labor force in ever higher proportions. Their careers remain largely contingent on the needs of husband and children, but they are not bound to the home.

For women, as for men, there is occupational payoff in high educational attainment. Among married women who have had a year or more of graduate train-ing, nearly two thirds were in the labor force in 1970, as against only a third of those with only a grade school education. And this despite the fact that the hus-bands of well-educated women far more often had jobs that made the wife's work-ing less necessary for the family income. On the other hand, many women with low levels of education had single-parent families and worked from necessity at meager wages, having no alternative.

The occupations at which most women work are disproportionately "women's jobs."[42] There tend to be two labor markets: the more or less fully competitive market for majority males and the restrictive market that allocates particular jobs for minorities. Despite some movement in recent years, women are employed most often in child-care occupations, teaching at the lower grades, nursing, secretarial and clerical work, and as semiskilled operatives in light manufacturing such as in textiles. In all these occupations they receive less pay than men in jobs calling for comparable skills, intelligence, and responsibility, as indeed they do even when they work in jobs that are not primarily "women's work."

Nevertheless, more women are now being trained for the professions, more are taking degrees in graduate schools of business administration and more are showing up at managerial levels in business and even on the boards of directors of some large corporations. The number of women lawyers and women physicians has at least tripled since 1960. Even larger gains, both relative and in absolute number of jobs, have occurred in the skilled trades, long exclusively male territory. Women have been employed as carpenters, plumbers, house painters, electricians, and auto mechanics in the past two decades, largely as a consequence of federal contracts that forbid discrimination (even as they became welders and assembly workers in shipyards and aircraft plants during World War II).[43]

Women who have orderly, uninterrupted careers by and large make a career decision early and, if they marry, either remain childless or have only one or at most two children.[44] A successful male business executive or professional has a wife to help him by entertaining guests, taking care of household management, and car-rying out the many little chores that everyday life entails. Few women can count on such help, so a woman who achieves a high level of occupational success must have phenomenal ability and energy. She is often called Superwoman.

For most women, occupational careers will be resumed after the children have reached the age when they can comfortably be left on their own. The job will offer less challenge than a full occupational career, and less chance for advance-ment, but it will be a source of real satisfaction. Partly because the job is a less cen-tral element in identity, the lack of outstanding rewards will be less crucial.

In the decades to come we may expect that more and more couples will come to share occupational roles and family roles more evenly. The dual career family has emerged as a viable pattern for some couples, with each member supporting the ef-forts of the other to achieve career success as well as a fulfilling family life. We shall examine such patterns in subsequent chapters.

Stages and Occupational Careers

As we have seen, some careers entail a sequence of rather clear-cut stages while others seem to develop haphazardly, largely dependent on the state of the economy at any given time. There is no evidence that most workers, men or women, go through a standard sequence of stages. Some start with dreams, some with well-developed plans and some with little idea of what they want to do occupationally. Some make commitments very early and never waiver in them. At the other extreme are those who never find a really satisfying occupational niche but who ultimately resign themselves to a particular occupation or employer.

The "settling down" stage, which Levinson proposed for the mid-thirties, may occur anywhere from age twenty to age forty, though for most men it probably occurs before they are thirty. As we have seen, professionals are far less likely to be tempted to shift fields than are workers who enter an occupation that does not require long preparation and strong commitment. Those who start graduate education in a given field and then find aspects of the field distasteful to them usually will not complete their studies.

At this point we can say that chronological age in itself does not seem to be strongly related to career commitments or career stages. Women's careers in particular will be influenced by their family commitments, and for many women strong involvement in an occupation will not come until well into their middle years. We shall return to examine how stage theories apply in Chapter 8.

NOTES

1. Valerie Oppenheimer, *Work and the Family: A Study in Social Demography* (New York: Academic Press, 1982).
2. *The Random House Dictionary of the English Language,* unabridged edition, s.v. "career."
3. Perhaps the fullest treatment of the topic is given by William J. Goode, *The Celebration of Heroes: Prestige as a Control System* (Berkeley, CA: The University of California Press, 1978).
4. Harold Wilensky, "Orderly Careers and Social Participation," *American Sociological Review,* 26 (1961), 521-39.
5. Ibid., 530-33.
6. John A. Clausen, "Studies of the Post-war Plans of Soldiers: A Problem in Prediction," in Samuel A. Stouffer et al., eds., *Measurement and Prediction* (Princeton, NJ: Princeton University Press, 1950), p. 637.
7. W. H. Form and D. G. Miller, "Occupational Career Patterns as a Sociological Instrument," *American Journal of Sociology,* 54 (1949), 317-29.
8. H. S. Becker, "Notes on the Concept of Commitment," *American Journal of Sociology,* 66 (1960), 32-40.
9. A classic study delineating stages in one professional field is Oswald Hall's "The Stages of Medical Career," *American Journal of Sociology,* 53 (1948), 327-36.
10. Melvin Kohn and Carmi Schooler, *Work and Personality: An Inquiry into the Impact of Social Stratification* (Norwood, NJ: Ablex Publishing Corp., 1983).
11. Seymour Wolfbein, *Work in American Society* (Glenview, IL: Scott, Foresman and Co., 1971), p. 46.

12. W. H. Miernyk, "The Changing Life Cycle at Work," in N. Datan and L. H. Ginsberg, eds., *Life Span Developmental Psychology: Normative Life Crises* (New York: Academic Press, 1975), pp. 279-85.

13. Natalie Rogoff, "The Decision to Study Medicine," in R. K. Merton, G. C. Reader, and P. Kendall, eds., *The Student Physician* (Cambridge, MA: Harvard University Press, 1957), pp. 109-29.

14. Dan C. Lortie, "Laymen to Lawmen: Law School, Careers and Professional Socialization," *Harvard Educational Review*, 29 (1959), 352-69.

15. How a child learns about his world from the conversations of grown-ups in the family is beautifully illustrated by Russell Baker's *Growing Up* (New York: St. Martins Press, 1982).

16. An excellent general description of the mechanisms and processes that shape occupational choice is provided by Cyril Sofer in his introduction to *Occupational Choice: A Selection of Papers from the Sociological Review*, ed. W. M. Williams (London: George Allen and Univen, Ltd., 1974), pp. 13-57.

17. Bureau of Labor Statistics, *Employment of High School Graduates and Drop-outs in 1982* (Washington, D. C.: U.S. Department of Labor, 1983).

18. The following are among the major contributions to this literature: E. Ginsberg et al., *Occupational Choice: An Approach to a General Theory* (New York: Columbia University Press, 1951); E. Ginsberg and J. L. Herma, *Talent and Performance* (New York: Columbia University Press, 1964); D. E. Super, "A Theory of Vocational Development," *American Psychologist*, 8 (1953), 185-90; P. M. Blau et al., "Occupational Choice: A Conceptual Framework," *Industrial and Labor Review*, 9 (1956), 531-43.

19. Daniel Levinson, *The Seasons of a Man's Life* (New York: Alfred A. Knopf, 1978), pp. 91-98.

20. Ginsberg and Herma, *Talent and Performance*, pp. 173-74.

21. Jeylan Mortimer, "Social Class, Work and the Family: Some Implications of Father's Occupation for Family Relationships and Sons' Career Decisions," *Journal of Marriage and the Family*, 38 (1976), 241-55.

22. Tamara Hareven, *Family Time and Industrial Time* (Cambridge, England: Cambridge University Press, 1982).

23. J. L. Holland, *Making Vocational Choices: A Theory of Vocational Personalities and Work Environments*, 2nd ed. (Englewood Cliffs, NJ: Prentice-Hall, Inc., 1985). See especially pages 47-57.

24. L. S. Gottfredson, "Aspiration-Job Match: Age Trends in a Large Nationally Representative Sample of Young Men," Report No. 268 (Baltimore, MD: Center for Social Organization of Schools, Johns Hopkins University, 1978).

25. J. G. Bachman, P. M. O'Malley, and J. Johnston, *Youth in Transition*, Vol. VI, *Adolescence to Adulthood: Change and Stability in the Lives of Young Men* (Ann Arbor, MI: Institute of Social Research, 1978).

26. Ibid., p. 61.

27. J. A. Clausen, "Men's Occupational Careers in the Middle Years," in *Present and Past in Middle Life*, D. E. Eichorn et al., eds. (New York: Academic Press, 1981), pp. 338-46.

28. Kohn and Schooler, *Work and Personality*.

29. H. J. Becker, "How Young People Find Jobs: A Review of the Literature," Report No. 241 (Baltimore, MD: Center for Social Organization of Schools, Johns Hopkins University, Dec. 1977).

30. Studs Terkel, *Working* (New York: Random House, 1972).

31. R. Blauner, *Alienation and Freedom: The Factory Worker and His Industry* (Chicago: IL: University of Chicago Press, 1964).

32. L. Rubin, *Worlds of Pain: Life in the Working Class Family* (New York: Basic Books, 1976).

33. R. Dubin has studied the meaning of work in terms of its centrality as a source of satisfying ties with others. Robert Dubin, "Industrial Workers' Worlds: A Study of Central Life Interests of Industrial Workers," *Social Problems*, 3 (1956), 131-42.

34. Following Hall's research, cited earlier, there have been a number of studies of medical training and practice. For a bibliography, see H. E. Freeman, S. Levine, and L. G. Reeder, eds., *Handbook of Medical Sociology,* 3rd ed. (Englewood Cliffs, NJ: Prentice-Hall, Inc., 1979).

35. W. H. Whyte, *The Organization Man* (New York: Simon and Schuster, 1956).

36. R. M. Kanter, *Men and Women of the Corporation* (New York: Basic Books, 1977).

37. M. S. Granovetter, *Getting a Job: A Study of Contacts and Careers* (Cambridge, MA: Harvard University Press, 1974).

38. Michael Maccoby, *The Gamesman* (New York: Bantam Books, 1978).

39. Clausen, "Men's Occupational Careers," p. 333.

40. It should be noted, however, that roughly a fourth did not marry at the turn of the century. Many daughters served as homemakers for their fathers, younger children, or other relatives. See Hareven, *Family Time and Industrial Time.*

41. H. Carter and P. Glick, *Marriage and Divorce: A Social and Economic Study* (Cambridge, MA: Harvard University Press, 1970).

42. H. Kahne, "Economic Research on Women and Families," *Signs: Journal of Women in Culture and Society,* 3 (1978), 652-65.

43. M. L. Walshok, *Blue Collar Women: Pioneers on the Male Frontier* (New York: Anchor Press/Doubleday, 1981).

44. J. G. Stroud, "Women's Careers: Work, Family and Personality," in *Present and Past in Middle Life,* pp. 356-90.

CHAPTER 7
MARRIAGE
AND
THE FAMILY CYCLE

(A good marriage) It is a pleasant associa-
tion for life, full of trust and confidence,
and with an infinite number of useful
functions and mutual obligations.
Montaigne, Essays, *1595*

Just as each generation repeats the cycle of life from birth to death, so families go through their own cycle. Marriage or the enduring life together of a couple begins a new family cycle which may be said to rise with the birth of children, to reach its peak when all the children are at home in later childhood and adolescence, and to decline as children leave to begin their own new family cycles.[1] The family may survive until the death of husband or wife or it may disintegrate or at least splinter with the divorce of the married pair. Many divorces occur early, before there are children, but a majority leave a residual family, headed at least for a time by a single parent.

Despite profound changes in patterns of sexual behavior and in the commitments made to marital partners during recent decades, most men and women still marry and rear children. Moreover, they do so in families that are only a little less stable than those of earlier eras. Whereas many families are now broken by divorce, many in the past were broken by the early death of husband or wife.[2] Divorce is not yet the norm, and, particularly among those who marry after the age of 21, family life offers a major stabilizing force on personal functioning for most adults in the United States even in the 1980s.

The family's own life cycle tends to define for husband and wife the expectations and requirements they must meet at different stages in their marriage, as children appear and progress along their own life courses. The parental ages associated with stages of the family cycle will vary somewhat, depending on cultural norms, on relative cohort size and events affecting each cohort, such as wars and depressions, on education and occupation of the father and the mother, and on individual choices as to the number and scheduling of children. If there are no children, we can hardly speak of a family cycle but only of the phases of a marriage.

Stages of the Family Cycle

The stages of the cycle that are highly salient for most families are at present the following:

Life as a pair (often with a period of living together before making a commitment to marriage)
Life with children in the home

Youngest child under 6 (preschool)
Youngest child 6–12 (preadolescent)
Youngest child 13–20 (adolescent)
Youngest child over 20 (unlaunched)

Empty nest—couple with no children at home
Life without a spouse—widowhood

The age of the youngest child is obviously important because of the constraints imposed by child care, constraints that most often bind the mother to the home. But the age of the youngest child will not define the stages if another child is seriously problematic, whether handicapped or dependent psychologically. Indeed, especially difficult periods may be defined by the inability of one or more children to meet expected levels of performance. Families may be broken at any stage of the cycle, but the constraints placed upon parents by the needs of their children continue to operate. Unlike the stages of occupational careers, which tend to be closely dependent upon the particular occupation pursued, the stages of the family cycle permit us to say a good deal about the circumstances of family life for persons from very diverse backgrounds. In general, there will be a fairly close relationship between the age of the husband and wife, the duration of the marriage, and stage of the family cycle. Where individuals depart to a marked degree from the age norms, however, the stage of the family cycle will often give us a better understanding of the family's functioning than will age or duration of the marriage.

Most of us spend roughly the first fourth of our lives in the parental home and the bulk of the remainder going through our own family cycle. But the duration of the various segments of the cycle has changed markedly in this century; the empty-nest stage in particular has increased dramatically. Until very recently, marriages came earlier than at the turn of the century, but first births were deferred slightly so that the age of parents at the start of child rearing has not changed much. The chief shifts in the family cycle have resulted from a shortened period of childbearing due to smaller families and increased life expectancy. As a consequence, the last child now most often leaves home when the mother is in her early fifties (about five years earlier than was the case 60 years ago), and the parents survive as a pair eight or 10 years longer than they did early in the century.[3] Hence the years with young children in the home are markedly reduced and the empty-nest stage prior to the death of one spouse has been lengthened from an average of about one year to an average of 15 years for couples who stay together in the 1980s.

Some social scientists would include under the rubric "family" the most diverse groupings of persons living in a household. There have always been households that were organized for purposes other than rearing children, but it is doubtful that they were considered to be families. Neither gay couples nor communes are families by the definition that delimits the scope of discussion here. A family is, above all else, the unit of social organization in which children are procreated and reared. There are obviously alternative life-styles that do not entail procreation and that have become more widespread in recent decades, but we shall not be able to consider these in any detail in the present treatment of the life course.

Single-parent families, in the sense of an absent father, have existed in many polygamous societies; the mother's kin usually play a significant role in child rearing in such societies. Only recently have divorce and unmarried motherhood replaced death as the major origins of single-parent families in the United States.[4] Ultimately, all societies demand that parents take some measure of responsibility for their offspring, and the social norms that define and enforce that responsibility (becoming moral imperatives) provide a basic structure to the family cycle. Moreover, in most societies the nucleus of the family, the husband and wife, have made a commitment to each other and established a household or begun to live together in a parental household before having children of their own.

ANTECEDENTS TO FORMING A FAMILY

From our earliest days we form impressions of the nature of relationships between husbands and wives, parents and children. Our conceptions of marriage are colored by such things as the names by which our parents addressed each other, what they said about each other when they were angry or upset, the extent to which they did things together, and whether or not they stood together when we were not on the same wavelength with one of them. If they seemed to enjoy each other as close friends and were solicitous of each other's needs and tastes, we felt warm and perhaps wondered if someday we would have a husband or wife who would be so wonderfully close. If they bickered over trivia or competed for tidbits at the dinner table, we may have felt that marriage was inevitably the battleground of the sexes. A man who for years had treated his mentally ill wife as a despised enemy commented: "I guess my marriage was about average; it wasn't too different from my parents' marriage." He had previously stated that his parents hated each other but stayed together.

So we may dream with pleasant anticipation of the family life we hope to have or may wonder if we want a marriage and family. Sometime in adolescence or early adulthood, however, most of us will have our dreams or musings replaced by the reality of a relationship with someone to whom we feel strongly attracted. For many, there will have been a succession of such attachments, providing zest to our activities but not a conviction that we want to spend the rest of our lives with the person to whom we are attracted.

As we noted in the chapter on adolescence, forming an intimate tie with a person of the opposite sex is itself an important developmental accomplishment, though it may seem to come much easier to some persons than to others. Many young men and women, especially those who do not have opposite-sex siblings, are unable to relax and be themselves in a person-to-person conversation with opposite-sex age mates. For some, the terror is dispelled once a mutually gratifying relationship has been established; for others, inability to establish a heterosexual relationship may persist. In some males it will be a sign of deep psychological vulnerability.[5] On the other hand, establishment of such a relationship appears for many adolescents to be a critical element in coming to have a strong sense of identity.

Trends in the Transition to Marriage

Although the transition from adolescence to full adulthood as manifest in marriage and a separate household is frequently described in popular articles as a longer and more difficult process than in earlier times, it appears to be more clearly scheduled now and to be accomplished in a much shorter time.[6] As previously noted, formal schooling lasts much longer and marriage tends to come earlier than it did a century ago. Although we do not have longitudinal data from a century ago to permit an accurate assessment of the sequence of school leaving, entering the labor market, leaving the parental home, marrying, and setting up a new household, we know from the analysis of census data that these several transitions were made over a much longer period and with greater variability between early and late movers. In 1880, many left school at 12 or 14 and went to work soon after. School leaving and entering the labor force tended to occur in quick succession then and now. In the 1880s, however, most young people stayed in the parental home and contributed their wages to family income until they were ready to marry. A tenth of males married by 20, but the average (median) age of marriage was 27 for males and 23 for females. There was, then, a much greater spread in the ages at which people married.[7] Moreover, marriage did not mean that the couple immediately set up their own household. They frequently lived in one or the other parental home for a year or two or boarded with another family before establishing a separate household. For many, this meant much longer subordination to parents; for others, it reflected having responsibility for support of a widowed mother and probably deferring marriage for some years as a consequence.

For men, the decision to marry depends largely on educational and occupational aspirations and the possibility of sustaining those aspirations if they marry. In general, the higher the educational level attained, the lower the proportion of men marrying at a young age. An employed wife may, nevertheless, be a great aid to completing professional training provided that the couple defers having children for some years. The feasibility of marriage will also depend on the level of earnings relative to the couple's aspirations for a given style of life. Men in relatively stable blue-collar jobs such as skilled workers and higher-level machine operatives are likely to marry early; those in "stop-gap" jobs such as lower-level operatives, laborers, or lower-level clerical and sales workers—jobs that are often taken for short periods between episodes of schooling or that represent the only kind of job available to the school dropout—will more often have to put off marriage, for their incomes will be markedly lower than those of craft workers.[8] Professionals and those beginning careers in management will aspire to a style of life that requires much higher expenditures than are typical of working-class families, and they will usually defer marriage longer still.

Valerie Oppenheimer has documented how differences in income expectation and in family expenditures among members of different occupational groups influence when people marry and whether wives work.[9] In recent decades the earnings of young males have declined relative to their midlife peak earnings. Moreover, inflation has markedly increased the cost of setting up a household, leading to a decline in the proportion of young marriages. The decline in earnings since the 1960s was most acute for those in lower-level white-collar jobs, which have been much less rewarded than blue-collar jobs of comparable level. Men in occupations with a steep gradient of earnings—that is, where one could expect substantial salary increases in the middle years—were much more likely to defer marriage than men in craft occupations where the earnings gradient was lower, so that their income was relatively high early in the career. These economic circumstances help to explain when families enter various stages of the family cycle.

Those Who Never Marry

In the face of rapid social change, it is difficult to extrapolate past trends and to estimate what proportion of men and women will choose to remain single, or, if they marry, to remain childless. Both patterns have been on the increase since World War II. Before that, both were quite rare in the United States. Roughly 95 percent of men and women born in the 1930s and 1940s could be expected to marry, and 90 percent could be expected to become parents.[10] These proportions, much higher than had been found earlier in the twentieth century, reflected favorable economic conditions, a high valuation on parenthood, and a fairly even balance in the sexes. Nevertheless, some men and women chose to remain single, either because they devoted themselves to the care of others, or never found anyone whom they wished to marry, or did not wish to undertake the commitments that are entailed in marriage.

Single men have always enjoyed much greater freedom than single women, and no great onus has attached to a man's remaining single. Men who did not marry have been viewed as "eligible bachelors" well into their middle years. Until recently, women remaining single beyond 30 were, however, seen as spinsters. They had for some reason "perversely" failed to accept the primary role proffered to women in any society, or else they were seen as having been too plain or unattractive to have received proposals of marriage. Yet over the past two centuries there have been a number of such women who have demonstrated extraordinary talents and made major social contributions despite the difficulty of finding acceptance in societies where women are expected to marry. And most have been no more "plain" than their sisters. Moreover, failure to marry is far more indicative of personal problems and vulnerability in a man than in a woman.

Increasingly, women who have been trained as professionals or who have made a heavy investment in a career (often after a failed marriage) are finding that life is much simpler when they can pursue their career interests without taking on a commitment to a husband and children. A wife is a far more helpful asset to a male executive than a husband is to a female one![11] If we consider the number of divorced women with career commitments and no intention of remarrying, it appears that unmarried status is neither as rare nor as problematic as it was a few decades ago.

What of married couples who do not have children? There has been little research on such couples, but again there is evidence that their number is increasing. A few men and women apparently decide by adolescence that they don't want children, though they do want a normal relationship with the opposite sex.[12] Some apparently agree explicitly, prior to marriage, that they will not have children, regularly using contraception and turning to abortion in the failure of contraceptive means. A larger proportion postpone having children for some years and then come to the conclusion (often after seeing the extent to which their friends with children are tied down and financially strapped) that there are great advantages to remaining childless. Particularly in the face of the world's population problem, there is no compelling reason to have children unless one genuinely expects to enjoy them.

There are, then, viable alternatives to setting the family cycle into motion. For the great majority of men and women at the present time, however, the alternatives do not seem as attractive as do marriage and parenthood. A great many highly educated women now defer childbearing until after age 30, enabling them to establish careers, but then have one or two children. Although a few writers repeatedly proclaim the end of the nuclear family of husband, wife, and children, the nuclear family is still the dominant pattern; there is little reason to think that the pattern will soon disappear.

THE TRANSITION TO MARRIAGE

The transition from single to married status is certainly one of the most fateful changes of status to occur during the whole life course. Moreover, the timing of this transition has significant consequences for both men and women. In Western society, women usually marry men slightly older than themselves. Among the reasons for this are the later biological and social maturing of males and the time taken for men to become economically ready to support a wife and potential family. A woman who marries very early tends to marry an older man, sometimes considerably older; she also is likely to marry a man from a background similar to her own, unless she has some special qualities or reputation that make her more widely known.[13] On the other hand, a woman who defers marriage until after most other women have married may find a relatively small pool of eligible and desirable marriage partners whose ages are slightly greater than her own. As a consequence, she is more likely to marry a somewhat younger man.[14] If she does not, she may well marry a man who has deferred marriage because of his own educational aspirations and relatively low income. The men that late-marrying women choose are often from somewhat lower social backgrounds, but they tend to be upwardly mobile in their own careers and to attain high occupational status.[15]

The age at which a person decides to marry depends on both subjective assessments and objective circumstances. Feeling ready for marriage—emotionally, financially, and in terms of life plans—does not insure that an appropriate partner is available. Moreover, obligations to parents or other relations (such as helping a younger sibling through college) may lead to deferring marriage longer than one would like, even if an ideal mate is waiting in the wings. As we have seen, the circumstances encountered by a particular cohort may also make a large difference. During periods of depression, marriage is especially likely to be deferred by working-class men and women, who generally marry at younger ages than do their middle-class counterparts.[16] Lillian Rubin comments that working-class teenagers tend to "chafe under living conditions that are oppressive and parental authority that feels repressive. Marriage often is seen as the only escape."[17]

Women will often marry early because of tensions in the parental home; men will more often leave home without marrying. A study of families of mental patients revealed that daughters of mentally ill mothers frequently left home as early as sixteen. Some sought permission to marry, threatening to become pregnant if it were not given. Several carried out the threat to escape from a home situation that they regarded as intolerable (as much because of their fathers' unreasonable demands as because of their mothers' illness).[18]

Whether they marry to escape from the parental home or to achieve their dreams of a family and life of their own, a large proportion of those who marry early find that maintaining a household is more demanding than they had realized. It is undoubtedly most demanding for those whose marriage was precipitated by pregnancy. Among young working-class wives whom Lillian Rubin interviewed, fully two fifths reported that they had been "caught" after having "fooled around."[19] Where this occurred, the couple had simultaneously to work out their mutual understandings as husband and wife, arrange for setting up a household or at least finding a place to live, and preparing for the birth of the child. Several large-scale studies linking birth certificates to marriage licenses have suggested that even in the 1950s and 1960s, between a fifth and a fourth of all marriages in the United States began with a pregnant bride. Not surprisingly, such marriages were least likely to endure. In recent years, however, it appears that pregnancy, even when carried to term, less often results in marriage. Nearly two fifths of all births to women under the age of 20 are to unmarried mothers. Most of these women will marry subsequently, but we do not yet know whether chances of marital stability will be enhanced by the postponement of marriage.

Many couples will, however, postpone having children until they have worked out their personal adaptations and feel economically and emotionally ready to face parenthood. Even under these circumstances, the young couple faces many adaptations in achieving the life-style that will be characteristic for them. Each will have come with distinctive family traditions, perhaps differing tastes in foods and cultural activities, unique personal habits, and some proclivities that are likely to seem odd or irrational to the partner. Courtship may have revealed some differences in behavior and perspective, but until they have lived together for a time, couples will not fully experience the meaning of their individual differences. Strong physical attraction and supportive emotional involvement will help in achieving mutually acceptable definitions, but there will nevertheless be issues still emerging over a period of years. Communication and continuing ties with families of orientation, visiting patterns at holidays, the preservation of areas of privacy as well as the sharing of tasks and the provision of support when both husband and wife may be out of sorts or experiencing stress or illness—all these will require negotiation and mutual understanding if persistent tensions are to be avoided.[20]

In the early years of marriage there are major economic investments to be made. If a couple is to set up housekeeping, they will need furniture, dishes, flatware, and a variety of kitchen appliances and linens, even if they can find rental quarters that contain stove, refrigerator, and other necessities. Young women no longer bring either dowries or hope chests to marriage, though parents may often help the couple get launched. Most often, however, young wives bring earning power, and the majority will work during the early years of marriage, especially among middle-class couples. As we shall see shortly, working-class and middle-class families face rather different "life-cycle squeezes" in trying to stretch finances, and these become most acute in the period when children enter the picture.

Despite the problems of adaptation required in marriage, the early years of marriage are for most persons a time of high hopes and much joy. There are stresses, but they are not totally unexpected. Even in relationships that may later sour, there can be growth; and in struggles to get a household established there can be genuine pleasure of accomplishment. Couples who postpone having children until they have achieved a good sharing relationship and have gotten economically established will have had a chance to enjoy each other's company with far less stress than those who must face parenthood almost immediately.

CHILDREN IN THE HOME

The transition to parenthood is for many persons, especially women, the most demanding role transition of the whole life course. Having primary responsibility for the care and rearing of an infant is, especially in the early stages, a 24-hour assignment. It is an assignment not easily combined with other roles, especially those that require adherence to a schedule. If pregnancy results from a couple's decision to have a child at a particular time, so that parenthood has been freely chosen, the experience may be a thrilling one; if, however, the first pregnancy is unplanned, and other roles had been given priority for the time being, parenting may be more onerous than thrilling.

Preschool Children

Alice Rossi has nicely delineated some of the more problematic aspects of the transition to parenthood.[21] It is an abrupt transition, more so than marriage. The married pair has had a chance during an engagement period to get to know each other better, to explore their own wishes and formulate plans based on their mutual needs. Marriage implements those plans. But pregnancy has little similarity to parenthood, and the infant whose appearance terminates pregnancy is wholly an unknown quantity. Moreover, it will be months and even years before he or she becomes really predictable to parents who have had only sporadic exposure to infants and children. Guidelines to child care are available in books and in classes for expectant parents, but they do not prepare parents for dealing with long periods of crying for no apparent reason, or for the incredible level of parental attentiveness that a crawling one-year-old or a toddling two-year-old will require in almost any setting.

When a man becomes a father, his esteem will in general be enhanced. His freedom will be somewhat curtailed, but performance of his occupational role will seldom be impaired unless he chooses, as a few men now do, to share child care or even to become the primary giver of child care. Men who take on the latter responsibility are still likely to lose some of the esteem they had acquired through becoming a father.

The great majority of women give up their jobs in the later stages of pregnancy and prepare for a period of full-time motherhood. Whereas more than three wives in five work prior to the birth of their first child, less than one in five works among those with children under age six.[22] Most women go from a period of active participation in the labor force and the community to a period of considerably constricted activity, chiefly in the home.

Family income is suddenly cut when the wife's salary is no longer available. If they have completed paying for furnishings and equipment while two salaries were available, the couple will be much better able to manage the squeeze that occurs when only one must suffice. If, however, an infant appears on the scene while they are still acquiring basic household equipment, they carry a heavy economic burden. Children require their own special equipment, not to mention the medical costs of delivery and health maintenance. In the absence of health insurance, the financial burden may become a major crisis, especially for families of low-income husbands and for those who are completing their student years.

One response to this economic squeeze is for the husband to work harder in striving to move up the ladder of his occupation. Professionals and businessmen invest heavily in their work, putting in longer hours or bringing work home with them. Some men, especially blue-collar workers or others whose primary jobs offer relatively little prospect of substantial pay increases, moonlight—that is, they take on a second job.[23]

An infant can usually be accommodated in an apartment without too much difficulty. Addition of a second child is likely to start the parents hunting for a larger apartment or, if they can afford it, a house. In past decades, when housing costs were much more moderate and mortgage interest rates were low enough so that the monthly cost of buying was not appreciably greater than the cost of renting, most couples could own a home by the time the husband was 35.[24] In the 1980s, it appears that only families with quite substantial incomes will be able to afford a home of their own during the first decade or so of marriage, especially in metropolitan areas. Many families who cannot afford to buy a house will move repeatedly, seeking more adequate quarters as the children grow in number and in years. Newness and convenience may be traded off for spaciousness, whether of an apartment or of a house.

Fathers are usually attentive to their very young infants and helpful to their wives at this time, especially during the infancy of the first child. Parents tend to be anxious with their first child and much more relaxed with the next. But with additional children, husbands are likely to be more driven to increase their income by investing themselves more heavily in their work. Even if their families are very important to them, they will often be less available around the house. Some women will thoroughly enjoy motherhood, especially when they have only one infant, but for those who must make do on very limited income and who have two or three children spaced only a couple of years apart, life can be grueling and isolating prior to the time when some of the children start school. An occasional evening off or some relief on the weekend are about all that many young mothers can hope for. Not surprisingly, the marital relationship will often be strained by competing demands for time and energy. Studies of general life satisfaction (not marital satisfaction) show a decline during this period of the family cycle. Especially for women with several children, it is often the low point; their life satisfaction is far less than that of women the same age who do not have children and also below that of women all of whose children are six and over.[25]

There is, to be sure, much variation in the stresses and satisfactions brought by children depending on whether they are planned, how closely together they come, and what resources the parents can draw upon. Couples who have had difficulty in conceiving will generally be overjoyed, as will those who put off their parenting until they were financially secure. Under such circumstances they are likely to have only one or two children, and these will not constitute a major burden. Where there are several children, the wife's satisfaction and her mental health will be significantly dependent on the amount of help and support she receives from her husband. Combining paid work with the care of small children, as does roughly one mother in five, will make child care more difficult and severely limit time for rest and relaxation, but several studies suggest that work which gets a mother into contact with others actually helps to prevent depression and low morale.[26] Positive effects will result particularly when the husband shares in child care and household tasks. If he does not, or if he objects to his wife's working, both husband and wife may experience psychological costs of her employment.[27]

Children of School Age

As the children reach school age, there is very frequently a sharper division of labor between husband and wife. She increasingly takes over the household tasks as the husband's assistance tends to diminish. If the family is renting, they may move to be near a school regarded as appropriate. Neighborhood now becomes as important as indoor space, and families that can afford it frequently move to the suburbs at this time to seek a home of their own.

The oldest child's entrance into school begins a phase of social participation on the part of many parents that derives from the needs of their children rather than from the parents' own interests. Particularly for the middle-class parent, there will be pressure to join the PTA, and perhaps to volunteer as a teacher's helper on field trips or for other special activities. Involvement in the Cub Scouts or Blue Birds comes a bit later for many mothers. Many couples will affiliate anew with a church congregation so that the children may attend Sunday school.

Middle-class suburban mothers will spend many hours a week chauffeuring children to and from school, movies, music lessons, and a host of other events and activities that today's children engage in. In the city, children can more often take public transportation. In general, working-class mothers and fathers will involve themselves less in such child-centered activities than will middle-class parents. But middle-class mothers can more often get their husbands to share their burdens on weekends.

Once all the children are in school, the mother may usually count on a few hours a day that are all her own. They may be largely taken up with a variety of chores, such as shopping and maintaining the home, but respite from the unremitting care of young children will be a source of considerable relief. Some mothers may return to work soon after the youngest child enters school, especially if they can make arrangements for child care in the after-school hours and can manage a relatively flexible schedule for their work. Some husbands will oppose their wives' working, but if the family income is meager, they may nevertheless accede. Divorced mothers of school-age children are very likely to take a job if they do not already hold one.

For mothers who return to work at this time, their schedule is likely to be as exhausting as it was when the children were small. Employed wives will most often prepare meals and carry the major portion of housekeeping tasks, though American husbands are becoming more helpful to their wives than they were a generation ago (and much more helpful than husbands are in the Soviet Union or in Japan).[28] Here again, when paid employment is combined with the role of wife and mother, women seem less acutely stressed when they have a job outside the home, for it often affords stimulating and supportive contacts with other adults.

Adolescent Children. Looking back from their late years, a large proportion of mothers and fathers in our longitudinal studies select adolescence as the period of child rearing that was most difficult for them. Although some parents found that the early period of child care was trying for them, especially if they had a handicapped or ill child, adolescence brought problems of coping with teenagers who were exploring a world their parents never knew, a world in which rock music, drugs, and sex often played a significant part. Adolescents challenge their parents in new ways; many parents find the period exciting, but few find it easy.

As we have already noted, adolescence poses economic as well as emotional problems. Groceries to satisfy the appetites of energetic teenagers, increased clothing costs, and expenses for the paraphernalia that late twentieth-century living demands all call for increases in the family budget. A second life-cycle squeeze occurs for many families. The more children in the family and the closer together they are in age, the greater the squeeze. And of course the younger the parents when they first have children, the earlier this squeeze occurs. Thus it comes sooner for the working class than for the middle class, and it will be far more acute for men in low-income occupations. The cost of maintaining a family with three children ranging in age into the adolescent years is roughly double that of maintaining the married pair.[29] If the children go on to higher education, the costs multiply far beyond this. The second life-cycle squeeze is very often the cause of the wife's return to the labor market, and substantially more than half the mothers of adolescent children are currently employed.

There are other problems to be faced in the children's adolescence. The adolescent's ability to argue, interest in new experience, and desire for a measure of autonomy all call for different parental responses than those employed with pre-adolescents. Husbands and wives may have quite different attitudes and feelings about the ways of coping with such problems as may arise. Parental tensions and conflicts relating to the children are often most severe in this period.[30] Often father or mother will be facing personal decisions that add to the difficulty of resolving differences between spouses. Their own parents may at this time be encountering serious illness or making the transition into retirement. Thus, the period of the children's adolescence is unlikely to be tranquil for most families.

In the next chapter we shall look more closely at the effects of parental aging and other role developments during the middle years on life satisfaction, stress, and coping. Here we must at least note that for families with adolescents, as for other stages, the age and education of the parents can make a considerable difference in how they understand their offspring and how they feel about life in general. Older parents may be more tired and less zestful, but they may also be less likely to be caught up in trying to compete with their adolescents in inappropriate ways. Better-educated parents are likely to have found the early years of child care relatively more difficult and to find dealing with late adolescence easier than do less-well-educated parents.[31]

Unlaunched Children over 18. Once they have completed their education, most young adults will aspire to having an apartment or home of their own. This will, of course, be more feasible for college graduates than for most high school graduates; both the offsprings' maturity and their occupational status will play a major role in parental willingness to give up supervision for offspring under 21. Fathers are notoriously unwilling to see their daughters share an apartment with other young women. Often there will be a good deal of tension before the young woman is given parental blessings to depart unless she is getting married. On the other hand, parents will be generally less involved in decisions for their older children and may more fully enjoy them as persons. Yet ultimately, sons and daughters are expected to make their own way in the world, and except in times of economic hardship, when the extra income provided by working children can be critically important, the children's departure is a signal that the parents have accomplished their nurturant roles.

The number of young men and women still living in the parental home after age 25 is not large, but such children are often a sign that all has not gone well. High dependency may be a sign of vulnerability to mental disorder. Inability to hold a job because of emotional problems or excessive alcohol or drug use not infrequently goes with a love-hate relationship between parents and children. They cannot live happily together, yet they cannot give up their efforts to do so. Studies of marital satisfaction through the family cycle often find that satisfaction is lowest among families with unlaunched children.[32]

In past generations, a daughter whose marriage was not working out went "home to mother." The pattern is certainly less frequent today, but both sons and daughters sometimes retreat to the parental home when they have met temporary defeat in their struggle to make a life of their own. Such returns may be disruptive of parental harmony in that they tend to give rise to recriminations and possibly coalitions.

The Empty Nest

During their young adult and early middle years, most men and women invest a good deal of their energy, their emotions, and their income in their children. If they have been fortunate enough to see their children avoid involvement in delinquency, drug use, or alcohol abuse during adolescence, they can watch them be launched into the adult world without great qualms. If the children have gone away to college, launching is a gradual affair. Summers and other vacation periods are times of reunion, but much of whatever parental tendency still exists to want to control their offspring will be blunted by the knowledge that they are more or less on their own most of the time.

Before we had systematic research evidence on marital satisfaction and life satisfaction at various stages of the life course, the prevailing wisdom about the "empty nest" was that it was a time of emotional depression for most mothers. Psychoanalysts proclaimed that once they had passed the menopause and their children had left home, women would despair. Depression over the loss of fertility was assumed to be almost inevitable. With research evidence now abundantly available, we know that for most women nothing could be further from the truth. In the next chapter we shall have more to say about the menopause, but neither this physiological transition nor the departure of the children is a cause for despair. Most mothers are glad to see their children launched. To be on their own is not, after all, to be lost to the family. If their relationships are close, as most are, they will be keeping in touch; it is best, however, that each live her or his own life, with the knowledge that the family still exists as a set of intimate ties.

This is not to say that the departure of the children doesn't produce any feeling of loss. Many wives will refer to the "bittersweet" nature of the children's departure. Where the child has been continuously at home, the wrenching will be strongest, especially for the close mother-daughter pair. Daughters are, however, more likely to marry relatively soon after completing their education. Counteracting the departure of the children is the greater freedom that parents can enjoy together. The house is theirs again. They can feel freer in their language (so often curbed so as to set a good example to the children) and in the expression of their sexuality. And now the wife and mother can usually be free to decide what she wants to do with the rest of her life. It is not surprising to find that both marital satisfaction and general life satisfaction go up when the children have been launched.[33]

Now comes the period prior to the husband's retirement when the family's economic position is most secure, barring recessions and depressions, a period of greater tranquillity and yet much active pleasure for those husbands and wives who have weathered the storms together. For some couples, however, the launching of their children brings to an end the main goal they had shared. If they find little pleasure in each other's company, divorce may bring down an early curtain on this last act.

One final word of caution regarding the generalization that the empty-nest period brings greater feelings of satisfaction than of loss. There are women whose children have been the major focus of their lives and their closest companions for many years. For those who do not have close friends or interests outside the home, the empty nest *can* bring depression and despair. But this is perhaps as much because the woman is confronted with the question of what she is going to do with the rest of her life as because of the departure of the children.[34]

Parenting over the Years

Family roles are never fixed for long. As children grow, they gain not only a general knowledge of their society, but specialized knowledge their parents never possessed. If they are given the opportunity, they can teach their parents many things, even as they themselves continue to learn from their parents. Ultimately, of course, most children become autonomous, independent of parental control, though few parents of any age can fully inhibit their desire to exert a measure of influence. But if parents are not coercive in their efforts, most can continue to provide a measure of guidance to their adult offspring based on their own experience in facing the same general problems their offspring face as parents, workers, or citizens of the community. And in their later years many parents will turn to their middle-aged offspring for advice and guidance that derive from the younger generation's participation in a vastly changed world. The role of the older person in less-developed societies is less threatened by the obsolescence of what was learned early in life, and parents may therefore tend to retain more authority and respect in such societies than in our industrial society.

DIVORCE AND REMARRIAGE

In the nineteenth century, many families were disrupted by the death of the mother or father in their middle years; few marriages ended in divorce. Widowhood declined markedly in the twentieth century; divorce increased from 1880 to 1920, then remained at a relatively stable level until the late 1960s. Two peaks of higher divorce rates followed World Wars I and II and the hasty marriages that they encouraged, but as recently as 1965, only about 1 percent of married couples were divorced in any given year. Today, the rate is at least double that; it now appears that close to one half of those entering marriage at the present time will eventually divorce. Most will not, however, remain single for long. If past trends continue, roughly three fourths of the women and four fifths of the men will again marry, most of them within three years of their divorce.[35]

For most men and women, the years surrounding a divorce tend to mark the low point in morale over the whole life course. Occasionally, in the early years of marriage, husband and wife can mutually recognize that what they want in life is quite different, and that the marriage was a mistake. They can agree to go their separate ways, perhaps even remaining friends. But when there are children to whom both parents are attached, the story is most often quite different. Often tensions arise over problems that the children are having or over the unequal participation of the spouses in the care and disciplining of the children. Couples are more likely to divorce if they came originally from different backgrounds, if they married very young, and if their marriage was in response to a pregnancy. Sometimes the divorce is caused by infidelity, though this seems to be less frequent in the early years of marriage than in the middle and later years.

Whatever the cause, the breaking of a marriage means that the family becomes subdivided, most often with the mother having custody of the children.[36] The divorce settlement usually provides that the husband shall contribute to the support of the children. Such support is seldom adequate for the maintenance of the family home, and many husbands default on their contributions. Even when husbands do contribute, however, divorce is usually a much better economic deal for husbands than for wives. In a seven-year longitudinal study of families, roughly one in fourteen experienced divorce or separation during the study years. Half had already remarried by the end of the study. Men who remained divorced or separated experienced some decline in income, but this was more than offset by the decline in their expenses; on the average they experienced a 30 percent *increase* in income relative to needs. For women who experienced divorce, separation, or widowhood, real income *fell* about 30 percent. Of those women who had not remarried at the end of the study period, nearly 80 percent were employed in the labor market, a far higher proportion than had been employed prior to the divorce.[37]

We have touched upon the consequences of divorce for children in an earlier chapter. The experience is a searing one for most husbands and wives. Why then do most divorced couples subsequently remarry? The reasons are many and diverse. Most men and women desire a reasonably stable relationship with a member of the opposite sex. For men, the benefits of having a wife who will be a helper and maintainer of the hearth are generally recognized. For women, especially if they already have children, having a man available to serve as a father and economic provider also may have obvious attractions. But not the least of the motivations of many who remarry is that they wish to demonstrate to themselves and to the world that they are winners, not losers. Many will recognize that the failure of their first marriage was a result of unwise decisions, often deriving from immaturity and from romantic notions of marriage. The second time around, they are more concerned with the judgment and maturity of the spouse than with appearances and romance. Second marriages tend to be more equalitarian than first marriages, and there will be far more discussion of a husband's responsibilities and chauvinistic attitudes than there might have been in the first marriage.[38]

If the couple is still relatively young at remarriage (and a high proportion will be in their late twenties or early thirties), they usually decide to have a child to cement their relationship. Yet unless the relationship is very satisfying, many husbands and wives are likely at first to be wary of anything that would make for greater complications if the marriage does not work out. Wives are more likely to work in second marriages than in first marriages.[39] And if things do not go well, second marriages are likely to end somewhat sooner than first marriages, once the telltale signs of strong conflict and its psychological costs are felt. Second marriages are slightly more likely to end in divorce than first marriages, but for many men and women the second time around produces a very satisfying relationship, one in which the family cycle can be completed in a normal way, with the launching of the children.

INTERRELATIONSHIPS OF WORK
AND FAMILY ROLES

In the past two decades the traditional sex role emphases of adult life—work for men and home and motherhood for women—have been markedly modified if not yet transformed. Most women now expect to work both before they marry and after their children are old enough to be left under the care of someone in whom the mother has confidence. Women born in the 1960s and 1970s (and the men they will marry) are being socialized to a new set of priorities. Those born in the 1920s, who came to adolescence in the Depression years, were perhaps the most domestically oriented generation in American history. When there were not enough jobs for men who had been the primary source of support for their families, strong feelings were expressed against women who worked unless they were themselves supporting families.

In the 1980s it may be difficult to imagine how completely taken for granted it was in most families, forty or fifty years ago, that daughters would not have any occupation other than wife and mother. As one college graduate in her early sixties described her early life plans: "I was programmed to get married. That is what you do. I had an opportunity for a job—everybody did during the war—and I was told that that would be embarrassing to my father; nice girls didn't do that." Or again, "It was understood that after your education you would get married. That was the way it was." Not surprisingly, with the great influx of women into the labor market in recent years—wives of executives as well as wives of salesmen and factory workers—many women of this earlier period have come in their later years to resent the system that denied them a chance to do something more with their abilities and talents. Motherhood was no longer enough.

Even those highly domestic daughters of the Depression era have gone to work in large numbers once their children were grown. In some families, husbands have strongly objected; in others, wives have been encouraged by their husbands. College graduates who felt they had made no use of their education during their child-rearing years have been especially eager entrants into the labor market. Where husbands have objected, or have been unwilling to share in household tasks, women who derived much satisfaction from their work may decide that life is more pleasant without the hassles that home life entails, especially after their children are well along in school. Among women heavily invested in work in their middle years in the Berkeley Guidance Study (women born at the start of the Great Depression), eight of 10 who had married became divorced by age 40; two other career women never married.[40] For that generation, heavy work investment by the wife and family stability seldom went together.

Until recently the usual expectation for women who combined marriage and a career has been for the wife's career to be subsidiary to her husband's. It was (and is) almost always the wife who stays home when a child is sick and must be cared for at home by one of the parents. It was almost always the location of the husband's job placement that determined where the family would live. This traditional pattern is now being reshaped somewhat by wives who are capable of greater occupational success than their husbands. Yet full equality is not easily attained. Some couples rotate the primary choice of occupational placement when new opportunities arise, but this hardly permits either one adequate freedom. So-called "dual-career couples" are not a new invention, but are more numerous than ever before. The marital relationship is likely to suffer if both are equally intent on occupational success.[41] Many men know that their wives are as bright and capable as they are;

but perhaps only a few are willing to admit to themselves that they have married an extraordinarily capable woman whose potential is far above their own.

A wife's employment can thus be threatening to a man. Several recent studies suggest that men whose wives work are more vulnerable to anxiety and depression.[42] This is especially the case when the husband has opposed his wife's employment. The dynamics are not entirely clear, but it would appear that tensions in the home, as well as guilt and feelings of inadequacy, may be implicated in this outcome. Husbands who help with housework and the care of children are somewhat less affected than those who make a sharp distinction between "men's work" and "women's work."

Men's Work Involvement and Family Participation

A young professional or business manager may be happy in marriage and still be so heavily engrossed in work as to be unavailable to his family at times when they need him. Many men in their thirties who are launched on markedly successful careers assume that they will be able to give more time to their families "next month, if not next week" or "next year, if not next month." Meanwhile they expect, or at least hope, that their wives will understand and be supportive. Being helpful and supportive often means taking care of everything that needs to be done at home, from looking after the children to seeing that the car gets taken for servicing, making minor household repairs, paying the bills, and much more. Many wives are indeed helpful and supportive. But if they understand their husband's work involvement, they also know that the children see far less of their father than would be desirable. They will often feel that they are not in control of their own lives; their plans and activities seem forever contingent on their husbands' careers.[43] Other wives will assert their needs and wishes, and the family may become a battleground, with the husband's time allocation as the major issue.

In our own Berkeley research (not yet published), we asked women in their later middle years, a decade or so after most of the children had left home, whether their husbands' unavailability earlier in their careers had been a problem to them. Roughly half said that it had. An even higher proportion of their husbands acknowledged that this was so. For many of the men, the realization of the costs of their work involvement to their wives and children came only after years of tension and recrimination. Suddenly the children were gone and the opportunity to know them intimately, as some had in the early days of childhood, had somehow evaporated. Several men acknowledged that their first marriages had been terminated as a consequence of their putting the job first, and roughly one in six reported serious and long-lasting problems such as alcoholism of wives and delinquency of children that they attributed to their own lack of availability. For most men the problem was most acute in their thirties and early forties, but its consequences often persisted as a gnawing sense of regret at 55 or 60.

Along in the middle years the work role appears to lose a bit of its salience for many men, at the same time that it is becoming more salient for their wives.

Other changes are taking place that also point to a softening of sex-role stereotypes and differences. Personalities change over the years just as occupational involvements and family composition do. And it is to the personal aspects of the middle years that we turn next. Before doing so, however, a further comment on cultural variation in the family cycle seems in order.

Culture and the Family Cycle

Within the United States, social class and economic prospects influence the age at which persons marry, the number of children they will have, and the probability that the marriage will endure and the family cycle be lived out. Economic factors play a part in shaping the family cycle in all societies, but cultural norms play an even larger part. In much of the world, marriage is not a consequence of courtship and personal choice on the part of the couple, but rather a matter of arrangement between families. When Mohandas Gandhi, the great Indian leader, was married at the age of 13 to his child bride, she was the third fiancée for whom his parents had contracted.[44] The two girls who had earlier been designated as brides-to-be had both died during childhood. The early marriage resulted from his father's desire that the ceremony be combined with that of an older brother. Arranged marriages are still the norm, even for highly educated persons in many Eastern cultures (including some who secure Ph.D.'s in American universities).

The traditional family in India, China, Japan, and in much of the Muslim world is either an extended family (with several generations living together) or a stem family (in which the oldest son brings his bride to his parents' home and ultimately inherits the home and heads the family). Where and how the couple live after marriage may depend, then, on whether the husband is the oldest son or a younger son. If he is the oldest son, his wife will enter the household subservient to her mother-in-law. Ill will between the two is frequent enough to be a major theme in folk tales. But a constraint is placed upon excessive harshness on the part of the mother-in-law by the knowledge that when her husband dies, her son will succeed him and her daughter-in-law will then be in the driver's seat.[45]

Where more than one generation shares the household, there can be much more flexibility in arranging for child care or outside employment. In the People's Republic of China, for example, it is regarded as the right of every older person (or couple) to reside with one of their children or to have one of the children reside in their household.[46] Grandparents, then, take over the role of primary child care so that mothers and fathers can be gainfully employed outside the home. Thus the family cycle takes many forms in different cultures.

Life-Course Theories
and the Family Cycle

Culture and social change thus influence the scheduling of phases of the family cycle, the structure of the family itself, and the functions served by the family. Yet in all societies there exist expectations as to when men and women should form more or less permanent relationships with mates, and all provide rites of passage to celebrate the arrival of children and enhance the status of parents. Even if marriage is not always celebrated ceremonially, it almost always leads to a change in status that has significant impact on the life course.

Marriage and parenthood are major forces for change in personal habits and often in values and goals as well. No other transitions, with the possible exception of divorce and widowhood, demand comparable adaptations. Identities may be called into question or affirmed in family life. Whether or not one wants to call marriage a *normative crisis,* it is likely that most marriages will encounter crisis situations. For some persons they come early, for some further along the way, as parenthood and/or changing relationships add new role demands. Nevertheless, for a substantial portion of the life course of most people, the round of daily life is patterned by marital and parental roles.

NOTES

1. The concept of the family cycle was first proposed many decades ago by Paul Glick, whose career was spent in the study of data on the family at the U.S. Census. For an overview, see Paul Glick, "Updating the Life Cycle of the Family," *Journal of Marriage and the Family,* 39 (1977), 5–13.
2. Tamara Hareven, "Family Time and Historical Time," *Daedalus* (Spring 1977), pp. 57–70.
3. Paul Glick, "Updating the Life Cycle," p. 7.
4. Each new statistical report in the last decade indicates a higher proportion of births to unmarried mothers. Divorce rates are more difficult to evaluate in the absence of longitudinal data, but they increased far more from 1965 to 1980 than in the previous 45 years.
5. Inability to establish a heterosexual relationship is highly typical of adolescent males who develop schizophrenia. Manfred Bleuler, *The Schizophrenic Disorders: Long-Term Patient and Family Studies* (New Haven, CT: Yale University Press, 1972).
6. John Modell, Frank Furstenberg, Jr., and Theodore Hershberg, "Social Change and Transitions to Adulthood in Historical Perspective," *Journal of Family History,* 1 (1976), 7–32.
7. Ibid., p. 16.
8. Valerie Oppenheimer, *Work and the Family: A Study in Social Demography* (New York: Academic Press, 1982), p. 150.
9. Ibid., pp. 135–62.
10. Hugh Carter and Paul Glick, *Marriage and Divorce: A Social and Economic Study* (Cambridge, MA: Harvard University Press, 1970), pp. 144–45.
11. See Rosabeth Moss Kanter, *Men and Women of the Corporation* (Cambridge, MA: Harvard University Press, 1977).
12. J. Veevers, "Voluntary Childlessness: A Review of the Issues and Evidence," *Marriage and Family Review,* 2 (1979), 1–26.
13. Oppenheimer, *Work and the Family.*
14. Glen Elder, Jr. and R. C. Rockwell, "Marital Timing in Women's Life Patterns," *Journal of Family History,* 1 (1976), 34–53.
15. Ibid., p. 41.
16. Oppenheimer, *Work and the Family.*
17. Lillian Rubin, *Worlds of Pain* (New York: Basic Books, 1976), p. 57.
18. J. A. Clausen and C. L. Huffine, "The Impact of Parental Mental Illness on the Children," in Roberta Simmons, ed., *Research in Community and Mental Health* (Greenwich, CT: JAI Press, 1979), p. 199.

19. Rubin, *Worlds of Pain,* p. 60.
20. Reuben Hill and Joan Aldous, "Socialization for Marriage and Parenthood," in David Goslin, ed., *Handbook of Socialization Theory and Research* (Chicago, IL: Rand McNally, 1969), pp. 885–950.
21. Alice Rossi, "The Transition to Parenthood," *Journal of Marriage and the Family,* 30 (1968), 26–39. For data on timing of the transition see R. R. Rindfuss, S. P. Morgan, and C. G. Swicegood, "The Transition to Motherhood," *American Sociological Review,* 49 (1984), 359–72.
22. Oppenheimer, *Work and the Family.*
23. Harold Wilensky, "The Moonlighter: A Product of Relative Deprivation," *Industrial Relations,* 3 (1963), 105–24.
24. Oppenheimer, *Work and the Family,* p. 127.
25. Angus Campbell, Philip Converse, and Willard Rodgers, *The Quality of American Life* (New York: Russell Sage Foundation, 1976), p. 335.
26. R. C. Kessler and J. A. McRae, Jr., "The Effect of Wives' Employment on the Mental Health of Married Men and Women," *American Sociological Review,* 47 (1982), 216–27. See also P. D. Cleary and D. Mechanic, "Sex Differences in Psychological Distress among Married People," *Journal of Health and Social Behavior,* 24 (1983), 111–21; and George Brown and Tirril Harris, *Social Origins of Depression* (New York: Free Press, 1978).
27. C. E. Ross, J. Mirowsky, and J. Haber, "Dividing Work, Sharing Work, and In-Between: Marriage Patterns and Depression," *American Sociological Review,* 48 (1983), 809–23.
28. See, for example, Gail Lapidus, *Women in Soviet Society* (Berkeley, CA: University of California Press, 1978), especially pp. 270–84; and Samuel Coleman, "The Tempo of Family Formation," in David Plath, ed., *Work and Life Course in Japan* (Albany, NY: State University of New York Press, 1983), pp. 138–214.
29. Oppenheimer, *Work and the Family.*
30. Robert Blood and Donald Wolfe, *Husbands and Wives: The Dynamics of Married Living* (New York: Free Press, 1960), p. 247.
31. Alice Rossi, "Aging and Parenthood in the Middle Years," in P. Baltes and O. G. Brim, Jr., eds., *Life Span Development and Behavior,* vol. 3 (New York: Academic Press, 1980), pp. 137–205.
32. Blood and Wolfe, *Husbands and Wives,* p. 266.
33. N. D. Glenn, "Psychological Well-Being in the Post-Parental Stage: Some Evidence from National Surveys," *Journal of Marriage and the Family,* 37 (1975), 105–10.
34. Lillian Rubin, "The Empty Nest: Beginning or Ending?" in L. A. Bond and J. C. Rosen, eds., *Competence and Coping during Adulthood* (Hanover, NH: University Press of New England, 1980). Also M. F. Lowenthal and D. Chiriboga, "Transition to the Empty Nest: Challenge or Relief?," *Archives of General Psychiatry,* 26 (1972), 8–14.
35. F. F. Furstenberg, Jr., "Conjugal Succession: Reentering Marriage after Divorce," in P. B. Baltes and O. G. Brim, Jr., eds., *Life Span Development and Behavior,* vol. 4 (New York: Academic Press, 1982), p. 110.
36. Until very recently, mothers were awarded custody almost automatically unless they were said to be "unfit."
37. S. Hoffman and J. Holmes, "Husbands, Wives and Divorce," in G. J. Duncan and J. N. Morgan, eds., *Five Thousand American Families: Patterns of Economic Progress* (Ann Arbor, MI: Institute for Social Research, 1976).
38. Furstenberg, "Conjugal Succession," pp. 127–39.
39. Oppenheimer, *Work and the Family.*
40. Janice Stroud, "Women's Careers: Work, Family and Personality," in D. Eichorn et al., eds., *Present and Past in Middle Life* (New York: Academic Press, 1981), pp. 356–90.
41. See Rhona Rapoport and Robert Rapoport, *Dual-Career Families Reexamined: New Integrations of Work and Family* (New York: Harper and Row, 1976).
42. Kessler and McRae, "Effect of Wives' Employment."

43. For a detailed examination of the wife's situation, see Janet Finch, *Married to the Job: Wives' Incorporation in Men's Work* (London: George Allen & Unwin, 1983).

44. See Erik H. Erikson, *Gandhi's Truth* (New York: Norton, 1969), p. 115.

45. To be touched upon further in Chapter 9. For a general account of the Japanese family system in the 1950s, see Ronald Dore, *City Life in Japan: A Study of a Tokyo Ward* (Berkeley, CA: University of California Press, 1958), pp. 91–135.

46. See Chapter 2, "The Chinese Family," in William Kessen, ed., *Childhood in China* (New Haven, CT: Yale University Press, 1975).

CHAPTER 8
THE MIDDLE YEARS

The young are slaves to dreams;
the old servants of regrets. Only
the middle-aged have all their five
senses in the keeping of their wits.
Hervey Allen. Anthony Adverse

This chapter might have been titled "Life After Forty." That age is commonly regarded in the United States as a watershed. The twenties and thirties bring major transitions and major commitments; they represent the high plateau of strength and vigor. By 40, downhill slides in energy and attractiveness often become evident. Women over 40 are admonished by advertisers to turn to cosmeticians in order to maintain their glamorous appeal. At 40 many men will be entering the period of their maximum occupational performance and power at the same time that thinning hair and a slight paunch attest to being past their physical prime. The young men who were seen as "comers" in their early thirties are expected to have demonstrated their promise by 40.

In the middle years, men and women are expected to become more stable. They may be less enthusiastic but also less excitable; they will presumably be wiser and more accepting of life. On the other hand, one reads a good deal in the popular press and even in the scientific literature about the "midlife crisis." In this chapter we begin to examine the changes that come about with advancing age. We look at what people are doing, how they feel about what they are doing, and what they want for themselves and their families. What leads to satisfaction and happiness in the middle years? What leads to crises and feelings of failure and bitterness?

MIDDLE AGE AND ITS TRANSITIONS

For our purposes we shall define the middle years as extending from roughly 40 or 45 to 60 or 65. We must recognize from the start, however, that thinking of oneself as middle-aged does not depend upon being 40 or 60 or any other age. How one views oneself will depend upon social-class background, on the degree to which physical strength and appearance are highly valued attributes, on actual physical condition and health, and on one's future prospects as compared with one's past accomplishments. Working-class men, who are likely to be concerned with physical strength and vigor, tend to see middle age as beginning at 35 and old age at 60; middle-class persons, on the other hand, much more often place the start of middle age at 45 and old age at 70.[1] Moreover, the connotations of middle age are much more negative for working-class men, who see this as a time of decline, than for middle-class men, who view this as a period of peak productivity and income.

The childhood and adolescent years are marked by such rites of passage as graduation, church confirmations or bar mitzvahs, initiation ceremonies in fraternities and clubs, and often by family ceremonies that symbolize the attainment of greater maturity. Early adulthood also has its major transitions that are celebrated by symbolic rites that serve as public affirmations of change, such as marriage and customary practices surrounding the birth of children (gifts, christenings). The middle years have no special rites of passage. A divorce is not usually celebrated, nor does a second marriage have quite the symbolic significance of the first one. And the departure of one's children from the family home seems just to happen, not to be the focus of a rite of passage.

Though scheduled transitions are few, there may be many unscheduled transitions beyond the early years of adulthood. Most men will change jobs and sometimes careers; most women will enter or leave the labor force, depending on their interests and their family's needs; many families will move to new communities where they will face the rebuilding of personal networks; major illnesses of parents, spouses, or children will lead to changes in life-styles for a significant number of middle-aged persons; and many other unanticipated contingencies will lead to disruptions and adaptations of major proportions. Again, they will be uncelebrated by formal rites, except as arrivals in certain positions will call for welcoming parties and permanent departures from some organizations may be the occasion for paying respects through going-away parties. But these transitions will bring about significant changes in roles, relationships, and the experience of both stress and satisfaction. Some persons will be largely in control of their lives and may experience a good deal of stability through the middle years; others may see their way of life threatened or transformed.

Time Perspectives in Midlife

More than half of normal life expectancy has been lived by the time one becomes 40. This has led some writers to stress the significance of becoming aware of mortality, of having to face the fact that death lies somewhere ahead. Apart from clinical evidence (largely the experience of psychiatrists with patients who fear death), there is little indication that fear of death poses any sort of crisis in the middle years. Yet in the middle years there does surely come an awareness that the amount of time left to accomplish one's aims and enjoy one's blessings is limited. As Bernice Neugarten has noted, there comes a shift in perspective; one looks within oneself more than before and one thinks in terms of time left to live.[2]

The contemplation of death does not seem to be a major problem for most persons either in middle age or in old age. In a study of four age groups facing transitions, ranging from high school students about to graduate to men about to retire, Marjorie Fiske Lowenthal and her colleagues found that age did not much affect how often people said they thought about death. It did influence the circumstances in which they thought about death and the emotions they felt.[3] Several studies suggest that what is most feared by mothers is that they may die before they have been able to launch their children, and what is feared by men is that they will die before they have been able to provide for their families. Death was most frightening to the young, for they thought of it in terms of an unexpected event occurring by virtue of accidents or catastrophes rather than as a natural process. The confrontation with death becomes more real in the later middle years precisely because death as a natural phenomenon is possible at any time. A major illness or the death of a friend brings stark awareness that one's time for accomplishment and enjoyment may be limited.

PHYSIOLOGICAL CHANGE
IN THE MIDDLE YEARS

During the early adult years, physical and intellectual strength and vigor remain essentially unchanged from their peaks in the early twenties. There are no sharp dividing lines between youth and early adulthood or between early adulthood and middle age. Professional athletes usually have to find another career between the ages of 35 and 40, though an occasional baseball pitcher can still dazzle batters when in his early forties. Along in their forties, most people become aware of some decline in speed if not in stamina. Those who put on a good deal of weight will tire more readily than they did a few years earlier, and many of those who started smoking cigarettes in adolescence will be showing some impairment of lung capacity.

Health and Disease

An average American who has survived until 40 can now expect to live beyond 70, but death rates begin to rise significantly in the forties. Men become subject to the threat of a heart attack even before their forties, though most women will be protected by their hormones for another decade or more. Between 45 and 64, roughly one person in three will die, most in the second decade, of course. Two fifths of all deaths will be attributable to cardiovascular diseases and another fourth will be due to cancer.[4] Hypertension, respiratory diseases, and accidents will account for half the remaining deaths in the age group.

Rates of chronic diseases and impairments go up even more sharply each decade than do death rates. Obesity and high blood pressure are perhaps the most serious of the physiological changes taking place, but gastrointestinal complaints, arthritis, and diabetes also occur with greatly increased frequency.[5] Nearly two thirds of the population (more women than men) will find their vision becoming blurry in the middle years, and one in 20 will have severe visual impairment even with the best correction eyeglasses can provide.[6] Dental problems also become widespread during the middle years: A fourth of the population will lose all their teeth prior to age 65, and nearly 90 percent of persons 45 to 64 develop diseases of the gums and mouth.[7] Most middle-aged persons will not be markedly affected by such impairments and diseases; these are nuisances, but one can live with them. Nevertheless, fully a fifth of persons in the 45-to-64 age group will have their activities limited to some degree because of chronic conditions, and for many these limitations will force them to change some of their normal major activities.[8] Such limitations are most likely to occur in the fifties and early sixties, but heavy smokers and heavy drinkers may experience marked impairment a decade or so before their peers.

Having noted that one middle-aged person in five will have his or her activities limited by health conditions, we should perhaps stress the corollary: Four out of five are able to keep on doing what they have been doing, though usually at a slower pace. Tennis players will usually shift at some point from singles to doubles, and joggers will become more concerned about their hip sockets and less given to sprinting.

At 40, the average adult's cardiac efficiency and breathing capacity are still roughly 90 percent of their maximum values; by 60, a number of basic physiological mechanisms will be down to somewhere between half and three quarters of their earlier values.[9] Some men and women will look and feel old at 60; others will still be resilient and fit. Much will depend on heredity, diet, and, by no means least in importance, exercise and other personal habits. Thus there are significant physical declines, but there are enormous differences in the degree to which they affect activities and interests.

The Psychological Meaning of Age and Aging

The meaning of age itself begins to become much more significant in the middle years. For much of our early lives we look forward to being older than we are. Then, when we are in our physical prime, we don't think much about age. But by 40 or certainly by 50, age is something we would like less of. Alice Rossi studied women in their late thirties to early fifties who had adolescent daughters in high school.[10] They were asked how old they felt, how old they would like to be if they could be any age they wanted, and until what age they would like to live. Mothers who were 44–56 wished, on the average, to be 15 years younger than they were, while mothers who were 33–43 wished on the average to be only six years younger than they were. Both groups regarded the mid-thirties as the best time of life for men and for women. No woman wanted to be older than she was.

But age in itself was not the most important determinant of how old these mothers would like to be. Indeed, it was far less important than whether feelings of competence and of freedom from stress characterized a mother's life. Women with larger families, those who had their children relatively late, those who had symptoms of aging (such as changes in body shape, eyesight, teeth, energy level, weight, or sex lives), and those with the lowest educational attainments wanted most to be younger than they were. Thus the meaning of age depends upon what one is called upon to do and how one's life has been scheduled previously.

Sexuality in the Middle Years

By their fifties, most married couples are making love only about half as often as they did in their early adult years.[11] There is less urgency to sex, but for many it remains a supremely rewarding experience well into the later years. Beyond the late forties most women will have lost the capacity to bear children but not the capacity to enjoy sex.

The Menopause.   Until recent decades, the menopause was viewed as an extraordinarily traumatic time for women. Any emotional upset in a woman in her late forties or early fifties was likely to be attributed to the menopause. The onset of menses at the start of puberty is sudden and unequivocal; the cessation of menses is more gradual and often irregular. Hormonal changes lead to periodic hot flushing—popularly referred to as "hot flashes"—in many women. Nervous tension and headaches may also occur. The symptoms are often annoying but seldom seriously debilitating. Subsequent to the menopause most women experience renewed feelings of well-being.[12]

As with the empty nest, the menopause has symbolic meanings, and these may be as important as the biological ones. Beyond this period, women can no longer bear children, and this feature was regarded by psychoanalysts as a serious psychological threat, particularly to those women who had not become mothers. The other side of the same coin, however, is that women who have not had available a completely reliable form of contraception now no longer need fear an unwanted pregnancy. Recent research suggests that relief at not having to worry about pregnancy is far more common than despair over loss of ability to bear children. Indeed, despair is far more likely to characterize the woman over age 40 who suddenly discovers herself pregnant when her other children are adolescents or young adults.

Sexual interest and enjoyment may actually increase after the menopause, for the hormonal changes that take place have only a slight relationship to sexual desire. In her study of middle-aged women, Lillian Rubin found a number who reported that their early fifties were a time of maximum sexual satisfaction, even a "second honeymoon."[13] Within the following decade, however, it appears that a decline in sexual interest and activity is common and comes earlier for women than for men.

The Male Climacteric. Men have no equivalent to the menopause, despite the fact that the term *climacteric* is frequently applied to men in late middle age. If men are healthy and interested, they may not only be sexually active but may continue to sire children into their eighties and perhaps nineties. For both men and women, loss of interest in sex is likely to be preceded by loss of closeness in the relationship. Also, continued interest and activity into old age tends to be associated with high sexual activity in the earlier years.[14]

Sex in the later middle years is highly contingent on the health and interest of marital partners or other potential sexual partners as well as on the individual's own health and interest. Particularly for older women who are widowed or whose husbands are in poor health, opportunities for sexual fulfillment are likely to be sharply limited. Cultural barriers have prevented us from learning in any depth about the place that sexual enjoyment on the one hand and deprivation of sexual expression on the other play in later middle age.[15]

To summarize this section as a whole, physiological changes in the middle years tend to be gradual and to have only a modest impact on activities except for that fraction of the population that has serious debilitating illnesses. The kinds of activities that people engage in tend to change slightly, but even very active sports can be pursued well beyond the middle years. What of intellectual capacity and vigor? Do we find a decline corresponding to that found in physical vigor? The answer is a resounding "no."

INTELLECTUAL CAPACITIES
IN THE MIDDLE YEARS

Intellectual ability is perhaps the most stable aspect of personal functioning in the middle years. From the late teens to the fifties, there is very little change in standard intelligence scores administered to the same individuals.[16] Until longitudinal data became available, it had been assumed that intelligence declined with each additional decade. Studies of cross sections of the population showed lower scores for 40-year-olds than for 30-year-olds, and for 50-year-olds than for 40-year-olds. The declines reflected cohort differences. The better-educated younger cohorts scored higher than the older cohorts (but not higher than older persons of comparable education). When we examine the same individuals over several decades, the data show no such declines in total scores.

IQ Change in the Middle Years

There are, nevertheless, some slight changes going on. Psychologists now distinguish "fluid intelligence" (defined as reasoning ability and the ability to perceive figural relationships not based on learning) from "crystallized intelligence," which is the result of accumulated knowledge available for problem solving (including such components as verbal comprehension, semantic relations, etc.).[17] Some components of fluid intelligence do indeed begin to decline in early adulthood; others, including intellectual flexibility, show little decline. Moreover, there is an increase in crystallized intelligence up to the seventies. In general, then, the various component capacities and skills that make up intelligence, including cognitive flexibility, show no appreciable change during the middle adult years except for a slight decrease in speed of response.

Influences on IQ Change

In the Berkeley longitudinal studies, average IQ's actually increased about six points from testing at age 17-18 to that at age 48 (age at last published report), and data currently in hand will almost certainly show that IQ's at 60 remain high.[18] These averages conceal the much more substantial gains of some and the significant IQ loss of others between adolescence and middle age. As might be expected, high educational attainment and other sources of intellectual stimulation tend to contribute to IQ gain beyond adolescence. Occupational attainment is substantially related to adolescent IQ, but does not explain gains in the adult years; educational attainment does.[19] The failure of occupational attainment to account for gains runs counter to Kohn's research (reported in Chapter 6) on the effects of the substantive complexity of occupational tasks on intellectual flexibility.[20] It may be that IQ inadequately assesses the concept of intellectual flexibility, but on the other hand, the testing of the Berkeley longitudinal subjects was far more carefully controlled and psychologically sophisticated than the assessments made by interviewers in the surveys on which the Kohn research was based.

Men and women tend to marry partners who are close to each other in IQ even if not in education. When they do not, their own IQ's are likely to change in the direction of their spouse's IQ. The Berkeley research found that men and women who married spouses with IQ's at least 10 points higher than their own were very likely to show substantial gains in IQ by their middle years. Conversely, however, those whose adult spouse scored 10 or more points below the study member's adolescent IQ were likely to show a loss by middle age.[21]

Personality also has a bearing on whether or not a person tends to gain or lose in IQ from adolescence to the middle years. IQ gainers had shown more self-control in adolescence and were more "cognitively invested"—that is, they valued intellectual matters, had high aspirations, and were more verbally fluent than those who failed to gain or even lost in IQ over the years.[22]

As we shall see, intellectual power may be retained well into the eighties and nineties. Much depends on the extent to which one's capacities are exercised, though the lack of exercise seems less crucial for intellectual functioning than for physical abilities. Serious illness may bring a marked drop, however. Heavy consumption of alcohol is also often associated with decline in IQ. Among "heavy" and "problem drinkers" in the Berkeley studies, more than two thirds were IQ decreasers and only one in eight showed IQ gains.[23] Moderate drinking, on the other hand, shows no association with IQ. It is not clear whether the effects of high alcohol consumption are a consequence of organic damage (which ultimately will occur) or of the psychological state of depression that characterizes most problem drinkers.

ROLE INVOLVEMENT
IN THE MIDDLE YEARS

Young adults tend to have more relationships with friends, neighbors, and colleagues than do the middle-aged. Studies of social networks suggest that in the middle years and beyond, social activities generally diminish, although middle-aged women are more sociable than men. With increasing age, social ties with kin tend to constitute a larger proportion of meaningful relationships for both men and women.[24]

Although most people tend to associate with others fairly near to their own ages, the middle-aged have ties both with their children's generation and with their parents. As their children become independent and less a source of immediate concern, their aging parents are likely to become more dependent on men and women in their forties and fifties. Many parents will, of course, have died before their offspring reach 50, but at least one grandparent in four is likely to live to 80.

Many men and women get to see their grandchildren married, and there are more great-grandparents than ever before. But as longevity increases, so do the serious illnesses of old age, especially mental disorders such as Alzheimer's disease, which leaves the body intact but the mind lost in memoryless space. It is the middle-aged offspring who then are most often faced with making arrangements for the care of infirm parents.

Gender Differences

As we have repeatedly noted, women are more concerned with and sensitive to interpersonal relationships than men. During the child-rearing years, however, they are constrained to have fewer friends and associates, to engage in fewer social activities than do men of the same age. They can less often count on the emotional support of others and as a consequence they are likely to find life especially stressful during these years. But once the children are in school or on their own, women can express their sociability in friendships and associations with other women. Men, on the other hand, especially if married, diminish the extent to which they confide in or have close ties to other men. For married men, it appears that their wives satisfy their needs for a close confidant.[25]

In their thirties, when the children are in school, mothers and fathers become much more involved in community activities than they were in their twenties. For some, involvement in organizations and associations tends to drop off after the children leave school, but for others the middle years are years of maximum participation. Among men, this is especially true of those who are highly successful.[26] And for middle-class mothers who do not take jobs when their children reach adolescence, there is time to join with others in programs for community betterment, in political involvement, and in a variety of leisure activities.

Whether women work at paid jobs or not, the lifelines of men and women tend to converge somewhat in the middle years. Change runs in opposite directions. Men tend to become somewhat less preoccupied with work, unless they are extremely successful, and women tend to become more preoccupied with an occupational role. The middle years are for many women the time of new opportunities, exciting prospects for the future. For many men they are the time when it becomes evident that they will not go as far as they might have hoped to go in their jobs, and they are likely therefore to turn more to being with their families and to leisure activities. Because of these differences, we shall consider the meaning of the middle years separately for the two sexes.

Women's Lives in the Middle Years

For the great bulk of women, the role of mother continues to be the primary role, so far as emotional involvement is concerned, as long as there are children at home (and indeed, for life), regardless of whether or not a woman has taken a job. It is the wife and mother who most often maintains family ties and links the generations. Children will in general have closer ties with their maternal grandparents, aunts, and uncles than with their paternal relatives. And it will be recalled that mothers are far more likely to be close confidants for children of both sexes than are fathers. This continues well into the children's adolescence and probably into their adult years as well.

The Midlife Search for New Meanings. Nevertheless, there comes a time when many women feel that they have something more to contribute than maternal nurturance. In *Women of a Certain Age: The Mid-life Search for Self,* Lillian Rubin reports on a study of women of middle age whom she interviewed. Most of them were, like herself, middle class.[27] Many of them wanted, as she did, to be something more than the symbolic mother, always nurturant, always available. Rubin's research and that of others attests to women's need for challenging, instrumental activities in the middle years. As we noted in the last chapter, the need is especially great among women who have had a college education before raising their families.

The search for new interests and activities can lead to feelings of excitement and a new sense of freedom or to a sense of loss and depression on the part of women who are unable to resolve the dilemma posed by the end of the child-rearing era. Further education is one mode of resolution; learning new skills, whether for work or for pleasure, is another. Work as a volunteer in behalf of good causes is yet another. But for a period many women will be perplexed and perhaps depressed. One cannot attribute the sense of freedom or the sense of loss directly to either the empty nest or to the menopause. These are merely markers, symbolically important though they be, indicating that it is time to find a new set of priorities that will enable the women to experience relatedness and accomplishment and that will sustain or build upon the identity that has developed in the years of being preeminently wife and mother.

Women's Work in the Middle Years

Middle-class wives are likely to work because they want to; working-class wives are more likely to work because they have to in order to help maintain the family. It is therefore much easier for a middle-class woman to be choosy in taking a job or ready to give up an unsatisfying job. By virtue of educational advantages, of course, middle-class wives are often in a position to secure more challenging and rewarding jobs.[28] Although the occupational role less often becomes the primary definer of identity for a woman than for a man, a fourth of the late-middle-aged women in our Berkeley studies rate that role at least equal to their family roles in influencing their sense of self. The work role is by no means a minor matter for most women in their fifties. Many report that for the first time in their lives, they feel that their competence as productive adults outside the home has been validated. When faced with challenges, most women rise to meet the challenges and overcome obstacles. If they have husbands who are unaccustomed to expressing appreciation for a wife's contributions, recognition outside the home is especially gratifying.

We are just beginning to learn about the interrelationships of careers of husbands and wives in the later years, but we know that a major factor in the morale of middle-aged women is the degree of consensus between husband and wife on how occupational and family roles are to be meshed. Husbands who object to their wives' working often have unhappy wives who stay at home or rebellious wives who take a job regardless of their wishes. And as previously noted, in the latter instance not only family tranquillity but the husband's own self-esteem is threatened.[29]

Even when they find work satisfying, however, most women do not plan to work as long as they possibly can. Retirement tends to take place before the age of 65, often when the husband retires, but even earlier if the job is not sufficiently rewarding. Wives are more likely to retire when their husbands do if their husbands receive high salaries or have good pensions.[30] On the other hand, they may continue to work on for years after their husbands retire if their husbands' wages were low and they have no pensions. A working wife's morale tends to be highest in families where husbands share in preparing meals and in household tasks. Joint activities of the spouses may be somewhat diminished where both work, but the time they spend together will usually be higher-quality time. Many husbands are ambivalent about their wives' working but recognize that their wives are happier. Others report increased tension over their wives' diminished availability.

Men's Lives in the Middle Years

By 40, the great majority of men are well settled in a particular occupation, though many will change employers several times before they retire. A large number of studies document the increasing stability of men's occupational careers as they move from their twenties into their thirties and forties.[31] The evidence indicates that each decade brings greater stability and, on the whole, also greater job satisfaction. Nevertheless, for many men investment in the job slackens off in the forties, particularly if prospects for further advancement seem relatively dim.[32] Differences between men in lower-level jobs (whether white-collar or blue-collar) and the upper ranks of managerial and professional personnel are very great in this respect. As would be expected, men in manual occupations achieve peak skill and job satisfaction somewhat earlier and have lower aspirations for advancement in the middle years.

By 40, few blue-collar workers expect to advance except in seniority, but most men in middle-class occupations still hope to move ahead. Some advance in the decade of the forties, but if they do not, by 50 they tend to be resigned to remaining in the slot they have occupied for some time. Among those men who do move up, a significant proportion change employers during their forties. Men who have moved up the occupational ladder are actually more likely to change employers than those who have stayed at the same level.[33] Moreover, job satisfaction and career satisfaction tend to be highest among those men who had earlier moved up from working-class backgrounds to middle-class jobs; many of them have come farther than they had ever expected. This is, of course, not merely a reflection of their superior abilities but also of the changing structure of the labor market; in the past generation, white-collar jobs have multiplied while blue-collar jobs have declined in number.[34] Under these circumstances, it is not surprising to find that men who had *not* advanced beyond the level of their fathers' occupations tend to be those least satisfied with their jobs at ages 40 and 50. At 40, some are investing themselves very heavily in their work; by 50, they tend to be resigned to their current status.

Middle age is a period in which some hopes are blighted, some opportunities are seen as forever lost. This has led to a proliferation of writing on the so-called "midlife crisis," almost all of it dealing with the male of the species. Orville Brim cites as an example of the genre the following statement from an article by Lear:

> The hormone production levels are dropping, the head is balding, the sexual vigor is diminishing, the stress is unending, the children are leaving, the parents are dying, the job horizons are narrowing, the friends are having their first heart attacks; the past floats by in a fog of hopes not realized, opportunities not grasped, women not bedded, potentials not fulfilled, and the future is a confrontation with one's own mortality.[35]

It seems desirable to consider at this point whether or not such a crisis is pervasive.

If so, when does it occur and what are the prime causes? If not, how are the lost opportunities and the blighted hopes dealt with?

Is There a Midlife Crisis?

The term *midlife crisis* has a nice ring to it. It is of fairly recent origin and seems to have initially achieved popularity through an article by a psychoanalyst, Elliott Jacques, on "Death and the Mid-life Crisis."[36] Jacques proposed that "the reality and inevitability of one's own eventual personal death . . . is the central and crucial feature of the midlife phase."[37] As we have noted, however, psychiatrists' conclusions based on anxious patients are not in general supported by data on the larger population. Moreover, most persons have had some occasion to consider their own mortality long before middle age. Anyone who has served in the military in wartime, or who has been involved in near misses or near-fatal crashes on the highway knows that death is always a possibility. Some persons will sense themselves as charmed, invulnerable, but most adults recognize their vulnerability. Surveys of the general population indicate that 85 percent report that they think it desirable to plan for death before it actually is at hand.[38]

There are a number of other reasons why the middle years may bring a sense of crisis. Endocrine changes and diminished sexual activity have been frequently cited, but as we have already noted, they are gradual and show great individual variation in their timing. The quality of the marital relationship probably far outweighs hormonal change in predicting midlife sexuality. For most men (and women) there is no standard period of crisis or despair regarding sexuality.

Levinson's theory of the life course offers yet a different explanation for a potential midlife crisis. He proposes a midlife transition between the ages of about 40 and 45 and states that it must begin no earlier than 38 and no later than 43.[39] He sees three major tasks to be accomplished during this transition: (1) terminating the era of early adulthood with a review and reappraisal of what has been done to date; (2) modifying the negative aspects of the present life structure and testing new choices; and (3) dealing with the polar issues of youth versus old age, destruction versus creativity, masculinity versus femininity, and attachment versus separation. According to Levinson, every man at midlife must come to terms with these issues, though no rationale is offered as to why this must be done around age 40 rather than all through the maturing years. Levinson states that "for the great majority of men this is a period of great struggle within the self and with the external world. This mid-life transition is a time of moderate or severe crisis."[40]

Life is full of transitions. As we have seen, most of them are linked to social roles. Some of them are directly linked to age, whether by law or by custom. Others are much more loosely linked to age, by virtue of bodily changes and physical health. If we are to talk of a midlife crisis, there should be some typical events that precipitate a crisis at a particular age or time, or some criteria that permit us to say that the crisis exists. Undoubtedly, some men and women do experience crises in their middle years; most do not appear to do so. Moreover, if there is a crisis it may occur at any time, not just around age 40.

Adaptations are called for whenever existing life patterns are inadequate to meet new demands, when they no longer bring satisfaction of basic needs, or when the patterns themselves cannot be sustained. Crises occur when the individual is unable to adapt or otherwise cannot resolve the dilemmas faced. New demands occur on a largely unscheduled basis during the middle years, except as family phases define periods of greater or lesser economic need or changing degrees of closeness in ties. It would seem that most of us attempt to cope with problems when we encounter them. We do not wait for an "age-40 transition" before we try to adapt. The systematic data we possess on the prevalence of depression and of alcoholism do not suggest any age-specific peaks in these phenomena. Depression has its peak prevalence among women prior to age 35, while among men the highest rates are for the age group 55–70.[41] Alcoholics show up in our mental hospitals in the middle years, but the great majority were drinking heavily in their early adult years. Indeed, many of those who are identified as alcoholics in the middle years were discernably problematic in their high school years.[42] Claims that these disorders result from a midlife crisis are thus easily refuted.

Levinson insists that any given "life structure" is satisfying for only a limited time. His concept of structure is at the root of the problem. We are organized persons, but we are constantly in the process of adapting, changing as situational requirements demand. We bend far more often than we break. Losing one's spouse or one's job in the middle years may be a shattering experience. Realizing that one has already lived most of one's allocated time or that one has not achieved all one hoped to do is seldom a shattering experience.

There are other reasons for doubts and regrets, as we have noted. But perhaps the midlife problem most often mentioned after those already discussed is disillusionment with one's career. We turn next to the issue of career satisfaction and career change in the middle years.

Career Change at Midlife. In Chapter 6 we noted that many careers entail an early period of searching for the right occupational niche. Professionals and higher-status managerial or technical workers tend to find that niche and remain highly committed over the whole of their work life. But some men and women later discover possibilities they had been unaware of or talents they did not know they had.

Until fairly recently, the emphasis in research on careers was on what Seymour Sarason has called the "one life—one career" theme.[43] It was assumed that for most persons a single career line, preferably orderly, was not only the dominant pattern but the preferred pattern. But Sarason, Gould, Levinson, and others have challenged this thesis, maintaining that at around age 40 many men will question what they have been doing. Some will change jobs or wives or both; others may become confirmed in their earlier commitments.

How many men do change careers at midlife? If one argues, as Sarason does, that career change occurs when a psychologist shifts from clinical work to teaching, when a lawyer becomes a judge, or when an account salesman becomes sales manager (i.e., executive), then career change is indeed a frequent occurrence in the middle years.[44] Much depends on whether people feel they are entering new careers or new phases of ongoing careers. In my own research (and indeed in my own life experience as a sociologist who has been a research worker and research administrator in government and in a university as well as becoming a teacher), one has the sense of being in a new phase of an ongoing career when one continues to draw upon the same fund of technical and professional knowledge. At the same time there is no denying that changes in emphasis that go with promotion or a new job assignment—as well as major career change—can make one's work more challenging and exciting. Such changes may be sought especially when people feel the need for greater rewards than they have been receiving, and not at any particular age.

One study, specifically designed to assess the frequency of occupational change over five-year periods, found relatively high change in the twenties, less in the thirties, and much less from the forties on. More than 75 percent of men and 70 percent of women over 40 were in the same occupation they had been in five years previously.[45] And of those who changed occupations, 60 percent were in the same type of occupation (using Holland's categories, noted in Chapter 6) as before. Thus only about 10 percent appear to have made substantial career changes. These findings are similar to those of a 10-year longitudinal study of middle-aged men by Parnes and his associates.[46]

Evidence from many studies indicates that each decade brings greater stability in occupational careers. There is no evidence of greater instability in the late thirties or early forties than there was five years earlier. Thus there is no basis for proclaiming a general midlife transition around age 40 in terms of occupational change. There are certainly men and women who experience great occupational transitions, but except for women entering the labor market, they do so with decreasing frequency in the later years.

Men Who Do Not Achieve Early Aspirations.   Most men aspire to greater success than they achieve. Early in their careers, most will move along at about the same pace, but some will be seen as "comers" and others will fall behind. Each decade, more will see themselves passed over for promotion or otherwise come to see that their prospects are limited. As we have noted, many will invest less heavily in their jobs.

Several intensive studies of men in middle-management jobs as well as studies of larger cross sections of middle-aged workers suggest that for only a small minority is failure to achieve early aspirations a serious problem. By their forties and fifties most men have made a realistic assessment of how much they want to put out in the way of effort and what they might gain from doing so. They see the costs as well as the benefits. Those who are not especially successful on the job appear to be no less happy or well adjusted than the men at the top.

A 20-year study of college graduates hired for management jobs by American Telephone & Telegraph found that the men who had moved up at least three levels of management during this period were much more heavily involved in their jobs than men who had advanced only one level, but those who had advanced most were no happier or better adjusted.[47] Moreover, the men who were well adjusted but less successful were judged equally intelligent, promising, and work-involved when first hired. But over the course of their early years with the company they had cut back in the intensity of their involvement. Clearly they were making choices.

Similar conclusions were derived from a study of British managers by Cyril Sofer.[48] The evidence is that people are constantly comparing themselves with others and evaluating their own performances. They do not wait for the turning of a decade, but raise or lower their sights or otherwise adapt as their life situations demand. Particularly as they move along into the later middle years, most men will be striving less and reflecting more. And their reflections will as often lead them to consider what they have accomplished—to look at the bright side—rather than what might have been.

Early Retirement.   Increasingly, in recent years, both men and women have been voluntarily retiring from the labor force while still in their later middle years. This had previously been a possibility only for the affluent few who had amassed large enough fortunes to live on their investment income. Now, however, it is a possibility for a much larger segment of the population, thanks to a generally much higher level of lifetime earnings and to the provisions of private and public pension plans. While we shall deal with the general topic of retirement in the next chapter, it is relevant to note that those who retire in their fifties and early sixties comprise two quite different groups: (1) those who have health problems that make it difficult for them to continue to work at their regular occupation and/or those who are out of work and are competitively disadvantaged (such as persons with little education and minority-group members); and (2) those who have sufficient resources to retire and who wish to enjoy nonremunerative activities such as recreation and travel.

Those who retire because of impairment or disadvantage are of course much less well off in retirement than they had been when employed, but they are not in a position to better themselves. As the longitudinal research of Parnes and his associates has demonstrated, poor health and disadvantaged position tend to go together. Retirement because of health is most frequent among the poorly educated, who are in the lower occupational strata and are most subject to perennial unemployment.[49] Men with very low educational attainment, low occupational status, and low earnings are likely to drop out of the labor force even if they are not in poor health. Social Security benefits for people meeting minimal requirements of coverage have increased rather sharply in recent decades, and Parnes's research suggests that this trend has induced some men to leave the labor force as soon as they become eligible for disability or other payments.[50]

Widowhood.   Since women now survive eight years longer than men, on the average, and since most women are married to men somewhat older than themselves, it is obvious that women are much more likely to become widows than men are to become widowers. Nearly a fourth of married women are widowed in their forties and fifties. The economic plight of widows is, in general, made more serious if their husbands have been incapacitated or have experienced some reduction in their ability to work during a period of months prior to death. Again, Parnes's longitudinal study of middle-aged males (followed up each year for a decade) produces evidence previously lacking: In the year before their deaths, men with a health problem who were under 65 when they died had worked less than half the number of hours worked by men without a health problem.[51] On the average, the health problems of the men who died had resulted in diminished labor-force participation and earnings for several years.

Both the men who die in the middle years and their widows tend to be drawn disproportionately from among those with low educational and occupational status, and therefore the widows have minimal resources for coping economically. After the deaths of their husbands there is only a slight increase in the labor-force participation of white widows and actually a decrease in that of black widows; the older widows tend to have obsolescent work skills and the younger ones to have children to care for. As a consequence, one third of white widows and two thirds of black widows have incomes below the poverty line, even counting pensions from Social Security and welfare benefits.

In the short term, bereavement by the death of a spouse is generally agreed to be the greatest stress one is likely to face in life. The younger the husband or wife who dies, the greater the anguish experienced. Men whose wives died at an early age are themselves at substantially greater risk of dying in the following two or three years; women who lose their husbands are more likely to develop drinking problems or mental disorders, but otherwise do not appear to suffer higher mortality rates.[52]

Women who are widowed in the later middle years are unlikely to marry. There are far fewer men available, and older men tend to choose much younger wives. For a great many women in our society, then, there is likely to be a decade or more in which they remain without a spouse; for those widowed in their forties, it may be half their lives. For most, however, widowhood will not come until they themselves are crossing the threshold of old age, so we shall postpone further discussion of widowhood until the next chapter.

Generativity versus Stagnation

In his formulation of stages of the life cycle, Erikson proposes that each stage entails increased vulnerability and at the same time heightened potential for development in some particular respect. Young adulthood saw the achievement of intimacy (or a sense of isolation). Middle adulthood (in Erikson's terms, simply *adulthood*) calls for the achievement of "generativity" (versus "stagnation"). Generativity, he writes, "is primarily the interest in establishing and guiding the next generation or whatever in a given case may become the absorbing object of a parental kind of responsibility."[53] It is the essence of mature adulthood to need to be needed, Erikson notes, and the provision of guidance and support to others, especially to those younger and dependent, is a crucial need if one is to avoid stagnation.

As we have seen, women seem to resolve the "crisis" of generativity versus stagnation much more easily and fully than men do. Erikson has certainly identified a major facet of concern in the middle years. As he notes, generativity does not necessarily require that one be a parent. A childless person may provide guidance and serve as a model for younger persons in productive, creative activities and may thereby achieve a strong sense of generativity. Whether or not this component of our sense of who we are in the middle years is *the* task of those years is a matter of value judgment. It is of some interest to note that several studies find childless, middle-aged persons reporting higher life satisfaction and happiness than parents of the same age. Loving care and guidance does not insure that one's children will become happy, well-adjusted adults in their own right (though it certainly helps). For those parents whose children become mentally ill, alcoholic, or merely unhappy and inept, there may be heartache rather than a sense of generativity. Some know that they failed to provide the guidance that was needed; others thought they had done well and ask, in their late middle years, "Where did we go wrong?" But here again, most parents will have done well enough to be able to derive deep satisfaction from their children and joy from their grandchildren.

PERSONALITY IN THE MIDDLE YEARS

Whether they have had one marriage or several, orderly careers or chaotic ones, most people have a strong sense that at 40 or 50 they have not changed much from what they were like at 20 or 30. As one woman put it when asked at age 50 whether she thought she had changed since early adulthood: "I'm fatter, lazier, and enjoying life more, but otherwise I'm the same me I used to be." Sense of identity seldom changes sharply in the middle years, yet often the person acquires interpersonal skills, confidence, and insight, imperceptibly yet cumulatively, so that over a decade or more the change in personality will be very striking to those who have not seen the person for some years. Role failures and personal disasters may also produce changes of a more negative sort.

Even though they are unaware of it, many people change over the years, some a little and some a lot. The Berkeley studies again give us the most compelling evidence in a series of reports covering change over the past 25 years, as additional assessments of the study members have been made.

In *Lives Through Time,* Block and Haan developed a typology that was based on the functioning of the study members in adolescence and in their thirties. About a fourth of the men and women were judged effective and well adjusted both in adolescence and in their thirties. In both periods they were seen as dependable, productive, poised, and sympathetic persons. Another group had had difficulties in adolescence (lacked controls, were negativistic, or were self-defensive), but became competent and dependable persons by midlife. Yet others who had had problems in adolescence continued to have difficulties as adults. Undercontrolled, rebellious adolescents who had had little insight into their motivations often dropped out of school early. Many seemed unable to find an appropriate job, and both men and women made conflictful marriages from which they subsequently divorced. By their thirties they began to look like losers. Some escaped into dependence on alcohol; others found other equally self-defeating modes of coping. Thus there were both elements of stability and elements of change between adolescent personality and personality in the late thirties.[54]

The same tendencies persist through the forties and fifties. It appears that there is somewhat more change in the thirties than in the forties, with individual stability highest on those dimensions of personality that relate to intellectual interest and values.[55] Even in their forties, however, some men and women "found themselves"—often thanks to a new marital partner—while a few seemed to deteriorate. Perhaps the sharpest change in the middle years, as evidenced in the Berkeley data, is an increase for both men and women in openness to knowing themselves, becoming more insightful, introspective, and less conventional and self-defensive.

Further evidence of change through the adult years comes from George Vaillant's study of Harvard men followed from their college years until their early fifties.[56] Many expressed markedly different views of themselves and of their values in later middle life than when at Harvard, but very few realized they had changed. In memory they reconstructed their early lives to fit their present views. Though most had been highly successful, not all were content with their lives. A few men were dissatisfied with their careers, others with their families. Some men had few friends and used alcohol and tranquillizers heavily.

Vaillant compared the men who had experienced warm family relationships and close friendships (we might call them "generative and friendly") with a small group who had neither successful marriages nor close friends ("isolated and lonely"), in terms of their early experience. Very few of the friendly men had been seen as maladjusted in adolescence, but nearly two thirds of the lonely ones had been so rated. The lonely men more often came from conflicted childhood family environments. They were more often distant from their parents and from their own children (but fewer had children). They were more driven; they far less often took vacations. They also were much more likely to suffer from chronic ailments and from psychiatric illness. Thus at age 52 there were persisting links with childhood and adolescence. Yet *some* of the friendly men had come from backgrounds that were more characteristic of the lonely, isolated men and vice versa. Personalities appear to change far more than the person's sense of identity, and such change goes on to some degree throughout life.

The demands of marriage, of parenting, and of occupational roles draw differentially on early life experience at different periods. In an analysis of "uses of the past," Peskin and Livson, drawing on the Berkeley data, have examined how characteristics measured in adolescence relate to the functioning of men and women at various stages of adult life.[57] They note that adolescent personality attributes are drawn upon more by mothers of young children who face a role toward which they were oriented in adolescence than by mothers whose children are older. Conversely, men at 30 are faced with occupational demands which have little resemblance to their adolescent orientations, and their adaptive strategies show little relationship to their adolescent personalities. Yet at 40 they show much greater use of their adolescent proclivities in adaptation. There is not, then, a simple, consistent relationship between early experience and later experience. Instead, there is a constant reweaving of personality dispositions to produce the patterned responses that characterize a given period or set of situational demands.

The findings from longitudinal research also strongly support the generalization drawn from cross-sectional studies that in the middle years men and women become more concerned with their inner life and less preoccupied with striving. There is evidence of another, related finding: Many men become more nurturant, more expressive of their feelings of tenderness, while women seem to shift in the opposite direction. This shift appears to begin in the middle years and to be accentuated in old age. We shall have more to say about it in the next chapter.

Leisure Activities

Leisure activities are pursued for the pleasures they bring, whether in self-expression, in escape from boredom or drudgery, or in simply seeking relaxation. Over the life course there will be shifts in many leisure activities and a fair degree of stability in others. In adolescence, a very high proportion of both sexes will participate in such activities as dancing, sports, vigorous outdoor activities, and attending movies. Surveys of the general population indicate that these activities will tend to diminish through the early and middle adult years, and indeed, the level of overall leisure-time activity for most individuals will never again equal that of adolescence.[58] But there are leisure activities that drop off only slightly over the life span, such as participation in discussions, television viewing, entertaining, and a variety of cultural activities.

A few activities peak in the early and middle adult years. These include club memberships, home embellishment (decorating, building, garden and yard work, etc.), and spectator sports. Solitary relaxation is one of the few leisure activities that shows a pronounced increase in the middle years. Cooking for pleasure is another, but only on the part of men. The middle years see a rising level of cooking by men and a declining level by women (but in every age group through 75 and up, women are nevertheless more likely to cook for themselves and for others).

Heavy involvement in leisure activities (as contrasted with work and family activities) tends to occur among men who have low occupational aspirations or who have given up the struggle to advance in their careers. They often turn to home hobbies or to relatively passive activities such as television watching. On the other hand, highly successful men are more heavily involved in organizations and in community activities, as previously noted.

Thus survey data that report frequencies of participation in leisure activities over the life course mask great individual and social-class differences. In general, we

can say that leisure activities tend to center more on the home in the middle years
and to be less intensely involving than at earlier periods of life.

Life Satisfaction and Happiness
in the Middle Years

For some men and women, especially in the upper-middle class, their forties
and early fifties are seen as the most satisfying time of life; for others, especially in
the working class, the forties and fifties are decidedly downhill. They are much
more likely to see their twenties as the best time of life. Studies of life satisfaction
and happiness over the whole adult life show some perplexing patterns. In general,
reported life satisfaction goes up with each decade, at least until the sixties. Yet
older people less often report themselves "very happy."[59] One might expect that
being satisfied would also mean being happy, but clearly the two words have different connotations. To be happy seems to imply zest and fun in life; to be satisfied is
to feel a reasonable balance between needs and need fullfillment. We might expect
that those who are healthy and reasonably well off in their later middle years would
be not only satisfied but happy as well. And this is indeed the case. The curve of
happiness stays high for these fortunate people.[60]

Life Stages in the Middle Years

It is difficult to recognize any clear-cut stages in the middle years. Physical
aging begins to affect health status and vigor; peak strength and energy begin to decline, but there are no critical events in the process. A woman may be referred to as
premenopausal or postmenopausal but that tells us little about her activities or life
satisfactions. Becoming a grandparent can be very important to some men and to
more women in the later middle years. In general, however, life satisfaction continues to rest largely on the current state of one's family and work roles and on
one's health and the health of one's spouse. Timetables become less important as
rites of passage become less frequent.

There is little indication of an age-40 transition or of an age-50 transition.
The transitions that are reported to be most significant to middle-aged men and
women in recent decades are divorce, job loss, long-distance moves that disrupt
close relationships (especially for women), and deaths of family members. Another
source of concern mentioned by many middle-aged men and women is that their
adolescent or young-adult children are having difficulty in finding themselves. None
of these transitions or concerns is tied to age as such: They may define periods of
lesser or greater satisfaction, but they do not define life stages.

Culture and Cohort Cautions

In discussing the middle years, I have confined attention almost exclusively
to the middle years in urban industrial society. Anthropological studies have dealt
much more fully with childhood, adolescence, early adulthood, and old age in other

societies than they have with middle age. We noted that the duration of middle age is itself a feature of urban industrial society. A majority of people now die in old age in the United States, but that is not true of most of the world's population.

We must note, moreover, that the roles available to men and women differ vastly in different societies, and the meanings and satisfactions of the middle years will vary accordingly. Cohort experiences may have like effects. A severe depression may displace millions of middle-aged workers, many of whom will never again have a secure job. A war that kills a high percentage of young men, as World War I did in France, Great Britain, and Germany and World War II did in Germany and Russia, will bring unfulfilled lives to many women, who can never hope to marry. The middle years will be very different from those here described.

The middle years are, in our society, the years when home becomes increasingly the center of leisure activity, the place of relaxation. Imperceptibly, the middle years shade into old age. For some, there is the beginning of drawing back from taxing involvements, often including retirement from work; for others there is the staving off of retirement itself. For all, there is the recognition that changes are coming.

NOTES

1. Bernice Neugarten, "Adult Personality: Toward a Psychology of the Life Cycle," in B. Neugarten, ed., *Middle Age and Aging* (Chicago: University of Chicago Press, 1968), p. 144.
2. Bernice Neugarten, "The Awareness of Middle Age," in Neugarten, ed., *Middle Age and Aging*, pp. 93–98.
3. Marjorie Fiske Lowenthal, Majda Thurner, and David Chiriboga, *Four Stages of Life* (San Francisco, CA: Jossey Bass Publishers, 1976), pp. 138–44.
4. Ruth B. Weg, "Changing Physiology of Aging: Normal and Pathological," in Diana S. Woodruff and James E. Birren, eds., *Aging: Scientific Perspectives and Social Issues* (New York: Van Nostrand Co., 1975), p. 233.
5. Ibid., p. 234.
6. Ethel Shanas and George L. Maddox, "Aging, Health and the Organization of Health Resources," in Robert Binstock and Ethel Shanas, eds., *Handbook of Aging and the Social Sciences* (New York: Van Nostrand Reinhold Co., 1976), p. 602.
7. Ibid.
8. Ibid., p. 603.
9. Weg, "Changing Physiology," p. 237.
10. Alice S. Rossi, "Aging and Parenthood in the Middle Years," in Paul Baltes and O. G. Brim, Jr., eds., *Life Span Development and Behavior,* vol. 3 (New York: Academic Press, 1980), pp. 137–205.
11. Alfred C. Kinsey, Wardell B. Pomeroy, and Clyde E. Martin, *Sexual Behavior in the Human Male* (Philadelphia: W. B. Saunders Co., 1948). See also William H. Masters and Virginia Johnson, *Human Sexual Response* (Boston: Little, Brown and Co., 1966).
12. Bernice L. Neugarten et al., "Women's Attitudes toward the Menopause," *Vita Humana,* 6 (1963), 140–51.
13. Lillian B. Rubin, *Women of a Certain Age: The Midlife Search for Self* (New York: Harper and Row, 1979), Chapter 4.
14. Masters and Johnson, *Human Sexual Response.*
15. Judith L. Laws, "Female Sexuality through the Life Span," in Baltes and Brim, eds., *Life Span Development,* pp. 207–52.

16. Dorothy Eichorn, Jane Hunt, and Marjorie Honzik, "Experience, Personality and IQ: Adolescence to Middle Age," in D. Eichorn et al., eds., *Present and Past in Middle Life* (New York: Academic Press, 1981), pp. 89–116.
17. Paul B. Baltes and Gisella Labouvie, "Adult Development of Intellectual Performance: Description, Explanation and Modification," in Carl Eisdorfer and M. P. Lawton, eds., *The Psychology of Adult Development and Aging* (Washington, D.C.: American Psychological Association, 1973), p. 166.
18. Eichorn et al., "Experience, Personality and IQ," p. 93.
19. Ibid., pp. 102–5.
20. Melvin L. Kohn and Carmi Schooler, *Work and Personality* (Norwood, NJ: Ablex Publishing Co., 1983).
21. Eichorn et al., eds., "Experience, Personality and IQ," p. 106.
22. Ibid., p. 112.
23. Ibid., p. 113.
24. Claude S. Fischer, *To Dwell Among Friends: Personal Networks in Town and City* (Chicago: University of Chicago Press, 1982).
25. Ibid., p. 253.
26. Harold Wilensky, "Life Cycle, Work Situation and Participation in Formal Organizations" in Robert Kleemeier, ed., *Aging and Leisure: Research Perspectives and the Meaningful Use of Time* (New York: Oxford Press, 1961), pp. 213–42.
27. Rubin, *Women of a Certain Age*. See especially the Preface.
28. Janice Stroud, "Women's Careers: Work, Family and Personality" in Eichorn et al., eds., *Present and Past*.
29. Ronald Kessler and James McRae, Jr., "The Effect of Wives' Employment on the Mental Health of Married Men and Women," *American Sociological Review*, 47 (1982), 216–27. Also Catherine Ross, John Mirowsky, and J. Haber, "Dividing Work, Sharing Work, and In-Between: Marriage Patterns and Depression," *American Sociological Review*, 48 (1983), 809–23.
30. John C. Henretta and Angela O'Rand, "Joint Retirement in the Dual Worker Family," *Social Forces*, 62 (1983), 504–20.
31. One of the largest studies is H. S. Parnes et al., *The Pre-Retirement Years*, vol. 4 (Washington, DC: U.S. Government Printing Office, 1975).
32. J. A. Clausen, "Men's Occupational Careers in the Middle Years," in Eichorn et al., eds., *Present and Past*, pp. 321-51.
33. Ibid. The same findings are reported in H. S. Parnes et al., *The Pre-Retirement Years: A Longitudinal Study of the Labor Market Experience of Men*, vol. 4 (Washington, DC: Government Printing Office, 1975), pp. 104-11.
34. See, for example, Seymour Wolfbein, *Work in American Society* (Glenview, IL: Scott, Foresman and Company, 1971), p. 46.
35. M. W. Lear, "Is There a Male Menopause?" *New York Times Magazine*, January 28, 1973. Cited by O. G. Brim, Jr., "Theories of the Male Mid-life Crisis," *Counseling Psychologist*, 6 (1976). Brim's review of the theories and evidence then available gives a well-balanced analysis. Much more evidence is now available, almost all of it raising serious doubts about the prevalence of a midlife crisis.
36. Elliott Jacques, "Death and the Mid-life Crisis," *International Journal of Psychoanalysis*, 46 (1965), 502-14.
37. Ibid., p. 506.
38. John Riley, "Death and the Meanings of Death: Sociological Inquiries" in *Annual Review of Sociology*, vol. 9 (Palo Alto, CA: Annual Reviews, Inc., 1983), p. 196.
39. Daniel J. Levinson, *The Seasons of a Man's Life* (New York: Alfred Knopf, 1978), p. 191.
40. Ibid., p. 60.
41. M. M. Weissman and J. K. Myers, "Rates and Risks of Depressive Symptoms in a United States Urban Community," *Acta Psychiatric Scandunavica*, 57 (1978), 219-31.

42. Mary C. Jones, "Midlife Drinking Patterns: Correlates and Antecedents," in Eichorn et al., eds., *Present and Past*, pp. 223–42.
43. Seymour B. Sarason, *Work, Aging and Social Change: Professionals and the One-Life-One Career Imperative* (New York: The Free Press, 1977).
44. Ibid., Chapter 11.
45. Gary Gottfredson, "Career Stability and Redirection in Adulthood," Report No. 219, Center for Social Organization of Schools (Baltimore: Johns Hopkins University, 1976).
46. Parnes et al., *The Pre-Retirement Years,* vol. 4, p. 120.
47. Douglas Bray and Ann Howard, "Career Success and Life Satisfactions of Middle-Aged Managers," in L. A. Bond and J. C. Rosen, eds., *Competence and Coping during Adulthood* (Hanover, NH: University Press of New England, 1980), pp. 258–87.
48. Cyril Sofer, *Men in Mid-Career, A Study of British Managers and Technical Specialists* (Cambridge, Eng.: Cambridge University Press, 1970).
49. H. S. Parnes, ed., *Work and Retirement: A Longitudinal Study of Men* (Cambridge, MA: The MIT Press, 1981), p. 207.
50. Ibid., p. 150.
51. Ibid., p. 206.
52. National Academy of Sciences, *Bereavement: Reactions, Consequences and Care* (Washington, DC: National Academy Press, 1984).
53. Erik Erikson, *Childhood and Society* (New York: Norton, 1950), p. 231.
54. Jack Block and Norma Haan, *Lives Through Time* (Berkeley, CA: Bancroft Press, 1972).
55. Norma Haan, "Common Dimensions of Personality Development: Early Adolescence to Middle Life," in Eichorn et al., eds., *Present and Past*, pp. 117–51.
56. George Vaillant, *Adaptation to Life* (Boston, MA: Little, Brown, and Co., 1977).
57. H. Peskin and N. Livson, "Uses of the Past in Adult Psychological Health," in Eichorn et al., eds., *Present and Past*, pp. 153–81.
58. Chad Gordon and C. M. Gaitz, "Leisure and Lives: Personal Expressivity Across the Life Span," in R. H. Binstock and E. Shanas, eds., *Handbook of Aging and the Social Sciences* (New York: Van Nostrand Reinhold Company, 1976), pp. 310–41.
59. A. Campbell, P. E. Converse, and W. L. Rogers, *The Quality of Life* (New York: Russell Sage Foundation, 1976), pp. 150–69.
60. Ibid., p. 167.

CHAPTER 9
THE LATER YEARS

Time goes, you say? Ah no!
Alas, time stays, we go.
Henry Austin Dobson

Throughout most of human existence, only a small proportion of men and women ever attained what we euphemistically call "the later years." Even today, in many less-developed societies, the average expectation of life at birth is less than 50 years. A fifth of all infants do not attain the age of one, and deaths from contagious diseases and injuries end many more lives before middle adulthood.

Only in recent years and in the most industrially developed nations does one find a majority of deaths occurring to persons over 65.[1] But it is not only the likelihood of survival that varies historically and culturally; the meaning of old age is itself subject to complete transformations in different cultures. The United States is a young nation, one that promotes youthful pursuits and glorifies youthful bodies. Old age is a nuisance, and old people themselves may be seen as nuisances. Yet in the half century since Franklin Roosevelt's New Deal provided for Social Security, and especially in the 20 years since older Americans became eligible for national medical insurance (Medicare), the status of the old has been changing. For one thing, there are now enough old people to have political clout, and they tend to use their votes. For another, the image of the older person has been changing from that of a relatively infirm, sexless, and all but useless hanger-on to an active, engaged, and still-contributing member of society.

As physical strength becomes less important in daily life, and as a higher proportion of old people have become economically self-sufficient, the old are less often a burden. Nevertheless, old age in the United States does not command the respect that it does in most Eastern cultures, where the old are revered for their wisdom and often retain authority over their adult children.[2] At the other extreme, however, there are societies—particularly nomadic societies—where the old present so great a problem that they are ultimately abandoned. Among the Siriono, for example, the old and infirm are simply left behind when resettlement is necessary because of depleted game and wild crops.[3]

Old Age as a Life Stage

From infancy through the middle years, most of the expectable transitions that go with increasing age entail learning new roles and reaping valued rewards. The socialization process continues from childhood into the later years. But for older persons there is less prospect of taking on new roles than of giving up roles long held, of yielding power and influence to younger cohorts or generations. Irving Rosow, a sociologist whose career has been largely devoted to the study of adult socialization and the aged, notes that the role changes anticipated with old age have largely negative consequences: The old are devalued; they are often seen as stereotypes rather than as individuals; they are excluded from many opportunities for social participation; they lose their major work and family roles through retirement and widowhood; and the primary role remaining to many such people is unstructured and ambiguous, not serving as a basis for maintaining a positive identity.[4] Moreover, few formal mechanisms of socialization are available to prepare people for their status of old man or old woman.

Roles entail obligations or tasks and privileges. Old age would seem to entail no special tasks except those required to maintain oneself, one's ties with others, and one's sense of identity and worth. And the privileges of the old are not derived from being old, but from being something more than old. Old age in itself tells us little about a person, nor does it define a role except as the role is ascribed by others. Many persons continue very active lives; some learn new skills and pursue new interests in old age. Creative contributions to the arts and sciences tend to come from young adults, yet Grandma Moses began to paint and became a world-famous artist in her eighties. Verdi wrote *Othello,* one of his greatest operas, at the age of 80. And in many nations political leaders have held top power into their late seventies and beyond.

To hold onto one's major roles and activities as long as possible is, then, one option for life in the late years. Another option is to disengage, to yield demanding roles and activities and to take life easy. The fortunate may seek relaxation and leisure, free from responsibility to all but their closest friends and family. The Sun Belt, and especially Florida and California, have absorbed millions of older Americans seeking not only to escape from cold winters but also to find a new style of relaxed living. Others choose to live in retirement communities in other areas of the country. Most, however, remain in the homes where they have spent their middle years.

Perhaps no other age stratum experiences as great a diversity of life-styles as do persons over 65 in modern industrial society. Many are economically comfortable, yet roughly one in seven falls below the poverty line in terms of income.[5] Groups of tourists largely comprised of older citizens fill the Sistine Chapel in Rome, wander through the Acropolis in Athens, and flock to hundreds of other sites that are daily ringed by tour buses. Yet other older folk seldom travel more than a few miles from the communities in which they have spent their lives. Some well-to-do older persons prefer to live in splendid isolation with like-minded "senior citizens." Others prefer to have contact with the young. Thus both preferences and actual life-styles vary so widely as to defy any blanket description. Some commentators deplore the plight of the elderly; others point out that for many older people, life was never more pleasant.

Life Expectancy and Societal Development

At the turn of the century, a child born in the United States had a life expectancy of about 50 years. Men and women differed little in how long they might expect to live. Relatively high birth rates, coupled with the moderately high death rate in the early and middle adult years, kept the proportion of persons over 65 relatively low—4.1 percent in 1900, and only 5.4 percent in 1930. By 1980, life expectancy had increased to 70 years for males and 78 years for females.[6] Concurrently, birth rates had dropped appreciably. As a consequence, persons over age 65 now make up over 10 percent of the population. And for every 100 men over 65 there are now 125 women. If present trends in differential life expectancy of men and women continue, by the year 2000 there will be 150 women per 100 men over 65 and 250 women per 100 men over 85.[7]

The aging of the population has been due largely to advances in public health and medicine. Fortunately, increased industrial productivity has made it possible to provide retirement benefits for most older workers, relieving them of the need to continue working. In 1900 less than 10 percent of workers over 65 had any kind of retirement pension; even in 1950, most men over 65 continued to work at a regular job. By 1980, a majority were retiring by age 65, and many even earlier. But as the proportion of older persons increases still further, and the proportion of the population of working age decreases, the economic burden of sustaining older persons will become much greater. We have all heard discussion of the problems of funding Social Security and Medicare over the long haul. They are just one part of the process of societal adaptation to our changing population structure and the impact it will have on future cohorts of Americans.

Housing needs of the aged will inevitably receive more attention in the future as the number of infirm survivors into the later years increases. The aged will constitute an increasingly important market for entrepreneurs of all types. The changes that take place in the general social fabric of the United States will be considerable, but those coming in the developing nations—somewhat later, it is true—will be even more far-reaching. We must keep in mind, throughout our consideration of the later years, that the life course will be lived out in a changing world, with many of the changes attributable directly to the increasing proportion of older persons.[8]

PHYSICAL AND PSYCHOLOGICAL CHANGE IN THE LATER YEARS

Life satisfaction at any given age or stage in life tends to be linked to successful accomplishment in the central roles and most salient tasks of that period. In early adulthood the establishment of competent autonomy and intimacy with the opposite sex is likely to be most highly related to general satisfaction. A little later, satisfaction in the occupational and marital roles accounts for the larger part of general life satisfaction. Health is largely taken for granted in early and middle adulthood, and it figures strongly in life satisfaction only for that small fraction of the population that suffers from serious disease or impairment. But in the later years, especially as major roles are impaired or lost, the perception of one's health becomes the single most important influence on life satisfaction.[9] Even if a person is in good health at 70, friends are crippled with arthritis, have heart problems or other conditions that limit activity, or they are dying at a rate that makes health a central concern.

A few lucky individuals maintain robust health into their eighties, with perhaps no deficit more serious than a hearing impairment. They still climb up one or even two flights of stairs rather than taking the elevator. They outperform men and women 20 years younger than themselves. But these are the rare ones. Far more often the aches and pains of an aging body lead to taking it easy, complaining a bit, but acknowledging that to be aching is still better than the alternative of no longer being a part of the scene.

Health and Illness after 65

As we noted in the previous chapter, chronic ailments and impairments tend to build up in the later middle years. Whereas less than a fifth of persons 45–64 experience significant restriction of activity, the proportion rises to roughly half in the 65-and-over group. Both the number of days per year that older persons are unable to carry out normal activities and days of confinement to bed roughly double in the 65-and-over group.[10] Women tend to have more illness and impairments than men, but they are also more likely to report themselves in good health. Older persons are somewhat less likely than younger ones to experience acute illnesses (such as respiratory infections, for example) but when they do get sick, the consequences tend to be more serious. Days of restricted activity due to acute illnesses are about the same for young and old, but are lower in the middle years.[11]

Chronic diseases of the heart and circulatory system afflict more than half of the over-65 population, with hypertensive heart disease (i.e., due to high blood pressure) and coronary artery disease most often involved.[12] Strokes (cerebral hemorrhages or blockages) also become a major cause of impairment and death, especially in the years beyond 75. Cancer also takes a high toll. Less life-threatening but almost as prevalent as heart disease is arthritis, which afflicts approximately half those over 65.

Despite the great increase in life-threatening conditions after age 65 or 70, most older people tend to view their health as reasonably good. Indeed, nearly two thirds regard themselves as better off than most of their peers![13] Symptoms and impairment influence older people's subjective assessments of their health, but having personal and social resources and being able to engage in at least some of the activities that are important to them substantially raises their ratings of their own health. It would seem that even when people have health problems, the mere fact of survival may lead them to see themselves as better off than they had anticipated.

This helps to explain why reports of life satisfaction tend to be high in the later years. Nothing else seems quite as important as feeling that one is reasonably healthy. Severely impaired persons or those suffering from persistent pain are, however, more likely to acknowledge that they are not in good health, and they are likely to report low life satisfaction as well. Severe impairment is frequently accompanied by bouts of psychological depression. Depression may also result from the loss of loved ones and from the feeling that one is useless. High rates of suicide tend to be one result. But the most vexing problems of ill health tend to be related to organic changes in the brain itself.

Mental disorders due to hardening of the arteries and other consequences of aging occur with high frequency among the very old, but perhaps no condition is more feared by the aged than Alzheimer's disease. Alzheimer's disease may occur at any age beyond the midforties, but is far more prevalent after 65.[14] The so-called functional psychoses are disorders of the young and middle adult years and occur with diminishing frequency in persons over 50. On the other hand, mental disorder due to degenerative diseases of the central nervous system (often in combination with life stress) account for more than three quarters of all dementia in persons 65 years of age and older.

The manifestations of Alzheimer's disease usually come gradually over a period of several years, beginning with a loss of memory for recent events and an inability to mobilize one's intellectual processes. Events that occurred only a few minutes earlier may be totally forgotten. Judgment is impaired. Simple tasks become increasingly difficult. Emotional upsets and paranoid delusions occur frequently. Ultimately, even one's closest loved ones may not be recognized. Yet the body may remain intact for years. The spouse, children, and friends of the patient will be those who suffer most as they see a beloved person gradually lose almost all human attributes. To all intents and purposes the later stages of Alzheimer's disease terminate the effective life course.

Change of life circumstances due to loss of a loved one, moving from a long-time home, and especially moving into a nursing home can trigger emotional and physiological responses that lead to a high probability of death.[15] In old age the homeostatic processes (self-regulating mechanisms) that maintain equilibrium within the organism become less effective. The older person is therefore more vulnerable to unexpected changes. For some older persons, maintaining a relatively invariant regime seems to offer a measure of security, but by the same token, such people are more threatened when they cannot hold to their routine activities.

Cognitive Abilities in the Later Years

As we noted in the previous chapter, cross-sectional studies show superior performance on intelligence tests by younger cohorts at any given age level through the middle years, but this differential disappears if we compare persons at the same educational and social status levels. This continues to be true even into the seventies. Intellectual power or reasoning ability diminishes only slightly if at all in the later years among persons in good health. Some show declines, but a few actually show gains beyond age 80. Again we note great variation among individuals. Some 80-year-olds are not only wise but are intellectually vigorous and creative. Others are intellectually uninvolved; they seem less interested in their world and less interesting to their associates. Hypertension—high blood pressure—appears to be a major factor in explaining why some persons show significant declines in measured intelligence in the later years. A 10-year follow-up study found that persons with high blood pressure (who would tend to suffer from arteriosclerosis) showed much greater declines in both verbal and performance areas of intelligence between their sixties and seventies than did those with normal blood pressure.[16]

Most older persons do substantially less well on tests requiring rapid completion. They appear to be less prone to guess answers about which they are unsure, which has been suggested as one explanation of their poorer performance.[17] There is also much evidence that retrieval of information from the brain's memory bank is a slower process, in which case responses inevitably take longer.[18]

Most older persons are aware of greater difficulty in recalling names and events from the past, though some report much sharper memories of their early lives. When those reported memories are compared with other available information derived from the period of their early lives that is in question, it is frequently found that the vivid memories are constructions of the later years, not valid representations of the past. As persons review their lives and reminisce about the past, they draw upon bits of information from a vast storehouse of memories. Unlike a computer tape or disk, the human brain does not have its data catalogued and organized in subfiles that can be easily distinguished. The running together of memories of different events and circumstances becomes most apparent when old-timers get together at reunions or when older husbands and wives reminisce about their lives together 40 or 50 years previously. Sometimes their faulty reconstructions can be a source of mutual hilarity; sometimes they can lead to anxiety about what may lie ahead.

It must be emphasized that when decrements in intelligence do occur, on the average in the seventies and eighties, they are often associated with poor health.

Survivors among those followed up for retesting generally prove to have had higher scores at the previous testing than those who died in the intervening period.[19] Indeed, for many persons, great declines appear to occur in the year or so preceding death. The human organism is a functioning whole, and body and mind are perhaps more closely linked in functional capacities as the end of life approaches.

RETIREMENT: THEME AND VARIATIONS

In the same sense in which 40 marks the beginning of middle age for many Americans, 65 marks the beginning of old age because it has come to be regarded as the age when a man's occupational career ends. For workers who have struggled through life in relatively unrewarding jobs, the prospect of being able to get along modestly well without working as they approach old age can be a heartening one in any society. In the People's Republic of China, more than a decade ago, I asked a retired factory worker (through an American interpreter) which was best, to be retired or to be working. His answer was more complex than I expected, for he explained that in the days before the liberation of China by Mao and his Communist forces, workers received no consideration and there was no possibility of retirement. But now, he said, a worker is respected while he works and is able to retire when he grows old. "In the old days, a day went like a year; now a year goes like a day." He was indeed glad he could retire, and if he added a political slant to his reply, it was stated gravely and with a deep sense of gratitude for the changes that had occurred.

Many elderly Americans felt that way, too, when the United States finally caught up with most of Western Europe by providing a governmental program of Social Security in the 1930s. Prior to that time only a few occupations carried retirement benefits, and these were largely within the domains of military or other governmental services, education, or at the upper echelons of business and industry. The meaning of retirement—whether a man or woman retires joyfully, with regret, or not at all—depends on the reasons for retirement, on a family's economic circumstances, and on the extent to which the person's sense of identity and of purpose in life was linked to the occupational role. As we noted in the last chapter, early retirement may occur when health is poor, or when a person is in good health, is reasonably well off, and has other activities in mind for the later years. Retirement at the "normal" age of 65 was until 1979 mandatory for many workers in industry, education, and state and local governments.[20] Federal workers could work until 70, but could also retire with full benefits as early as 62. In 1979 a federal law was enacted raising to 70 the age of mandatory retirement for most workers in the private sector. But even under the earlier ages for mandatory retirement that prevailed prior to 1982, only a very small proportion of men were forced out of work against their wishes. The great majority who retired at the time specified for mandatory retirement were apparently ready for this major transition. Only about one in 20 expressed interest in staying on the job full-time or seeking another job. Despite the high level of job satisfaction expressed by most older men, termination of this central role was not highly stressful, probably because it was an expected transition and one that promised increased leisure and relaxed enjoyment of the years remaining.

Most retirees now report that they are pleased with their experience after retirement, but those who retired because of poor health are obviously less pleased than those who retain good health. Men whose jobs have been the primary source of purpose in life are likely either to arrange to work part-time or to find some other significant activity in which to invest themselves. Some work as volunteers, some continue to practice their professions on a reduced schedule or to serve as consultants, some establish their own small-scale business enterprises (though this occurs more often among men who retire early). The higher a man's or a woman's educational level and occupational status, the more likely they are to stay active in the labor market, but even among those with a college education, fewer than one man in four or one woman in 10 in the age 65-to-70 bracket continues to work full-time.[21]

Beyond 70, only those whose work is a major source of personal satisfaction are likely to be found in the labor force, and they will usually be working on their own terms, often after a formal retirement. Those who continue to practice rewarding professions or to hold positions of high prestige in business or government have a good deal of latitude in how heavily they remain involved. A physician who says, "I cannot think of myself except as a physician and I cannot imagine ever totally giving up the practice of medicine" may nevertheless take in a younger partner or, if already in a group practice, may begin to take off several days each week. An emeritus professor can teach an occasional course (often at some other university than the one from which he retired), can continue research, or perhaps write a textbook.

Accepting retirement may be most difficult for those men who hold great power. In the business world a few men hold on as board chairmen well into their seventies, often exerting a controlling influence on the choice and tenure of corporation officers, ousting men much younger than themselves. And in the Congress of the United States one finds both senators and representatives who seek reelection well into their seventies and eighties, despite the grueling requirements of campaigning and the pressures of the offices themselves. Some men and women who have held high office do, of course, decide that they have had their say. The high proportion who seek to hold on, however, suggests that either the quest for power or a sense of mission has been of extraordinary importance to those oldsters who continue to seek elective office.

ASPECTS OF SUCCESSFUL AGING

The yielding of one's occupational role does not appear to threaten one's sense of identity or self-esteem except for a very small group of men and women, though some will feel less useful after retirement. But other role losses and situational changes must be faced, and they are not predictable in the way that retirement is. Beyond age 65, one's friends begin to disappear from the scene. By 75, roughly seven women in ten will have become widows, and one man in four will have lost his wife. Ill health becomes even more likely. Many older persons must leave the homes they had built or had at least furnished to suit their needs and tastes. They take up residence in quarters easier to maintain, and some will move to institutional settings where they can be looked after by others. All these losses are highly stressful, and the margin of reserve for dealing with stress is constantly diminishing.

Successful aging would seem to call for a combination of good fortune and good adaptive capacity. Older persons have fewer options than younger ones to change their life situations. In the later years a great many difficult situations will be encountered about which nothing can be done. Adaptation is required, and in the last analysis, adaptation demands acceptance, even resignation, without yielding one's sense of who one is and what one's life has been.

Integrity versus Despair

Erikson writes of the critical task of old age as entailing the resolution of *integrity* versus *despair*. The more fortunate a person is in maintaining health, having loved ones available, and being respected for past accomplishments, the easier it is to keep a sense of integrity. Personality remains embedded in a social network to the end, but obviously the network alone does not insure integrity. A pain-wracked body or a mind drifting in distant memories may betray the most beloved and revered person. Yet up to that point, social supports help to maintain the integrity and identity of earlier years.

Strength in the aged takes the form of wisdom, Erikson notes. One continues to draw on one's experience, aware of the relativity of that experience, maintaining mature judgment and understanding. We must be able to accept our own lives, without bitterness or rancor, even when we know we have made mistakes or have been treated badly. In Erikson's words: "Wisdom . . . is a detached and yet active concern with life in the face of death."[22]

Under what circumstances are men and women most likely to experience a sense of integrity and to avoid despair in their later years? Here students of old age have somewhat diverse opinions. There are several issues to consider. Perhaps the one that has been of greatest concern to theorists is the question of continued high involvement versus "disengagement" in the later years.

Social Involvement versus Disengagement

In 1961, a sociologist, Elaine Cumming, and a psychologist, William Henry, set forth a bold theory stating that successful aging, both from the individual's perspective and that of the society, required gradual withdrawal from social ties and activities.[23] Disengagement, they said, served society by making way for succeeding cohorts to take over. It served individuals by releasing them from normative demands that otherwise would become more onerous as personality changes of the later years set in. Older people needed to be able to escape time constraints, pressures for neatness and cleanliness, and proper decorum.

Many, indeed most, students of aging disagreed with Cumming and Henry.[24] Role loss in old age is to a degree inevitable, but most research suggests that mental health and life satisfaction are higher among people who remain firmly integrated into society than among the isolated and disengaged. But the adage "different strokes for different folks" holds for older persons as it does for younger. A measure of disengagement suits some people very well, while others would be miserable. A major problem is that too many older persons, especially those who have lost their husbands or wives and who are no longer employed, find that their main ties to the society no longer exist.

Older men and women with few active social roles or a low level of interaction with others show a substantially higher level of psychiatric impairment and much lower life satisfaction than those who are more active socially or who occupy meaningful roles.[25] Yet if the less active have at least one person with whom they can talk intimately about themselves and their problems, role loss and low levels of interaction with others are of little consequence. It does not matter whether it is a friend, a husband or wife, or a son or daughter; a close confidant is perhaps the best insurance against feeling depressed and useless that can be found. The probability of having a confidant is of course enhanced by having one's children nearby or living in a community where there are lots of other persons of similar age.

Housing and Living Arrangements

By age 60, more than 70 percent of the population live in homes that they own (though some will still be making mortage payments).[26] Most older couples will have acquired a house in their thirties or forties. As a consequence, most live in older houses that are in less good condition and have a lower value than houses being acquired by persons in their middle years.

Residential mobility is highest in the early adult years but drops off in later middle age; only about a third of the population aged 55–64 moves in a five-year period, as against nearly 80 percent through the twenties. High residential stability continues for survivors into the seventies and eighties, but some older persons give up their homes and go into rented apartments or smaller condominiums. Widows may move in with children (most often with daughters) or other relatives. Maintenance of a house may require a considerable measure of physical well-being if income is insufficient to hire help. Men and women who have lost a spouse are considerably more likely to move than those whose marriages are intact.

Most older people try to maintain an independent household as long as possible, and they are reluctant to move from homes they have occupied for many years.[27] The round of daily life is tied in with neighborhood friends and institutions. For people who have occupied their own homes for more than 20 years (as a high proportion of the 65-and-over population has), there is not only the matter of a known quality of life, but also memories of happy times when the children were growing up. Moreover, the tasks of household maintenance and perhaps a garden in which to exercise creative interests as well as bodies help give structure and even a bit of challenge to life. The extra space available in a home that no longer regularly houses children can permit visits by children who live at a distance.

Ultimately, most persons who live well beyond 80 will give up their homes, but the psychological wrench then is likely to be very severe. Identity has often become closely tied not only to persons but to a place and a way of life that must now be given up.

Widowhood

In the last chapter we noted that roughly a fourth of all married women will become widows before their sixty-fifth birthday. Half the remaining married women will be widowed between 65 and 75. In the same age span one man in five will lose his wife.[28] For women, then, who can expect to live into the late seventies, widowhood must be considered a phase of the expectable life course. To be widowed in the later years is to suffer a serious threat to one's way of life, but because it is something that most women have had to recognize as a probable event in their lives, it appears to be less devastating than early widowhood.

In most societies, including our own even after the advent of the women's movement, a woman's status and her sense of identity are strongly linked to the status and to the person of her husband.[29] Husbands have most often been the primary source of economic security and have usually performed the heavier tasks of household maintenance and repair. Moreover, once their children are grown, many women lavish care and attention upon their husbands, nursing them through illnesses, keeping them comfortable, buttressing their egos against the assaults of old age. Suddenly they are deprived of the role that has given structure and purpose to much of their adult lives. They are faced with difficult decisions such as whether to try on their own to maintain the family home or to make some other living arrangement. They must become financial managers if they are fortunate and seek additional income if they are not so fortunate. And these new demands confront them at a time when they may be almost immobilized by grief.

A generation ago, many women had not learned to drive a car; their ability to get around was dependent on public transportation or on their husbands. This is still the case in many countries. Even in societies where older persons reportedly have high status, such as India, once an older woman is widowed her status changes markedly. Her eldest son becomes head of the household, and her daughter-in-law (who may have long resented her) gains authority. The son may then tell his mother, "You will have to live particularly and quietly. . . . Otherwise take your clothes and go wherever you like."[30]

In the United States the economic plight of the widow of a retired worker is greatly eased by the provisions of Social Security and other pension programs that provide for continuing payments to widows and other dependents. This permits an ever larger proportion of widows to maintain independent residences. In recent decades the proportion of older women living with relatives other than their husbands has been cut in half, while the number living alone or in unrelated households has nearly doubled.

Modern industrial society coupled with the welfare state has permitted a much wider range of alternative living arrangements to the elderly than had previously been available. Perhaps no other group of persons has experienced greater enhancement of the quality of life than elderly widows, many of whom can now maintain a degree of autonomy rather than being wholly dependent upon their children for care and emotional support.

Older widows are much less likely than widowers to remarry, for they greatly outnumber eligible males. Substantial numbers of widows are world travelers; others live in enclaves where they can enjoy a rich social life. A good example of such an enclave is given in Arlie Hochschild's book *The Unexpected Community,* which describes the social integration of a group of widows living in a small housing project in the San Francisco Bay Area.[31] While maintaining ties with kin, they forged for themselves new ties and new shared understandings that provided collective support and a continued sense of integrity and self-expression. Such communities of age peers offer a major source of life satisfaction for many older persons. They provide appropriate in-group norms and rituals, including rites of passage, that enhance self-esteem and self-confidence.[32] In such groups older people know that they matter to someone else.

In contrast to patterns found in most industrial nations, Japanese widows still look to their children for aid and living arrangements, but in Japan, too, the pattern is changing. A few decades ago widows would by and large continue to live in the household headed by their eldest son upon his father's death.[33] While the eldest son is still seen as having somewhat greater responsibility for his parents than other children, many widows live serially with each of their children. Increasingly, they seem to be turning to the households of their daughters, for here there will be little of the tension that often exists with the wives of their oldest sons. And nearly a third of elderly parents express the desire to remain independent, though they do not look to their government to provide for them.[34]

Thus there are many contingencies that influence how an elderly woman who survives her husband will live out her days. In most societies kin will surround her and provide for her needs, though they will not necessarily honor her or make life easy. In urban industrial society there are both greater possibilities for maintaining a measure of autonomy in planning activities and living arrangements and greater dangers of being isolated and abandoned.

Widowers

Some men outlive their wives, of course. When they do, they face a rather different set of problems than do widows. Widowers are likely to have an easier time economically, partly by virtue of pension arrangements and partly by virtue of easier access to opportunities for additional earning. On the other hand, men (in American society, at least) tend to be far more dependent on their wives for emotional support than wives are on their husbands.[35] Men may suffer intense grief at the loss of their wives but tend to grieve less long. Perhaps because they reach out to women for comfort, and because there are so many eligible widows, men are much more likely to remarry after losing their wives. Whereas less than one percent of new widows aged 65–74 marry, roughly a fourth of the men who lose their wives at this age will remarry.[36]

Institutional Living

As longevity has increased, so too has the number and perhaps the proportion of older people who are not able to care for themselves. Some are physically impaired, some mentally confused or senile (the word is often avoided by scholars, for it can be used as an epithet, but it connotes mental incompetence that may derive from a variety of conditions associated with advanced age). King Lear, reduced in the end to episodes of pitiful "senile" babbling, epitomizes the state brought about by such grievous stresses that the older person can no longer maintain a grasp on reality.

In the nineteenth century, older Americans no longer able to manage on their own usually went to live with children. Housing was far more adequate in the United States than in most of the countries from which our population was drawn, and outside our urban centers adult children could usually absorb an elderly parent in their household. If the parent was in reasonably good health, she (less often he) could help care for the grandchildren, help in the kitchen, and generally be a contributor to the household. If in poor health, an aged parent could be maintained in a spare room or one given up by one of the children. But as the size of dwelling units diminished and there was less an aged parent could do to be helpful, homes for the aged appeared in greater numbers. Initially they were primarily run by religious or charitable organizations or by county governments, though small private boardinghouses also existed. More recently the nursing home has become a money-maker for corporations as well as for small entrepreneurs.

In 1950 roughly three of every 100 persons over age 65 lived in an institutional setting. More than a third were in state mental hospitals; most of the rest were in homes for the aged and dependent. By 1980, by virtue of the deinstitutionalization movement, there were far fewer older people in our state hospitals, but the proportion in homes for the aged and dependent had more than doubled.[37] One type of institution simply replaced another. Among older women, six in every 100 were in institutions, most of them in nursing homes. The pattern of life afforded is most difficult for the mentally intact but infirm patient who is surrounded by peers incapable of meaningful communication. In such settings it is extraordinarily difficult to maintain one's personal integrity; despair is a frequent mood.

Personality Change in the Later Years

We have repeatedly noted that older people tend to become more reflective and introspective, in American society at least. How they express themselves appears to depend a good deal on cultural norms—whether old people are exempted from some of the constraints of polite society or are expected to be more prim and proper as they grow old, whether they are encouraged to speak up or to hold their views to themselves. In the United States there has been a considerable easing up of constraints on the elderly in the past 60 to 80 years, especially for older women. Grandmothers in many circles do many things that would have been frowned on in the past—even enjoying an off-color joke, an indelicacy they would have been well shielded from early in the century.

There is a good deal of evidence from a number of societies that women tend to become more assertive and less submissive in their later years, while men become more accepting of feelings of tenderness and of their own emotions. An older man no longer needs to prove his masculinity; an older woman no longer needs to be so strongly oriented to pleasing others. But it appears that the move toward "unisex" in emotional expression begins well before old age. David Guttman has proposed that becoming a parent has the effect on most men (in all societies) of making them more aware of their sense of caring for others.[38] Erikson's "generativity" would imply the same tendency. Hormonal changes may also be involved. In any event, older men do become much less aggressive and more concerned with their connections with others, even though they still lag behind women in establishing close ties with peers.

Yet there remain continuities in personality that persist far into the later years. Mothers of members of one of the Berkeley longitudinal studies were themselves seen over a period of roughly 40 years. In their seventies they retained some of the attributes they had shown in their thirties.[39] Those who had been talkative 40 years earlier still tended to be talkative. Those who seemed most alert at 30 tended to be seen as alert in their seventies. The same is true of assessments of intelligence, verbal fluency, frankness, and self-esteem. Cheerfulness showed a fair measure of continuity over time, as did excitability and the tendency to worry about things.

Continuities in cognitive abilities, in temperament, and in modes of coping and of relating all suggest that there are significant features of personality that persist even though social roles and life-style may have changed greatly. The life-styles of these same parents of Berkeley Guidance Study members were studied by Maas and Kuypers.[40] They found some continuities in life-style on the part of fathers—particularly in their activities and relationships with their children and their wives—but much less continuity for the mothers. There was surprisingly little relationship between the life-styles of husbands and wives, perhaps because a very substantial proportion were less pleased with their marriages at 70 than they had been at 30 (if they stayed together).

It may be noted parenthetically that we know less about marital closeness and satisfaction in old age than we do about the empty-nest stage or any earlier stage. Some couples remain extremely close, but there is accumulating evidence that marital satisfaction tends to drop in the later years. Several writers have noted that as older men and women become more dependent on one another and on others, they struggle harder to preserve their sense of personal autonomy and to protect time for themselves.[41] Anxiety that they will become unable to maintain control of their lives may affect relationships between husband and wife or parent and child.

Maas and Kuypers found that on the whole most of these older men and women were functioning effectively, though the women were somewhat more impaired by poor health and psychological distress.[42] Among both men and women, those most prone to ill health at age 70 had more often reported health problems at age 30. To the extent that life stresses or constitutional vulnerabilities were manifest in somatic complaints early in adulthood, it appears that such problems are likely to appear in the later years as well. Yet it must be emphasized that the statistical analyses show *tendencies,* not inevitable continuities. Some of the women who had been most distressed in poor marriages at 30 were subsequently divorced or widowed. Those who became involved in work careers—along with other women who remained married but also held jobs that were satisfying to them—were among the most satisfied, healthiest, and most active of the parents.[43] Unfortunately, we cannot assess the causal relationships that lead to continuity or change except at the clinical, individual level. Early competence is the best predictor of later competence, but some people grow in judgment and maturity even in their later years, and others are beset by losses and setbacks that may unhinge them even though they had earlier seemed solidly in control of their lives.

Reminiscence and Life Review

Early in our adult lives we tend to be future-oriented. Our histories are short but our futures stretch far ahead. It is not that we can't tell the story of our youth, but rather that we are less preoccupied with our youth than with what is to come. As we grow older, we increasingly draw upon past experience when we encounter problems that resemble those we have faced before. Often we review that past experience for present purposes. As we noted in the last chapter, there may be apparent discontinuities as well as continuities in the way we draw on the past. Yet we manage to incorporate shifting mixes of experience into a more or less coherent life story. The past is constantly being recreated for present purposes; if memories are not always accurate, they are nevertheless real in their consequences for the present.

Many students of the life course have stressed the importance of the personal narrative for achieving a sense of coherence and integrity.[44] Most of us experience unexpected events—sometimes new opportunities, sometimes dashed hopes—that change the course of our lives at some point or points, yet we accommodate to these events once we have assimilated them, and most of them, at least, seem to fit naturally. Or if they bring a major change in our conceptions of self, as sometimes happens, we develop explanations that make us feel we understand where we are and how we got there.

In the later years, reminiscence serves other functions. As roles are lost and usefulness becomes less manifest in everyday life, the older person reviews the past as a means of holding on to the identity that was forged through the years of heavy involvement as parent, spouse, worker, friend, and "free spirit" or "responsible citizen," that is, as custodian of a unique life course. Robert Butler, a psychiatrist who has spent most of his career in the study of older persons, healthy as well as mentally ill, emphasizes the important function that the "life review" has for the older man or woman.[45] Ultimately, as death begins to be seen as a shadow behind a tree not far ahead in the path of life, the life review becomes a means of settling accounts. But the review is not a single episode in which one experiences one's past; it is a constant process of going back, of trying to hold in mind the moments of fulfillment or to resolve the doubts and regrets when a person knows that there is no more time to make up for past mistakes. Butler suggests that the more intense the unresolved life conflicts, the more work remains to be accomplished toward reintegration. Reminiscence as a form of stock-taking begins long before old age, but undoubtedly it becomes more urgent as death looms nearer and nearer. Often others will receive new clues as to important elements in the identity of the older person from the latter's reminiscences.

LAST ACT OF ALL

Death may come swiftly or slowly. When it comes and how it comes are matters of great concern both to the person whose life course is ended and to those who hold that person dear. Most lives in the past were truncated long before old age. Death was often unexpected and swift.

As public health measures and medical interventions have become much more effective in recent decades, dying has become a more drawn-out process for many persons. It is frequently noted that death and dying have been sanitized in modern America. Less than a fourth of deaths in the United States now occur at home; nearly three fourths occur in institutions. The bodies of the deceased seldom lie in an open casket in the living room, while relatives hold a wake before the funeral. These developments have sometimes been interpreted as signs of a denial of death, though they may also be interpreted as consequences of entrepreneurial ingenuity and technological developments along with a decline in traditional practices surrounding death. Births as well as deaths have been removed from the home. Recent developments have perhaps begun to reverse both trends.

The Process of Dying

The increasing proportion of deaths occurring in hospitals has given impetus to research on the process of dying. Outsiders have now been designated to care for the dying, and they do so within the context of bureaucratically organized institutions. Hospital staffs must schedule their operations, and this is true even when a patient is regarded as possibly or probably terminal. Glaser and Strauss have studied how staffs manage their relationships with patient and family and how they handle this "nonscheduled status passage."[46]

To the extent that the staff believes a death is likely to occur, there is a sequence of decision points and modes of operating. The primary issues are the degree of certainty that death will occur and the degree to which the timing of death can be predicted. From the patient's perspective, the important issues are awareness that death is about to occur and the opportunity to settle any accounts that are outstanding, from financial matters to personal quarrels. When the patient is aged, and knows that death is near, family and staff have an easier time helping the patient than where the likelihood of death has been denied. Often, of course, family members want to be encouraging; they tell the patient there is hope, even though they have been told by the physician that there is none. The patient may know that there is none and may be quite prepared to die, but may go along with the fiction of denial. This makes the staff's task—and ultimately the patient's—more difficult, for it may prevent the patient from making the kind of exit that he or she would like to make, with good-byes said and a sense that death is the right, true end of life.

No one has studied death more closely than Elisabeth Kübler-Ross, who has been instrumental in communicating the dying patient's point of view and need to share thoughts about death.[47] Ross has proposed that persons who suffer a long terminal illness go through a series of stages: (1) denial and isolation from others; (2) anger and resentment; (3) bargaining and an effort to postpone; (4) depression and a sense of loss; and finally, (5) acceptance. Others would say that most of these emotions or states can be present from moment to moment.

Denial of death is probably much less frequent among the elderly, especially if they are already weak or wracked with pain. Anger and resentment and efforts to bargain seem most evident among the young or middle-aged who have responsibilities and commitments they will be unable to meet. Among the old, especially those suffering from a painful disease, anger and a sense of bewilderment may come when technology is put to work to keep them alive: "Why won't they let me die?"

The death of an older person is obviously less disruptive to the family and to the community than is the death of a person in the prime of life. Death can bring an affirmation of solidarity among survivors, a coming together of a community of those whose lives were touched. Even those who mourn most deeply can feel a sense of relief that the period of suffering is past and a sense of joy in a life that enriched the lives of others.

While funeral services are not, by and large, the major events they once were in American society, they are still important rites of passage. Perhaps the memorial service, in which happy memories are shared, will in time replace the wake. Particularly for those who are themselves nearing an expectable death, the collective recognition of a passage is an important link to the world of the living.

A Final Note on Old Age

The later years, or more bluntly, old age, is an open-ended period. For some men and more women, it will last longer than their middle years. It will inevitably become a period of declining strength, health, and energy. The world in which the old operate will become smaller, circumscribed by their ability to drive, to take public transportation, to walk more than short distances. Yet, even in decline, the older person may experience rich and varied relationships with more mobile, younger friends, as well as with children and grandchildren. If older persons often tend to be garrulous, they can nevertheless at times be good listeners. If they cannot be actors on center stage, they can be willing and even enthralled spectators of the lives they themselves have set upon that stage. And they can enjoy their declining years thanks to developments in health care, to inventions that have increased their mobility and their comfort, and, most important of all, to the scientific and technological developments that permit a fraction of the population at the height of its capacities to produce enough goods and wealth to sustain the elderly in independent comfort. The life course could never before be so pleasantly lived out.

THE LIFE COURSE—LOOKING BACK

By now it will have become evident that no single theory can take us very far toward understanding the entire life span when we must take into account the effects of social position and social change as well as those of aging. We are organisms who reach maturity only after a long period of dependency, protected and nurtured by our caretakers, learning through language and precept an intricate socio-cultural system that will provide guidelines through life. The sources of possible influence are so numerous that we cannot hope to encompass them in any simple model or theory. Instead, we must try to identify those features or variables that tend to exert strong effects at particular times or in particular circumstances or that tend to give structure and substance to the life course.

Some theories and perspectives are more helpful than others. Early in life maturation and socialization go hand-in-hand as preeminent influences; socialization continues as long as we live. Theories of learning help us to understand how the infant and child master the process of reasoning and account for some of the differences among individuals. Theories of psychosocial development like that of Erikson sensitize us to problems requiring resolution along the way, although the evidence available does not suggest that they have to be resolved in a set order.

Other theories posit tasks or themes for which we have found little evidence,

Gould's *Transformations,* for example, proposes that the attainment of maturity rests on being able to discard a number of false assumptions arising from dependency on our parents. These assumptions may be characteristic of many psychiatric patients, but they are not characteristic of any substantial proportion of the general population. Levinson's *Seasons of a Man's Life* contains many insightful observations about careers and lives, but the basic premise that the phasing of lives is closely tied to the decades of aging is simply not supported by data from long-term longitudinal studies.

The formulation that I have found most congenial is that the life course in modern industrial societies is best understood by focusing on the major roles that most often express individual purpose and commitment—the occupational, marital, and parental roles. The evidence suggests that adequate socialization and preparation for these roles—knowing what they may entail and what one wants in each—can greatly facilitate long-term successful functioning in them.

In presenting this account of what we know about the life course viewed chronologically, I have touched repeatedly, if often lightly, on the importance of personal choice, major transitions and the adaptations they call for, continuities and discontinuities from one period to another, and the development and maintenance of a sense of identity. My primary objective has been to draw on the best available evidence to give an accurate picture of what we know about the life course, particularly as that evidence bears on major theoretical issues, but in the compass of a brief text it has not been feasible to spell out the theoretical implications as fully as might be desirable.

Having the evidence in hand, and I hope in head, you may find it useful to go back to chapters one and two and ask how the various formulations fit the data. Most important, ask yourself how well the formulations fit your own life and the lives of your parents and other older persons whom you know well. You will almost certainly become aware of cohort differences in scheduling and in the goals that seem most important. I hope you will also find it useful in thinking about the opportunities that exist for you, the social roles you will occupy, what you want to accomplish, and how you can best achieve your goals.

NOTES

1. Matilda White Riley, "Women, Men and the Lengthening Life Course," in Alice Rossi, ed., *Gender and the Life Course* (Chicago, IL: Aldine Publishing Co., 1984), pp. 333-47.
2. See, for example, Francis L. K. Hsu, *Americans and Chinese: Two Ways of Life* (New York: Henry Schuman, 1953).
3. Allen Holmberg, *Nomads of the Long Bow. The Siriono of Eastern Bolivia* (Garden City, NY: The Natural History Press, 1969).
4. Irving Rosow, *Socialization to Old Age* (Berkeley, CA: University of California Press, 1974).
5. As Social Security benefits have risen in recent years, however, the proportion of older persons below the poverty line has dropped and is much lower than the proportion among children under 18 (many of whom are in single-parent households). See Samuel H. Preston,

"Children and the Elderly in the United States," *Scientific American,* 251, no. 6 (Dec. 1984), 449.

6. Riley, "The Lengthening Life Course," p. 335.

7. Ibid., p. 336.

8. See P. M. Hauser, "Aging and World-Wide Population Change," in R. H. Binstock and E. Shanas, eds., *Handbook of Aging and the Social Sciences* (New York: Van Nostrand Reinhold Co., 1976), pp. 59–86.

9. Angus Campbell, *The Sense of Well-Being in America: Recent Patterns and Trends* (New York: McGraw-Hill Book Co., 1981), pp. 206–208.

10. Ethel Shanas and G. L. Maddox, "Aging, Health, and the Organization of Health Resources," in Binstock and Shanas, eds., *Handbook of Aging,* p. 605.

11. E. H. Estes, "Health Experience in the Elderly," in E. W. Busse and E. Pfeiffer, eds., *Behavior and Adaptation in Later Life* (Boston: Little, Brown and Co., 1969), p. 115.

12. Ibid., p. 117.

13. E. P. Stoller, "Self-Assessments of Health by the Elderly: The Impact of Informal Assistance," *Journal of Health and Social Behavior,* 25 (1984), 260–70.

14. The sharply increasing prevalence of this condition with our aging population has given rise to a great increase in research, and new knowledge is constantly accruing. For a number of vignettes describing the plight of patient and family, see *Newsweek* magazine, December 3, 1984. A review of recent research is given in Richard Wurtman, "Alzheimer's Disease," *Scientific American,* 252, no. 1 (January 1985), 62–74.

15. B. F. Turner, G. S. Tobin, and M. A. Lieberman, "Personality Traits as Predictors of Institutional Adaptation among the Aged," *Journal of Gerontology,* 27 (1972), 61–68.

16. Carl Eisdorfer, "Intellectual and Cognitive Changes in the Aged," in Busse and Pfeiffer, eds., *Behavior and Adaptation.*

17. K. W. Schaie, "Age Changes in Adult Intelligence," in D. S. Woodruff and J. E. Birren, eds., *Aging: Scientific Perspectives and Social Issues* (New York: D. Van Nostrand Co., 1975), p. 122.

18. D. A. Walsh, "Age Differences in Learning and Memory," in Woodruff and Birren, eds., *Aging: Scientific Perspectives,* p. 138.

19. Schaie, "Age Changes," p. 120.

20. Nearly half of all workers were in jobs providing for mandatory retirement at some stated age, and for seven in 10 of these workers, that age was 65. H. S. Parnes, ed., *Work and Retirement, A Longitudinal Study of Men* (Cambridge, MA: The MIT Press, 1981), p. 194.

21. H. L. Sheppard, "Work and Retirement," in Binstock and Shanas, eds., *Handbook of Aging.*

22. Erik Erikson, "Life Cycle," in David Sills, ed., *Encyclopedia of the Social Sciences,* vol. 9 (New York: The Macmillan Company and the Free Press, 1968), p. 292.

23. Elaine Cumming and William Henry, *Growing Old: The Process of Disengagement* (New York: Basic Books, 1961).

24. A cogent evaluation of the theory is given by Arlie Hochschild, "Disengagement Theory: A Critique and Proposal," *American Sociological Review,* 40 (1975), 553–69.

25. Marjorie Fiske Lowenthal and C. Haven, "Interaction and Adaptation: Intimacy as the Critical Variable," *American Sociological Review,* 33 (1968), 20–30.

26. Francis M. Carp, "Housing and Living-Environments of Older People," in Binstock and Shanas, eds., *Handbook of Aging,* p. 251.

27. Beth Soldo, "The Living Arrangements of the Elderly in the Near Future," in Sara Kiesler, J. N. Morgan, and V. K. Oppenheimer, eds., *Aging: Social Change* (New York: Academic Press, 1981), p. 491.

28. Linda George, *Role Transitions in Later Life* (Monterey, CA: Brooks/Cole Publishing Company, 1980), pp. 88–89.

29. Helena Z. Lopata, *Women as Widows: Support Systems* (New York: Elsevier, 1979).

30. The quote is from William H. Harlan, "Social Status of the Aged in Three Indian Villages,"

in Bernice Neugarten, ed., *Middle Age and Aging* (Chicago: University of Chicago Press, 1968), p. 474.

31. Arlie R. Hochschild, *The Unexpected Community* (Englewood Cliffs, NJ: Prentice-Hall, Inc., 1973).

32. Rosow, *Socialization to Old Age.* See especially Chapter 9.

33. Ronald Dore, *City Life in Japan: A Study of a Tokyo Ward* (Berkeley, CA: University of California Press, 1958), pp. 132-33.

34. Ibid., p. 131.

35. Lowenthal and Haven, "Interaction and Adaptation," p. 28.

36. W. P. Cleveland and D. T. Gianturco, "Remarriage Probability after Widowhood: A Retrospective Method," *Journal of Gerontology,* 31 (1976), 100.

37. U.S. Bureau of the Census: Population in Institutions, 1983.

38. David Gutmann, "Parenthood: A Key to the Comparative Study of the Life Cycle," in N. Datan and L. Ginsberg, eds., *Life Span Developmental Psychology* (New York: Academic Press, 1975), pp. 167-84.

39. P. Mussen et al., "Continuity and Change in Women's Characteristics over Four Decades," *International Journal of Behavioral Development,* 3 (1980), 333-47.

40. Henry S. Maas and J. A. Kuypers, *From Thirty to Seventy* (San Francisco: Jossey-Bass Publishers, 1974).

41. Bertram J. Cohler, "Autonomy and Interdependence in the Family of Adulthood: A Psychological Perspective," *The Gerontologist,* 23 (1983), 33-39.

42. Maas and Kuypers, *From Thirty to Seventy,* Chapter 9.

43. Ibid., p. 204.

44. See, for example, Bertram J. Cohler, "Personal Narrative and the Life Course," in P. B. Baltes and O. G. Brim, Jr., eds., *Life Span Development and Behavior,* vol. 4 (New York: Academic Press, 1982), pp. 205-41.

45. Robert Butler, "The Life Review: An Interpretation of Reminiscence in the Aged," *Psychiatry, Journal for the Study of Interpersonal Processes,* 26, no. 1 (1963).

46. B. G. Glaser and A. L. Strauss, *Awareness of Dying* (Chicago: Aldine Publishing Co., 1965). Also by the same authors, *Time for Dying* (Chicago: Aldine Publishing Company, 1968). The hospice movement, spurred by the work of Cicely Saunders and her followers, offers an alternative to death in the impersonal hospital setting. For a description of the aims and programs of hospices, see T. H. Koff, *Hospice, A Caring Community* (Cambridge, MA: Winthrop Publishers, Inc., 1980).

47. Elisabeth Kübler-Ross, *On Death and Dying* (New York: Macmillan, 1969).

AUTHOR INDEX

A

Adorno, T. W., 84
Ainsworth, Mary, 61
Aldous, Joan, 149
Alexander, Karl, 107
Allen, Hervey, 151
Allison, Paul D., 84
Asher, Steven, 84

B

Bachman, J. G., 107, 127
Baker, Russell, 127
Balswick, J. O., 107
Baltes, Paul B., 172
Baumrind, Diana, 75, 84
Becker, Howard S., 41, 126-27
Benedict, Ruth, 6, 14
Berger, Bennett, 107
Blau, P. M., 127
Blauner, Robert, 119, 127
Bleuler, Manfred, 148
Block, Jack, 63, 107, 167, 173
Blood, Robert, 149
Bloom, Benjamin S., 83
Blyth, D. A., 106
Boocock, Sarane, 15
Bouthelet, Lorraine, 84
Bowlby, John, 62
Bowles, S., 84
Bray, Douglas, 173
Brim, Orville G., Jr., 40, 41, 161, 172
Bronfenbrenner, Urie, 41, 84

Bronson, Wanda, 62
Brown, Roger, 62, 83
Buhler, Charlotte, 19-20, 32, 40
Butler, Robert, 189, 194

C

Caldwell, Bettye M., 62
Campbell, Angus, 149, 173, 193
Carp, Francis M., 193
Carter, Hugh, 128, 148
Chess, S., 62
Chiriboga, David, 41, 149, 171
Chodorow, Nancy, 80, 84
Clausen, J. A., 40, 55-57, 62, 83, 106,
    126-28, 148, 172
Cleary, P. D., 149
Cleveland, W. P., 194
Cobb, Sydney, 84
Cohler, Bertram J., 194
Coleman, James, 92-93, 106
Coleman, Samuel, 149
Conger, J. J., 83
Converse, Philip, 149, 173
Cross, Catherine, 84
Cumming, Elaine, 182, 183, 193

D

Dale, P., 83
Darwin, Charles, 92, 106
Datan, Nancy, 40
Demos, John, 15

Denzin, Norman, 14
deTocqueville, Alexis, 75
Di Virgilio, L., 62
Dobson, Henry Austin, 174
Dobzhansky, Theodosius, 61
Donne, John, 1
Dore, Ronald, 150, 194
Dubin, Robert, 33, 41, 120, 127

E

Eichorn, Dorothy, 172
Einstein, Albert, 92, 106
Eisdorfer, Carl, 41, 193
Ekland, Bruce, 107
Elder, Glen H., Jr., 8, 14, 84, 107, 148
Elliott, G. R., 41
Entwisle, Doris R., 84
Erikson, Erik, 18, 22, 35, 40, 58, 79, 101–2,
    108, 150, 166, 167, 173, 182, 193
Estes, E. H., 193

F

Featherman, D. L., 41, 107
Finch, Janet, 150
Fischer, Claude S., 172
Fiske, Marjorie (see Lowenthal, Marjorie
    Fiske)
Form, W. H., 126
Freeman, H. E., 128
Freud, Anna, 106
Freud, Sigmund, 21, 40, 58, 79, 80
Furstenberg, Frank F., Jr., 84, 107–8,
    148, 149

G

Gaitz, C. M., 173
George, Linda, 41, 193
Gianturco, D. R., 194
Gibbs, J. T., 107
Gilligan, Carol, 80, 84, 91, 106
Ginsberg, Leon, 40, 127
Gintes, H., 84
Glasner, B. G., 190, 194
Glenn, Norval, 14, 149
Glick, P., 128, 148
Goethals, George W., 108
Goode, William J., 126
Gordon, Chad, 173
Gottfredson, Gary, 173
Gottfredson, Linda S., 127, 173
Gould, Roger, 25, 40, 104, 108, 163, 192
Granovetter, M. S., 123, 128
Guttman, David, 187, 194

H

Haan, Norma, 63, 106–7, 167, 173
Haber, J., 149, 172
Hall, Oswald, 126
Hannan, M. T., 41
Hareven, Tamara, 116, 127, 128, 148
Harlan, William H., 193
Harlow, Harry, 49, 62, 76, 84
Harlow, Margaret, 84
Hauser, Robert M., 15, 107, 193
Haven, C., 193, 194
Havighurst, Robert J., 106
Hayduk, Leslie A., 84
Henretta, John C., 172
Henry, William, 108, 182, 183, 193
Herma, J. L., 127
Hershberg, Theodore, 108, 148
Hess, Robert D., 83
Hetherington, Mavis, 84
Hill, Daniel, 108
Hill, Martha, 108
Hill, Reuben, 41, 149
Hochschild, Arlie, 185, 193, 194
Hoffman, S., 149
Hogan, D. P., 41
Holland, J. L., 116–17, 127
Holmberg, Allen, 192
Holmes, J., 149
Honzik, Marjorie, 172
Howard, Ann, 173
Hsu, Francis L. K., 192
Huffine, Carol L., 148
Hunt, Jane, 172

I

Inkeles, Alex, 62, 83, 103, 108

J

Jacques, Elliott, 162, 172
James, William, 20, 40, 41
Jennings, M. K., 107
Johnson, Virginia, 171
Johnston, J., 127
Jones, Mary Cover, 106, 173

K

Kagan, Jerome, 19, 40, 47, 61, 62, 83
Kahn, Robert, 14
Kahne, Hilda, 128
Kandel, Denise, 94, 107
Kanter, Rosabeth M., 16, 122, 125, 128,
    148

Kaplan, Abraham, 16, 40
Kaplan, R., 63
Karp, David A., 41
Kearsley, Richard, 61, 62
Keating, Daniel P., 106
Keniston, Kenneth, 107
Kerckhoff, Alan, 83
Kessen, William, 62
Kessler, Ronald C., 149, 172
King, Karl, 107
Kinsey, Alfred C., 94–95, 107, 171
Koff, T. H., 194
Kohlberg, Lawrence, 71–72, 83, 91, 106
Kohn, Melvin, 73–74, 83, 111, 118, 126–27, 157, 172
Konecni, V. J., 63
Kübler-Ross, Elisabeth, 190, 194
Kuypers, J. A., 187, 188, 194

L

Labovie, Gisella, 172
Lapidus, Gail, 149
Laws, Judith L., 171
Lazar, J., 84
Lear, M. W., 161, 172
Lesser, Gerald, 94, 107
Lever, Janet, 80, 84
Levine, S., 128
Levinson, Daniel, 18, 24–25, 40, 115, 126–27, 162, 163, 172, 192
Lewin, Kurt, 16
Lidz, T., 40, 85, 105
Lieberman, M. A., 193
Liker, Jeffrey K., 84
Livson, Norman, 168, 173
Lopata, Helena Z., 193
Lortie, Dan C., 127
Lowenthal, Marjorie Fiske, 32, 41, 149, 153, 171, 193, 194
Luker, Kristin, 107
Lynn, David B., 84

M

Maas, Henry S., 84, 187, 188, 194
Maccoby, Michael, 123, 128
Maddox, G. L., 171, 193
Mange, A. P., 61
Mange, E. J., 61
Mannheim, Karl, 8, 14
Marini, M. M., 107
Martin, Clyde E., 107, 171
Maslow, Abraham, 41
Masters, William H., 171
Mattesick, P., 41
McKinney, K. L., 106

McRae, James A., Jr., 149, 172
Mead, George Herbert, 52, 62
Mead, Margaret, 86, 87, 105
Mechanic, David, 149
Miernyk, W. H., 127
Miller, D. G., 126
Mirowsky, John, 149, 172
Modell, John, 108, 148
Montaigne, Michel Eyquem, 129
Morgan, S. P., 149
Mortimer, Jeylan, 127
Moss, Howard, 62
Murphey, E. B., 108
Mussen, Paul, 61, 62, 83, 194
Myers, J. K., 172

N

Neugarten, Bernice, 14, 40, 153, 171
Niemi, Richard, 107
Novaco, R. W., 63

O

O'Malley, P. M., 107, 127
Oppenheimer, Valerie, 126, 133, 148, 149
O'Rand, Angela, 172
Orlansky, Howard, 62

P

Parnes, H. S., 164, 166, 172, 173, 193
Pearl, David, 84
Pearlin, L. I., 41
Peskin, Harvey, 106, 168, 173
Piaget, Jean, 20, 21, 40, 47–48, 62, 70–71, 83, 90
Pomeroy, Wardell, 107
Pope, Alexander, 42
Preston, Samuel H., 192
Proust, Marcel, 14

R

Rapoport, Rhona, 149
Rapoport, Robert, 149
Rathburn, C., 62
Redl, Fritz, 63
Reeder, L. G., 128
Renshaw, Peter, 84
Rheingold, Harriet, 54, 62
Riley, John, 172
Riley, Matilda White, 192, 193
Rindfuss, R. R., 149
Robinson, J. E., 107

Rodgers, Willard, 149, 173
Rodriguez, Richard, 78, 84
Rogoff, Natalie, 127
Rosow, Irving, 41, 175, 192, 193
Ross, C. E., 149, 172
Rossi, Alice, 62, 137, 149, 154, 171
Rubin, Lillian, 120, 127, 135, 148, 149,
    155, 159, 171, 172
Runyan, William McKinley, 37, 41
Ryder, Norman, 14

S

Sarason, Seymour, 163, 173
Schaie, K. W., 193
Schooler, C., 41, 83, 118, 126–27, 172
Sells, Lucy, 107
Sewell, William, 15, 98, 107
Shah, Vimal P., 98, 107
Shakespeare, William, 40, 85
Shanas, Ethel, 171, 193
Sheldon, William, 66, 83
Sheppard, H. L., 193
Shipman, Virginia, 83
Simmons, R. G., 90, 106
Smith, D. H., 83
Smith, M. B., 107
Smith, R. S., 61
Sofer, Cyril, 127, 165, 173
Soldo, Beth, 193
Sorenson, A. B., 41
Stevenson, Robert Louis, 85
Stoller, E. P., 193
Strauss, A. L., 41, 190, 194
Stroud, Janice G., 128, 149, 172
Super, D. E., 127
Swicegood, C. G., 149

T

Tanner, James M., 106
Terkel, Studs, 119, 127

Thomas, A., 62
Thurner, M., 41, 171
Tobin, G. S., 193
Tuma, N. B., 41
Turner, B. F., 193

V

Vaillant, George, 34, 35, 40–41, 168, 173
Veevers, J., 148
Vygotsky, L. S., 62

W

Waldfogel, S., 62
Walsh, D. A., 193
Walshok, M. L., 128
Weg, Ruth B., 171
Weissman, M. M., 172
Werner, Emmy E., 61, 83
Wheeler, S., 41
Whiting, Beatrice, 62
Whyte, William H., Jr., 122–23, 128
Wilensky, Harold, 126, 149, 172
Williams, Judith, 84
Wineman, David, 63
Wissler, Clark, 106
Wolfbein, Seymour, 126, 172
Wolfe, Donald, 149
Wordsworth, William, 80
Wurtman, Richard, 193

Y

Yarrow, Marian Radke, 12, 15
Yoels, C., 41

Z

Zelazo, Philip, 61, 62

SUBJECT INDEX

A

adaptation
  to changing circumstances, 163, 169
  as general perspective, 17
  life stress and, 18, 33–34
  in old age, 182
adolescence
  boundaries of, 87
  challenge to parents, 140
  developmental tasks of, 87–88
  economic costs to family, 140
  personality in, 101–3
  as recent discovery, 85, 87
  transition to adulthood, 103–4
adolescent society, 92–94
age norms, 7
age vs. cohort effects, 11–12
Alzheimer's disease, 158, 178
athletics, as path to adult attainment,
  66, 98
attachment, 48–49
autonomy, 104

B

birth, 46
body build and behavior, 65–67

C

central life interests, 33, 120, 122
childlessness, 134

D

child-rearing practices (*see also* parenthood;
  socialization)
  authoritarian vs. permissive, 75
children
  and care of older parents, 158
  in family cycle, 136–41
climacteric, male, 156
cognitive development, 20–21, 47–49,
  67–71, 90–92
cohort
  defined, 8
  differences in IQ, 156
  influences, 7–8, 38, 82, 170–71, 174,
  176, 186
continuity, discontinuity (*see* stability
  and change)
contraception
  in adolescence, 95
  and childlessness, 134
culture
  defined, 6–7
  and family cycle, 137, 147
  and gender differences, 57
  and life expectations, 10, 38–39, 131,
  171, 174
  as source of goals, 6–7, 10, 32–33
  and views of human nature, 53

day care centers, 61
death
  causes in later years, 177–78
  causes in middle years, 153

death (*cont.*)
  confrontation with, 153, 189–90
  stages in, 190
  as status passage, 190
dependency, of older children, 141
depression, economic
  effects on parenting, 81
  effects on women's roles, 145
depression, psychological
  age prevalence, 163
  in later years, 178
  and maternal role, 139
developmental perspective, 17, 19–26
developmental tasks
  in adolescence, 87–88
  in early childhood, 23, 79
  in later childhood, 78–80
diseases, chronic, 152, 154, 177–78
disengagement, 182
divorce, 129, 143–44
  consequences for children, 81, 144
  and economic problems of wives,
    143–44
  and remarriage, 144

E

educational attainment
  and occupational attainment, 96
  predictors of, 97–98
emotional development, 60–61, 81–82
empty nest, 130, 141–42

F

family, 129–50
  single parent, 131
family cycle, 30, 129–48
  defined, 129–30
  stages in, 130
father absence, effects of, 81
fatherhood, 137–38
friendships, 76–77, 158–59

G

gender differences
  in early maturing, 90
  in life expectancy, 176
  in middle years, 153–56,
    158–59
  sources of, 57–58, 80–81, 99
generativity vs. stagnation,
  166–67
genetic influences, 4, 43–45
growth, physical, 65

H

health
  in later years, 177–79
  in middle years, 153–54
heredity, 43–45
home ownership, 138, 183–84

I

identity, 22–23, 35, 101–2, 159–60
  achievement of, 101–2
  defined, 35
  and intimacy, 102
  and occupational role, 122, 125
  in old age, 182, 188–89
impairment, 5–6, 165
inequality between sexes
  educational, 99
  occupational, 125, 145
infancy, 42–49
  importance of, 58–61
  and parenting, 54
institutional living, in old age, 186
integrity vs. despair, 24, 182
intelligence
  crystallized vs. fluid, 156–57
  influences on, 59–60, 157–58
  stability of, 59, 157, 179
  tests of, 59, 156–57, 179–80
IQ change
  in middle years, 156–58
  in old age, 179–80

L

language, early development, 50–52
leisure activities, 169–70
life-cycle squeeze, 136, 137, 140
life expectancy, 1, 174, 176–77
life histories
  determinants of, 9–10
  subjective accounts, 11
life review, 188–89
life satisfaction
  effect of young children, 138
  in later years, 177
  in middle years, 170
longitudinal studies, 12

M

marital satisfaction, 138, 140, 141, 145–46,
  160, 188
marriage
  age at, 133, 135

early, 99, 135
  transition to, 134–35
  trends in, 132
maternal role
  in early childhood, 55, 61
  through family cycle, 136–42
  in middle years, 159
maturation, 4, 47–49
maturing, early vs. late, 5, 47, 89–90
memory, 48, 69–70, 179–80
  recognition and retrieval, 48, 67, 69
menopause, 141–42, 155–56
mesomorphy, 66, 89
mid-life crisis, 151, 162–65
minority status, effects of, 10, 74, 78,
    98–99, 107
mobility
  occupational, 98, 111, 117, 120, 124,
      164–65
  residential, 104, 123, 138, 183–84
moral development, 71–72, 91

N

normative crises, 18, 148

O

occupational careers, 30
  blue-collar, 119–20
  as central life interest, 120, 122
  change at mid-life, 163
  in management, 122–24
  in middle years, 160
  mobility in, 111
  professional, 120–22
  stages of, 126
  women's, 124–26, 160, 188
occupational choice
  and educational attainment, 96–99,
      117
  major influences on, 115–16
  personality correlates, 116–18
  theories of, 114–15
Oedipus complex, 22, 78–79
old age, 174–91

P

parental values, 73–75
parenthood
  changing roles in, 142–43
  societal expectations, 53–55
  transition to, 136–37
peer relationships, 76–77
perception, 69

personality, 101–3
  in adolescence, 102
  and careers, 116–18
  and cultural norms, 6, 28–30, 187
  in later years, 187–88
  in middle years, 167–69
  and modernity, 103
  stability and change, 102–3, 167–69,
      187–88
physical change
  in later years, 177–78
  in middle years, 158–59
physical development, 5, 47, 65–67, 88–91
  prenatal, 45–46
  stages of, 19–20
play, 57–58
political orientations, 99–101
pregnancy, premarital, 95–96, 137
prematurity, 46
puberty, 88

R

race (*see* minority status)
remarriage, 144
reminiscence, 188–89
retirement, 160, 165, 180–81
retrospective bias, 12
rites of passage, 13, 15, 37, 148, 152
  at death, 191
  defined, 37
  in middle years, 152
  school, 77–78
role, social
  changes in old age, 175
  defined, 27–28
  gain and loss, 31, 175
  involvement in middle years, 158–67
  sequences in life course, 26–31

S

scheduling, 3, 7, 18, 36, 96–99, 103–4,
    132–33, 147–48, 158–59, 161, 165
schema, 47–48
  defined, 68
school
  social class and performance, 78
  as source of parent's activities, 139
  and student role, 77–78
self-concept, development of, 32, 52,
    101–2
self-realization, 32
sensorimotor stage, 48
sexual behavior, 94–95, 155–56
singlehood, 133–34
Siriono, treatment of old and infirm, 175

social change (*see also* cohort, influences)
in employment experience, 112–13
and life expectancy, 176–77
in transition to adulthood, 103–4
in transition to marriage, 132–33
social class, defined, 74
social class differences
in meaning of physique, 89–90
in opportunities, 9–10
in parental values, 73–74
in school performance, 77–78
in verbal skills, 51
socialization, 6, 9, 28–30, 53–58, 72–75, 175
defined, 6
in family, 72–77
intergenerational, 143
in later years, 175
for marriage, 131–32
as perspective, 17
tasks of early, 55–57
stability and change
of early temperament, 58–59
in IQ, 59–60, 156–58, 179–80
in leisure activities, 169–70
in life organization and roles, 24, 29–31, 36, 158–59, 182–83, 189
occupational, 82, 111–12, 117, 120, 125, 163, 180–81
of personality, 102–3, 167–69, 187–88
stages
in adolescence, 105
biological development, 19–20
career, 111, 126
cognitive, 20–21
defined, 19
of family cycle, 130
in middle years, 170
psychosexual, 21–22
psychosocial, 21–26
stress
and adaptation, 33–35
defined, 33
in maternal role, 138–40
student activism, 100
suicide, 178
supports, social, 10, 34, 158
symbols and concepts, 68

T

temperament, stability of, 58–59
time
dimensions of, 2–4
historical, 3, 7–8
social, 2
timing-of-events model, 18
transitions
to adulthood, 103–4
to marriage, 134–35
in middle age, unscheduled, 152
to parenthood, 136–37
twins, identical and fraternal, 44

V

values
parental, 73–74
societal, 53

W

widowhood, 165–66, 184–86
wisdom, 182
women's occupational involvement
changing patterns, 124–25
class differences, 160
effect on husbands, 146, 160
and family size, 125
and marriage, 144–46
in middle years, 160
work and family, 144–47, 158–60